The cowboy.

THE STORY

OF THE COWBOY

Emerson Hough

LITERATURE HOUSE / GREGG PRESS
Upper Saddle River, N. J.

Republished in 1970 by

LITERATURE HOUSE

an imprint of The Gregg Press

121 Pleasant Avenue

Upper Saddle River, N. J. 07458

Standard Book Number–8398-0791-0

Library of Congress Card–77-104488

Printed in United States of America

EMERSON HOUGH

Emerson Hough was born in 1857 in Newton, Iowa, and died in 1923. His father was a schoolmaster who had emigrated to the Midwest from Virginia. After graduation from the Newton High School (there were three students in his class), Hough studied law at the University of Iowa, was admitted to the bar, and for a while practiced in Whiteoaks, New Mexico. But he had always loved the outdoors, and found office work too confining. He closed up shop and began a life of wandering, camping in the wilderness areas of the United States and Canada, and occasionally writing about his experiences. He worked on newspapers in Sandusky and Des Moines, and was branch manager of *Field and Stream* in Chicago. His first book, *The Singing Mouse Stories*, appeared in 1895, followed shortly by *The Story of the Cowboy*. With the publication of *The Mississippi Bubble* came success, and enough money to support him while he wrote subsequent books. This sensational novel, based on an eighteenth-century financial debacle, was not his best, and is out of print, whereas *The Covered Wagon, North of Thirty-Six,* and *The Passing of the Frontier* are still popular. *The Covered Wagon* was filmed, and was extremely profitable.

In 1897 Hough married Charlotte A. Cheseborough. He made his home in Chicago, but spent as little time as he could in the city, preferring to live a nomadic existence. For several years he headed the "Out-of-Doors-Department" of the *Saturday Evening Post*. Hough was active in his support of the Conservationist movement, and because of his patriotism, love of the strenuous life, and provincialism, was admired by Theodore Roosevelt. His specialty was historical fiction dealing with the winning of the West. He was not as good a writer as Winston Churchill, but like Churchill he gave careful attention to factual accuracy, and was extremely partial toward the rough but generally honorable men who conquered the wilderness.

The Story of the Cowboy is not, as one would think from the title, a novel. It is an historical and social study—a complete documentation, written with sympathy and firsthand knowledge of the subject. It is filled with fascinating details concerning cowboy life—details which would be too banal for the sensational novelist and of no interest to the historian writing about great battles and social forces, but which illuminate for us the realities of frontier life. Every aspect of cowboy life is covered—from the drive and the roundup, to his amusements, culinary likes and dislikes, and superstitions.

Upper Saddle River, N. J.   F. C. S.
May, 1969

EDITOR'S PREFACE.

LIKE everything peculiarly distinctive, the life of the cowboy through its very raciness has lent itself to literary abuse, and the cowboy has been freely pictured by indolent and unscrupulous pens as an embodiment of license and uproarious iniquity. If he were only this, the great business which he has conducted on the plains could never have grown to its imposing proportions. With the cowboy, as with the Indian, it is essential to disabuse ourselves of illusions. Picturesque the cowboy assuredly is, easily superior, so far as effectiveness is concerned, to the *guacho* of South America and, from an Anglo-Saxon point of view, to the bedizened *vaquero* of Mexico. Beyond this picturesqueness of effect and environment very few have cared to go, and therefore Americans have had little actual realization of the vastness of the cowboy's kingdom, the magnitude of the interests in his care, or the fortitude, resolution, and instant readiness essential to his daily life. The American cowboy is the most gallant modern representative of a human industry second to very few in antiquity. I use the present tense, but, like the other typical figures of the country west of the Missouri, the cowboy is already receding into the shadows of past years. The cattle, wild descendants of Andalusian stock, which he.herded in Texas and, later, drove to the North, have been bred to the ways of civilization, with a distinct gain to their comeliness, if not to their agility. The long trails have been blocked, the ranges traversed by barbed wire, and the superb freedom of the unowned plains is exchanged for the bounds and limits of exact ownership.

Such a chapter of American history demands preservation for reasons æsthetic and practical alike, and it is a happy circumstance that the demand is so aptly met in the union of actual knowledge and graphic expression presented in Mr. Hough's Story of the Cowboy. This is not a bare record, not a summary of industrial results, but a living picture of a type often heroic and always invested with an individual interest, and it is a picture also which brings before us the sweep and majesty and splendid atmosphere of the plains.

INTRODUCTION.

In a certain Western city there is the studio of a sculptor whose ambition in life has been to perpetuate the memory of the West. He has sought to put into lasting form the types of that unique and rugged era of our national growth when the soldier and plains-man, the Indian and the cowboy were the citizens of that vast and unknown region. In the following out of that idea he has made in clay and bronze many things entitled to be called curious and beautiful. It is the fancy of this artist at times to take some of these forms and play at pictures with them for the entertainment of his guests. A revolving pedestal is placed in the centre of the room in such way that the light of the fire or of the candles may cast a shadow from it upon the farther wall. Upon the pedestal is placed some figure which appears much magnified upon the white surface beyond, albeit somewhat blurred and softened in its lines. Now it is the likeness of the grizzly bear, now that of the buffalo, while again one sees the lean gray wolf, the tense figure of the flying antelope, or the reaching neck and cut chin of the panther. At one time a mounted Indian may flit upon the wall, or the soldier with sabre and spur. These things, curious and beautiful, form a wild and moving spectacle, coming as they do from a time which may now almost be said to belong to the past.

Upon a certain night this artist had played long
with his pictures, when he picked up another figure, holding it for a moment somewhat lovingly, it
seemed, before he placed it upon the little monument.
" Look! " said he. There upon the wall, of the size of
life, jaunty, erect, was the virile figure of a mounted
man. He stood straight in the stirrups of his heavy
saddle, but lightly and well poised. A coil of rope
hung at his saddlebow. A loose belt swung a revolver low down upon his hip. A wide hat blew up and
back a bit with the air of his travelling, and a deep
kerchief fluttered at his neck. His arm, held lax and
high, offered support to the slack reins so little needed
in his riding. The small and sinewy steed beneath
him was alert and vigorous as he. It was a figure vivid,
keen, remarkable. Those who saw it gave it quick ap-
plause. When it vanished there was silence, for perhaps here were those who thought upon the story that
had been told.

The story of the West is a story of the time of heroes.
Of all those who appear large upon the fading page of
that day, none may claim greater stature than the chief
figure of the cattle range. Cowboy, cattle man, cowpuncher, it matters not what name others have given
him, he has remained—himself. From the half-tropic
to the half-arctic country he has ridden, his type, his
costume, his characteristics practically unchanged, one
of the most dominant and self-sufficient figures in the
history of the land. He never dreamed he was a hero,
therefore perhaps he was one. He would scoff at monument or record, therefore perhaps he deserves them.

Either chiselled or written record may distort if it
merely extol. For this central figure of the cattle days,
this early rider of the range, it is best to hope that he
may not commonly be seen as thrown up on the air in a

mirage, huge, grotesque, fantastic, but that he may rather be viewed clear cut against the Western sky, a glorious silhouette of the open air. Before many years have passed the original of such a picture will have disappeared. We shall listen in vain for the jingle of his spurs, or the creak of his leather gear, or the whipping of his scarf end on the wind. Tinkle and creak even now die away in the distance beyond. An explorer, a surveyor, a guide, a scout, a fighting man, he passed this way. If we study him, we shall study also the day in which he lived, more especially that early day which saw the opening and the climax of that drama of commerce—the cattle industry of the West.

So great an industry could exist only over a vast extent of country. Therefore, although its methods and its followers have had a curious permanency of type, it was foregone that locality should determine a certain variety in its practical customs. Obviously a just estimate of the entire industry or of its leading figure must include alike the dissimilar and the common points of view. This is not easily done, for the vocation of the cattle rancher, once curiously without section, has now become much sectionalized, and has been much modified by agricultural influx—the latter an influence which will produce still greater change in the coming generation, when all the possible farming lands shall have been tapped and tested, and when the farming man shall have begun to look about him and to travel more in a day of cheaper transportation. In the attempt to arrive at an estimate which should be representative and fair, the writer has found his own experience very much aided by that of many rancher friends living or owning property over a wide area of the cattle range. The counsel of these friends has been desirable and valuable in an undertaking such as that

in hand. Especial thanks for critical suggestions are
due Mr. George Bird Grinnell, author of the Story of
the Indian. Mr. Grinnell's experience in the old and
the new West has been a wide one, and his observation has extended to the small as well as the large features of practical ranch life, so that his aid has been
matter of good fortune. The writer concludes his
labour with a sense of the inadequacy of the result,
but feeling none the less that the theme itself is an interesting and worthy one.

E. Hough.

Chicago, Ill., *Dec. 10, 1896.*

CONTENTS.

THE STORY OF THE COWBOY.

CHAPTER I.

THE LONG TRAIL.

It lies like a long rope thrown idly on the ground, abandoned by the hand that used it. Its strands are unbraided and have fallen apart, lying loose and forgotten upon the sandy soil. The wind is blowing dust across these disconnected threads, and the grasses are seeking to cover them, and the waters have in places washed them quite away. The frayed ends are disappearing. Soon the entire cord will have disappeared. The Long Trail of the cattle range will then be but a memory.

The braiding of a hundred minor pathways, the Long Trail lay like a vast rope connecting the cattle country of the South with that of the North. Lying loose or coiling, it ran for more than two thousand miles along the eastern edge of the Rocky Mountains, sometimes close in at their feet, again hundreds of miles away across the hard table-lands or the well-flowered prairies. It traversed in a fair line the vast land of Texas, curled over the Indian Nations, over Kansas, Colorado, Nebraska, Wyoming, and Montana, and bent in wide overlapping circles as far west as Utah and Nevada; as far east as Missouri, Iowa,

1

even Illinois; and as far north as the British possessions. Even to-day you may trace plainly its former course, from its faint beginnings in the lazy land of Mexico, the Ararat of the cattle range. It is distinct across Texas, and multifold still in the Indian lands. Its many intermingling paths still scar the iron surface of the Neutral Strip, and the plows have not buried all the old furrows in the plains of Kansas. Parts of the path still remain visible in the mountain lands of the far North. You may see the ribbons banding the hillsides to-day along the valley of the Stillwater, and along the Yellowstone and toward the source of the Missouri. The hoof marks are beyond the Musselshell, over the Bad Lands and the *coulees* and the flat prairies; and far up into the land of the long cold you may see, even to-day if you like, the shadow of that unparalleled pathway, the Long Trail of the cattle range. History has no other like it.

The Long Trail was surveyed and constructed in a century and a day. Over the Red River of the South, a stream even to-day perhaps known but vaguely in the minds of many inhabitants of the country, there appeared, almost without warning, vast processions of strange horned kine—processions of enormous wealth, owned by kings who paid no tribute, and guarded by men who never knew a master. Whither these were bound, what had conjured them forth, whence they came, were questions in the minds of the majority of the population of the North and East to whom the phenomenon appeared as the product of a day. The answer to these questions lay deep in the laws of civilization, and extended far back into that civilization's history. The Long Trail was finished in a day. It was begun more than a century before that day, and came forward along the very appointed ways of time.

Señor José Montero, let us say, lived long ago, far down in the sunny land of Mexico. The mountains rose up blue beyond the *hacienda*, and before it the valleys lay wide and pleasant. Life here was very calm, alike for the *haciendado* and the barefoot *peons* who made a servile army about him. There was a little grain, there were a few fruits, and there were herds of cattle. Yes, there were the cattle, and there they had always been, longer than José Montero or his father could remember. It might be that they had always been there, though to be sure there was talk of one Cortez. The cattle might have come from another land, at another time. *Quien sabe?* In the splendid savagery of that land and time it made small difference when or whence they came. There they were, these cattle, lean of flank, broad of horn, clean-limbed, muscular, active, fierce, simply wild animals that knew no care save the hand of force. They produced food, and above all they produced hide and leather.

The sons of José Montero moved slowly north in course of years, and edged into the Indian country lying above the Rio Grande. The priests went with them, to teach them the management of *los Indios reducidos.* The horses and the herds of cattle went slowly north with their owners. Thus, far down in the vague Southwest, at some distant time, in some distant portion of old, mysterious Mexico, there fell into line the hoof prints which made the first faint beginnings of the Long Trail, merely the path of a half-nomadic movement along the line of the least resistance.

The descendants of José Montero's sons spread out over the warm country on both sides of the Rio Grande, and they grew and their herds grew. Many years of peace and quiet passed, broken only by such troubles

as were caused by the Indians, with whom the sons of
Montero fared for the most part understandingly. But
one day, more than three quarters of a century ago,
there appeared in that country men of fierce-bearded
faces, many of blue eyes, and all of size and courage.
There was war, long years of bitter, relentless, un-
recorded war, a war of pillage and assassination, of theft
and ambush. The fierce strangers from the North
would not be driven back. They increased, they became more formidable. At times they even crossed the
Rio Grande and drove away herds to their *ranchos*
to the north, these being little less than fortresses or
barricades, their life one of armed but undaunted so-
licitude. In turn the sons of Montero made raids and
sallies, and killed men and captured women, and drove
away herds. The Long Trail began to deepen and
extend. It received then, as it did later, a baptism
of human blood such as no other pathway of the continent has known.

The nomadic and the warlike days passed, and there
ensued a more quiet and pastoral time. The fierce
strangers, perhaps reticent in regard to the methods
by which they had obtained what they liked, now held
that which they chose to call their own. It was the
beginning of a feudalism of the range, a baronry rude
enough, but a glorious one, albeit it began, like all
feudalism, in large-handed theft and generous mur-
dering. The flocks of these strong men, carelessly in-
terlapping, increased and multiplied amazingly. They
were hardly looked upon as wealth. The people could
not eat a tithe of the beef, they could not use a hun-
dredth of the leather. Over hundreds and hundreds
of miles of ownerless grass lands, by the rapid waters of
the mountains, by the slow streams of the plains or the
long and dark lagoons of the low coast country, the

herds of tens grew into droves of hundreds and thousands and hundreds of thousands.

Texas had become a republic and a State before a certain obvious and useful phenomenon in the economics of Nature had been generally recognised. Yet at some time and under some condition of observation it had been discovered that the short gray grass of the northern plains of Texas, which the buffalo loved so well, would rear cattle to a much greater size than those of the coast range. A cow of the hot and low country might not weigh more than five or six hundred pounds, whereas if driven north and allowed to range on the sun-cured short grasses, the buffalo grass, the gramma grass or the mesquite grass, the weight might increase fairly by one third. It was the simplest thing in the world to gain this increased value by driving the cattle from the lower to the upper ranges of the great State—always subject to the consent or to the enterprise of the savage tribes which then occupied that region.

This was really the dawning of the American cattle industry. The Long Trail thus received a gradual but unmistakable extension, always to the north, and along the line of the intermingling of the products of the Spanish and the Anglo-Saxon civilizations. Sometimes these fatter cattle were driven back and sold in Old Mexico, but there was no real market there. The thrust was always to the north. Chips and flakes of the great Southwestern herd began to be seen in the Northern States. As early as 1857 Texas cattle were driven to Illinois. In 1861 Louisiana was tried as an outlet without success. In 1867 a venturous drover took a herd across the Indian Nations, bound for California, and only abandoned the project because the plains Indians were then very bad in the country to the north. In 1869 several herds were driven from Texas to Nevada.

2

These were side trails of the main cattle road. It seemed clear that a great population in the North needed the cheap beef of Texas, and the main question appeared to be one of transportation. No proper means for this offered. At Rockport and one or two other harborless towns on the Texas coast it was sought to establish canneries for the product of the range, but all these projects failed. A rapacious steamship line undertook to build up a carrying trade between Texas and New Orleans or Mobile, but this also failed. The civil war stopped almost all plans to market the range cattle, and the close of that war found the vast grazing lands of Texas covered fairly with millions of cattle which had no actual or determinate value. They were sorted and branded and herded after a fashion, but neither they nor their increase could be converted into anything but more cattle. The cry for a market became imperative.

Meantime the Anglo-Saxon civilization was rolling swiftly toward the upper West. The Indians were being driven from the plains. A solid army was pressing behind the vanguard of soldier, scout, and plainsman. The railroads were pushing out into a new and untracked empire. They carried the market with them. The market halted, much nearer, though still some hundreds of miles to the north of the great herd. The Long Trail tapped no more at the door of Illinois, Missouri, Arkansas, but leaped north again definitely, this time springing across the Red River and up to the railroads, along sharp and well-defined channels deepened in the year of 1866 alone by the hoofs of more than a quarter of a million cattle. In 1871, only five years later, over six hundred thousand cattle crossed the Red River for the Northern markets. Abilene, Newton, Wichita, Ellsworth, Great Bend, " Dodge," flared out into a swift and sometime evil blossoming. The coming of the markets did not make more fortunes than it lost for the Southern cattle owners, for the advent of the long-horned herds was bitterly contested in many sections of the North, but in spite of all a new industry was swiftly and surely established. Thus the men of the North first came to hear of the Long Trail and the men who made it, though really it had begun long ago and had been foreordained to grow.

By this time,1867 and 1868,the northern portions of the region immediately to the east of the Rocky Mountains had been sufficiently cleared of their wild inhabitants to admit a gradual though precarious settlement. It had been learned yet again that the buffalo grass and the sweet waters of the far North would fatten a range broadhorn to a stature far beyond any it could attain on the southern range. The Long Trail pushed rapidly still further to the north, where there still remained " free grass " and a new market. The territorial ranges needed many thousands of cattle for their stocking, and this demand took a large part of the Texas drive which came to Abilene, Great Bend, and Fort Dodge. Moreover, the Government was now feeding thousands of its new red wards, and these Indians needed thousands of beeves for rations, which were driven from the southern range to the upper army posts and reservations. Between this Government demand and that of the territorial stock ranges there was occupation for the men who made the saddle their home. The Long Trail, which long ago had found the black corn lands of Illinois and Missouri, now crowded to the West, until it had reached Utah and Nevada, and penetrated every open park and *mesa* and valley of Colorado, and found all the high plains of Wyoming. Cheyenne and Laramie became common words now,

and drovers spoke as wisely of the dangers of the Platte
as a year before they had mentioned those of the Red
River or the Arkansas. Nor did the Trail pause in its
irresistible push to the north until it had found the last
of the five great transcontinental lines, far in the British
provinces, where in spite of a long season of ice and snow
the uttermost edges of the great herd might survive, in
a certain per cent at least, each year in an almost unassisted struggle for existence, under conditions different
enough, it would seem, from those obtaining at the opposite extreme of the wild roadway over which they came.

The Long Trail of the cattle range was done. By
magic the cattle industry had spread over the entire
West. To-day many men think of that industry as
belonging only to the Southwest, and many would consider that it was transferred to the North. Really it
was not transferred but extended, and the trail of the
old drive marks the line of that extension. To-day the
Long Trail is replaced by other trails, product of the
swift development of the West, and it remains as the
connection, now for the most part historical only, between two phases of an industry which, in spite of differences of climate and condition, retain a similarity in all
essential features. When the last steer of the first herd
was driven into the corral at the Ultima Thule of the
range, it was the pony of the American cowboy which
squatted and wheeled under the spur and burst down
the straggling street of the little frontier town. Before
that time, and since that time, it was and has been
the same pony, the same man, who have travelled the
range, guarding and guiding the wild herds, from the
romantic up to the commonplace days of the West.
The American cowboy and the American cattle industry have been and are one and inseparable. The story
of one is the story of the other.

CHAPTER II.

THE RANCH IN THE SOUTH.

DESCRIPTION of the Western cattle industry, whether in regard to its features, its characters, or its environments, must be largely a matter of generalization.
The cattle country itself covers a third of the entire
territory of the United States. We have sought roughly to divide it into the two sections of the North and
South, but it would trouble one to say where even a
broad and indefinite line should be drawn which should
act as a fair boundary between the two. Should we
place that boundary, loosely speaking, somewhere at the
central or southern line of the State of Kansas, we
shall have established a demarcation at best arbitrary
and in many ways inconclusive and inaccurate. Even
if we presume that this indefinite line be sufficiently
accurate, we shall have left, for our Southern ranch region, a domain many times larger than the entire territory of Great Britain, with a few of her choice provinces
thrown into the bargain.

Over so large a region there must prevail some
divergence of people and things; and in turn we
must remember that all these people and things, more
especially as they pertain to the story of the cattle
man, have in late years been subject to much change.
It would be very natural for any one who had but
a partial acquaintance, or one limited to a few sec-

9

tions of so large a region, to consider as incorrect
any specialized description which did not tally with
his own observation in his own locality. Still more
inaccurate might such an observer consider a description
which covered accurately twenty years ago a section
which he first sees to-day, in the last quarter of the
century. For instance, a citizen of the type our friend
the cowpuncher is wont to term a " pilgrim," might
go to-day to some railroad point in the vast State of
Texas, expecting to find there in full swing the rude
ways of the past. He might expect to see the ranchman an uncouth personage, clad in the border garb once
pictured in lurid literature or still more lurid drama,
his speech full of strange oaths, his home a dugout or a
shanty. Much surprised might this stranger be to dis-
cover his ranchman a comfortable individual, of well-
cut business dress, guiltless of obvious weaponry, and
plain and simple in speech. Still more surprised he
might be to learn that this ranchman does not live
upon his ranch at all, but in the town or city, perhaps
many miles therefrom. The ranchman may have an
office in the bank, and may be chief stockholder in
that institution and other leading concerns of his town.
He may be a member of the Legislature, or sheriff of
his county, or candidate for higher office. His family may have a son in college, a daughter in the art
school of a distant city. The ranch itself, if discovered,
may be simply a vast and partly tilled farm, with white-
painted buildings, with busy tenantry, and much modern machinery in intelligent use. This would be accurate description of a ranch in the South to-day. But
it would be accurate only in particular, not in general,
and it would never satisfy the inquirer who knows
something of what ranch life once was and is to-day in
a wide and wild portion of the Western region.

If we sought to be more general in the outlook for
a ranch fit to be called typically Southern, we should
certainly have much latitude afforded us. Suppose it
to be in the Indian Nations, taking it at that time before the Indians had grown wise in their day and generation, and before the United States Government had
evicted many of those opulent tenants, the cattle men of
the nations. Let us picture our ranch as lying along
some timbered stream, such as the Cimarron, which
flows just above the " black-jack " country of the Cheyennes and Arapahoes. Here the land lies in long swell-
ing rolls and ridges, with hills of short oak scrub, and
wide intervals of prairie. Into the main stream of
the river flow many smaller tributaries, and among
these are some little creeks heading back among the
hills in fresh, unfailing springs, whose waters flow always sweet and abundant throughout the year. Fancy
some such little nook, well up in the hills, a half mile
from the river, and in imagination surround it with
the forest trees which should grow at such a spot. Well
down the hillside, sheltered alike by the hill and by
the forest from the cold winds which come from the
north in winter, stands the ranch house. It is made of
logs, much in the style of the lumberman's log house in
the pine woods, except that the structure is more careless and less finished. The door is made of a single
thickness of unplaned and unmatched boards. It hangs
loose upon its rough wooden hinges, and its lock is a
rude wooden latch the string whereof literally hangs
upon the outside. Wide cracks are open about the
edges of the door and about the windows and between
the logs at the sides and ends of the room—for there
is but one great room in the ranch house proper. Along
the wall of this vast apartment are built sleeping
bunks, similar to those used by the cabin dwellers of

the pine woods. There is little furniture except a rough table or two, and a few stools or broken chairs. The clothing of the men lies under the bunks or hangs on pegs driven in the wall; for trunks, wardrobes, or private places for individual properties are unknown and unnecessary. The saddles, bridles, ropes, and other gear hang on strong pegs in the covered hallway or open-front room which connects the ranch room with the cook house. This connecting room or open hall is also the lounging place of the many dogs and hounds which make part of the live stock of the place. These dogs are used in the constant wolfing operations, and are a necessity on the ranch, but with them a continual feud is waged alike by the cook from whom they steal, and the foreman with whom they continually endeavour to sleep at night—this by reason of an affection much misplaced; for the foreman is a man of stern ideas of life. The cook house is also the dining hall, and here the same rude arrangements prevail as in the main apartment. There is a long pine table, two or three long wooden benches, perhaps a chair or two. There is a good cook stove, and the dishes are serviceable and clean, though not new or expensive. The cook has his bunk in the kitchen, and is left alone in his own domain, being held a man with whom it were not well to trifle.

The country of the Nations has a climate hot in summer, though not extremely cold in winter, except for occasional cold storms of wind and snow. Such a storm is called a " norther " ; by which we may know that we are upon a Southern ranch or one manned by Southern cowmen. In the North the same storm would be a " blizzard." On this range shelter for the cattle is never considered, and they fare well in the timbered hollows even in the roughest weather. Hay is of course

something little known. It is a wild country, and game
is abundant. The nearest railway point is one hundred
miles to the north, let us say, at least at the time of our
visit. The ranchmen do not see civilization more than
once a year. They are lonely and glad of the company
of an occasional deer hunter who may blunder down
into the forbidden Indian lands. All men are welcome
at the ranch, and no questions are asked of them. Every
visitor goes to the table without invitation, and there
all men eat in silence. One has seen at such a meal
a hunter, a neighbouring ranchman bound for his place
fifty miles below, and two suspected horse thieves, bound
for some point not stated. No questions were asked
of any of them. In this region, where news is the
scarcest of commodities, the idea of gossip is unknown.
The habit or the etiquette of the cowboy is not to talk.
He is silent as an Indian. The ranch boss is the most
taciturn of all. The visitor, when he comes to take his
departure, if he is acquainted with the ways and the
etiquette of ranch life, does not think of offering pay,
no matter whether his stay has been for days, weeks, or
months. If he be plainsman and not " pilgrim," no
matter whether he be hunter, ranchman, or horse thief,
he simply mounts, says " So long," and rides away.
The taciturn foreman says " So long," and goes back
to work. The foreman's name may be Jim, never anything more, about the place and among his own men.
On the neighbouring ranges or at the round-up he is
known perhaps as the " foreman on the Bar Y." Some
of the cowboys on the Bar Y may be diagnosed to have
come from Texas or some Southern cattle country.
The foreman may once have lived in Texas. It is not
etiquette to ask him. It is certain that he is a good
cowman.

This may indicate one phase of ranch life south

of our imaginary boundary line. It is, however, not comprehensive, and indeed perhaps not typically Southern. Let us suppose that the traveller has fared far to the south of the Indian Nations into the country along the Gulf coast of Texas. Here he is still on the cattle range, but among surroundings distinctly different from those of the Indian Nations. The hardwood groves have disappeared and their place is taken by " mottes " of live oaks, whose boughs are draped in the dismal gray of the funereal Spanish moss. There is no word now of swamp or brush or timber, but we hear of chaparral and cactus and mesquite. We are at the southern extremity of the great cattle range. Here the cattle even to-day are not so large as those of the North. They run wild through a tangle of thorn and branch and brier. For miles and leagues—for here we shall hear also of " leagues "—the wilderness stretches away, dry, desolate, abominable. Water is here a prize, a luxury. A few scanty streams trickle down to the arms of the salt bays. Across some such small stream the cattle man has thrown a great dam, costing perhaps a small fortune, and built by an engineer not afraid to use masonry, for he knows what the sudden Southern floods may mean. Thus is formed a vast " tank," at which the cattle water, coming from unknown distances to quench a thirst not stayed completely by the cactus leaves whose thorns line their mouths as they do those of the wild deer of the region. These tanks are the abode of vast swarms of wild fowl which come in from the sea. About them crowds all the wild game of the country. In the mud along their trampled banks one sees the footprint of the cougar, of the " leopard cat," of the wild deer, the wild turkey, the wild hogs, and peccaries, all these blending with the tread of the many wading or swimming birds which find

here their daily rendezvous. Sometimes such tanks run
far into the open country back of the "wet prairie,"
as the sea marsh is generally called, and again they may
run close down to the salt bays which make in from the
Gulf. Sometimes this artificial water supply of the
ranch is supplemented by a few natural lagoons of
fresh water, which rarely go entirely dry. These lakes
or lagoons or broken pond holes may run for miles
through the swales in the coast forest—a forest the
most forbidding of any in this whole great country in its
ominous gray desolation of twisted trees covered with
great festoons of that devil's decoration, the Spanish
moss. It is a thirsty land, this of the brooding Southwest, this land of warmth and plenty, where life grows
swiftly and is swiftly cut down. Here the cattle mature
and breed more rapidly than in the North. They range
over many miles of country, many of them forever unknown and uncounted, for the round-up in no part of
the Western range is more trying than in the pathless
thorny chaparral, where the rider can see but a few
yards about him and where no general view is ever
possible. Water is the one needful thing, and water is
the loadstone which draws to view the cattle man's
wealth as nothing else could do; for the cattle must
drink.

They must drink, even though the suns of summer
dry up the water pools till they are but masses of slime
and mud, till they are worse than dry—till they have
become traps and pitfalls more deadly than any that
human ingenuity could devise. Into these treacherous
abysses of bottomless and sticky mud the famished
creatures wade, seeking a touch of water for their
tongues. Weakened already by their long thirst, they
struggle and plunge hopelessly in their attempt to get
back to solid land. The hands of the waterless bogs

hold them down. For a day the creature holds its
head clear of the mud. Then its head sinks down.
Lucky is it if there be water enough to make the mud
soft, so that it soon covers the nostrils and cuts off
the toiling breath. Above these traps of death clouds of
buzzards are always soaring. Others drape the dismal
live oaks in lines of sombre black, blending fitly with
the sombre gray of the hanging moss. Along the banks
of such dried water holes there are always lying hundreds of skeletons. The loss of life is unknown and
uncounted. Horses, cows, calves, all the animals of the
range perish here yearly in unestimated numbers. The
loss of wealth is frightful in the aggregate, yet it is one
of the ways of the cattle trade never to regard it and
to take no means of preventing it. Indeed, nothing can
be done to prevent it. It is the way of Nature. The
rancher of the southern range will say to you that you
shall have as your own property every horse you shall
pull out of the mud, every horned head that you shall
save from death in the depth of the waterless bogs. But
though you take pony and rope and drag out helpless
victim after victim, what then shall you do? They
die upon the banks because they can not travel to other
water, if indeed there be any other water within many
miles. The tragedy goes on year after year, to what
extent no one knows. The rancher comes to be entirely careless of it. The business of cattle ranching is
primarily but a rude overlapping of the ways of Nature,
and to Nature's care and protection are left the creatures
whose lives are only partially taken in charge by their
human owners.

These untrodden wildernesses of the coast range
are now, strange to say, threaded by long lines of wire
fence. A " pasture " is an inclosed tract of land perhaps forty or fifty miles square. In the long wire

boundary fence there may not be a gate for twenty miles. The hunter who is lost there feels fortunate if he finds one of these long fences. Yet many a hunter, and many a new man on the range has found such a fence and followed it until he fell, mad with a thirst which he found no way of appeasing. The gray oaks and the evil cacti and the curled mesquite smile bitterly to-day over many such unfound wanderers. The native cowboys and range men know where the trail goes, where the gates are, where the ranch house is—far back, let us suppose, on the high prairie, where the windmills furnish sweet water in an unfailing supply. This house may be built of boards, simply and modestly, and it possibly is left unpainted. The house itself is a long and low one, with but a single story, and constructed with a wide hall extending through, so that the wind may blow in with what coolness it can claim in the torrid summer days. The rooms are large and airy, and the furniture is comfortable. There are green trees about this house, cottonwoods that have grown up tall and thin at the edge of the slender streams of water wasted from the windmill, and some audacious hand has actually planted flowers about a small plat of precious green. Apart from the house of the owner, which is at times occupied by himself and family, there is another and larger building of ruder furnishing. Here we find an interior not widely different from that of the ranch in the Indian Nations. We may find here, too, perhaps, a foreman whose only name is Jim. He has been foreman on the Star D for many years.

This country of the Texas coast is very hot, except in winter when the " northers " come, which chill the blood so strangely and which often kill hundreds of the weaker cattle with their mysterious, penetrating cold. Snow is never known here, and of winter as it is understood in the North there is practically none. The rainfall during the summer is extremely scant. All about the ranch house, miles and miles, as far as the eye can reach, the surface of the earth is gray and cheerless, with few trees inside the range of the low coast timber or chaparral. The hot sun in summer sets all the surface of the earth a-tremble, so that it moves and heaves and writhes. On the horizon float the strange pictures of the mirage. All men know there is no water where the mirage beckons. The water, rare, small, precious, is here, a jewel in this circle of green, this oasis in the apparent desert of the range.

Such is another ranch of the South. But with description so partial and imperfect we shall not even yet have covered our text sufficiently well to entitle us to leave it. We shall have left untouched and unindicated a vast territory of the Southern range where the cattle industry flourished for generations before it was dreamed of in the North. Suppose we move yet some hundreds of miles into the far Southwest, coming to that long arm of Spanish civilization which projects up from Mexico into the United States, last and lax hold upon a region which once bore the flag of Spain. Here, if anywhere to-day upon the cattle range, the ways of the past prevail, and here we shall find an environment as odd and picturesque as any. The Pecos and the Rio Grande rivers bound a vast and ill-known region, which has mountains and plains untraversed by the foot of the American tourist. Here we shall find villages unmarked on any map. We shall find men who in all their lives have never seen a railroad train nor heard the sound of the church-going bell. Life here, beyond that of any section of the United States, is ancient, simple, unprogressive, and truly pastoral in its features. In this far-away corner of the land the ways of modern life are slow to penetrate. The impact of Anglo-Saxon civilization is taken up by the *vis inertiæ* of the old Spanish ways. The vigorous Northerner becomes in a few years a slow-spoken and deliberate New Mexican. The cloudless blue sky, the soft warm air, the unvarying equanimity of Nature will have none of haste or worry. The country makes all men its own. It softens and blends and harmonizes all things and all men into its own indifferent calm.

The tone of our landscape here is not light, but deep in tint, a rich red brown which shades off into the plains and back into the darker colours of the mountains. You would call absolutely barren these wide tracts of land which lie shimmering and throbbing in the unscreened sun. The soil appears to be worthless sand or coarse baked earth. As you look out over such a country you can not believe it possible that it would support any animate life, unless it were this lizard upon the rock, or this hideous horned toad which crawls away from under foot, or these noisy prairie dogs which yelp here as they do upon the northern range. Yet this soil carries the rich gramma grass, whose little scattered tufts, not so large or so gray as those of the buffalo grass, cure and curl down upon the ground and form a range food of wondrous fattening quality.

We are in a mountain country here. The table-lands on which the cattle graze are more than four thousand feet above the level of the sea. The smaller table-lands or *mesas* are still more lofty. The foothills run up above six thousand feet, and back of these are mountains, sometimes low and brown, sometimes black with the heavy growth of piñons, sometimes high enough to have white tops for many months in winter. Snow never falls at this latitude over the lower valleys and *mesas*. Hay is rarely seen, except as imported in

bales. The native Mexican sometimes makes a faint
effort to cut a little hay, but does his mowing with a
clumsy hoe. His grainfields are but little patches, and
the reaping is done altogether with a sickle. In every
way this is an ancient and pastoral land.

We are far down in the lower end of the great Rocky
range, and at a point where little detached ranges and
spurs run out from the main chain and make small
mountain systems, each with a Spanish name of its own.
We hear of the San Miguels, the Oscuras, the Sacra-
mentos, the Magdalenas, the Capitans, the Nogales, the
Bonitos, the Blancos, the Patos, the Carrizos. Out of
each of these little subranges runs some one or more
mountain streams, each stream called a *rio*, or river,
no matter how small it may be. This high table-land
is a waterless country. It may be that only one or two
scant water holes are known in a space of a hundred or
two hundred miles. A tiny well is a treasure. A *rio* is
a fortune. In this region of rainless skies water is the
one priceless thing.

The small river tumbles swiftly down out of the
mountains, as any mountain stream, and it bears the
mountain trout as do the waters of the upper ranges;
yet after it has emerged from the mountains and passed
through the foothills its course is very brief. In a few
miles, perhaps twenty, forty, or fifty miles, it sinks and
is lost forever in the sands of the plains. Many miles
beyond there may be another river arising from the
sand and struggling on a little way in the attempt to
reach the Pecos or the Rio Grande. Without doubt
these waters are connected with the great sheet of water
which underlies all that region, and which will sometime be brought up by man to make this desert blossom.
What there may be beneath the surface of the earth,
however, does not concern our Mexican *ranchero*. It

is enough for him that his father and his father's father
held the land and owned the cattle. Bills of sale recording the curious old Spanish brands have been in his
family for a long time.

This is an old cattle country. Countless *rodeos* have
crossed these hills. Innumerable branding irons have
been heated in the piñon fires of these corrals. None
the less, this is in America, and hither the American cattle man was sure to come, in search of opportunity to
follow the calling which offered to him so much of
wealth and so much of fascination. His money or his
methods were sure to make him a place even in so old
and well-covered a country.

Let us suppose that we have come upon some such
modern ranch, down in this ancient part of the cattle
range. Back of the home ranch house there is a mountain range, which seems to be only a few miles away,
but which is really more than fifty miles distant. It
may be that the presence of the mountains has something to do with the water supply of the ranch. There
are known to be several springs up in the mountains,
and indeed the ranch owner has also purchased these,
and has erected near them log houses from the timber
of the mountains near at hand, each house being
the home of its own party of the range riders. Between
the foot of these mountains and the "home ranch" there
is no stream of water nor any sign of one, nothing but
a dreary expanse of brown and gray desolation. Yet
here, by the ranch house, protected by a heavy fence
from the intrusion of the animals, there bursts up out
of the ground a strong spring of fresh water, strongly
alkaline to be sure, but exceedingly valuable. This
spring is the *raison d'être* of the ranch house at this
point, out on the wide plain, and far from the shelter
of the arms of the mountain.

3

The waters of the great spring, carefully led and utilized, form at a distance of a mile or so from the house a shallow expanse or pool to which the cattle, over a range of probably twenty-five or thirty miles, come regularly to drink. The range near the water is much eaten down, so the animals go far out upon the plains to feed. They do not come to water every day, perhaps sometimes not even so often as once in every other day. An idler at the water pool, lying in wait for the antelope which often come in to water with the cattle, may see far away upon the horizon, toward the middle of the day, long trails and columns of dust, which grow more distinct as the moments pass, until they are seen to be caused by the hurrying squads of cattle coming in to water. They depart as they came, upon a rapid gallop, and their habit is one of the most singular things of the cattle range. Northern farm cattle would perish here, but these are animals seasoned for generations to this environment.

The ranch house here is an edifice entirely distinct in type, the adobe, typical dwelling of the Spanish Southwest. Never was human habitation more nicely adapted than this to the necessities of the country which produced it. No heat can penetrate these walls, more than three feet thick, of the sun-dried native brick or " 'dobe." The building is exactly the color of the surrounding earth, and stands square and flat topped, like a great box thrown upon the ground. The roof, which has but the slightest slant from ridge to eaves, is made of heavy beams which hold up a covering, two or three feet in thickness, of hard, dry earth. This roof serves to turn the rain during the short rainy season of midsummer, and moreover it stops the vivid rays of the half-tropic sun. Within the 'dobe it is always cool,

for it is a peculiarity of this climate that the heat is felt
only when one is exposed directly to the sun.

The interior of this ranch house is rather attractive,
with its walls whitewashed with gypsum, its deep window embrasures, and its hard dirt floor swept clean, as
though it were made of wood. A former owner, let us
say a wild young man whose family wished him to settle
down, but who could not long remain settled at anything, once sought to beautify this place. He put lace
curtains at the windows, and at great expense brought
out a piano from the railroad, one hundred and fifty
miles away. He even essayed rugs and pictures. Other
times have brought other customs. The present owner
cares more for his water front than for his curtains.
The cowboys are welcome to come into this house.
They throw their saddles down upon the bed or into
the bath tub which once the former owner cherished.
They go to sleep under the piano. One has seen their
spurs, as they slept, tangled in the lace curtains of the
windows. There is no one to order otherwise or to care
otherwise. Lace curtains have little to do with raising
cattle. There is no woman about the place. Nearly a
dozen men live here. The head of the domestic economy is the cook, a German who was once a sailor. The
responsible man of the outfit is the foreman, whose name
is Jim, and who may have come from Texas. One does
not know his other name. Jim is dark-haired, broad-
shouldered, taciturn, direct of gaze.

A second building, also of adobe, stands at a little
distance from the main ranch house, and this serves
as general quarters for the men as well as for kitch-
en and dining hall. The structure, oddly enough,
follows very closely the plan of the ranch house seen
in the Indian Nations. There are really two buildings,
connected by a covered way or open-air hall, which is

open in front, and which serves as saddle room and storage place for odds and ends. The beds are merely bunks where the men unroll their blankets. In this country no man travels without taking his blankets with him. The furniture of the kitchen is simple, the dishes mostly of tin or ironstone china. The cook, who was a sailor, never learned to cook. To suit the local taste he makes feeble efforts at the peppery Spanish methods. Butter and milk are, of course, unknown on this ranch, as they are on all the ranches of the genuine cattle range, although thousands of cows are all about. There is no historical record of any such event as a cowboy being asked to milk a cow, nor is it likely that anything so improbable ever happened, for had it occurred, the cowboy must surely have evidenced his feelings over such a request in a manner interesting enough to be preserved among the traditions of the range.

At table each man takes off his " gun," this being one of the little courtesies of the land, but no one removes his hat of deliberate intention. It is polite for a stranger arriving at the ranch to leave his belt and revolver hanging on the pommel of his saddle, or to lay them aside upon entering the house. This is delicate proof that he is not "looking for any one." The country at the time of which we write is wild and lawless, and human life is very cheap. Each cowpuncher rides on his daily work with a Winchester in the holster under his leg, and carries at his hip the inevitable .45 revolver. The latter he may use for a chance shot at an antelope or deer, a coyote or a wolf, and it is handy for the killing of an occasional rattlesnake—whose presence, curled up under the shade of a Spanish bayonet plant, the cow pony is sure to detect and indicate by jumps and snorts of the most intense dislike. In the hands of the cowpuncher the revolver is a practical weapon. One recalls that one evening a cowboy came into camp with the tails of four " crogers " (cougar— the mountain lion) which he said he had met in a body at a little piece of chaparral. He seemed to think he had done nothing extraordinary in killing these animals with his revolver. At times the foreman, Jim, has been known to bring home an antelope which he has killed with his " six-shooter," but this is a feat rarely performed, and only to be attempted successfully by a master of the weapon.

Each home ranch has a corral, and the corral of the Circle Arrow outfit is worthy of our consideration. It is constructed of the most picturesquely crooked cedar logs, and there is not a nail in its whole composition. It is lashed together with rawhide at each joint or fastening, the hide being put on wet, and drying afterward into a rigid and steellike binding, which nothing less than a cataclysm could shake loose or tear apart. We are here upon the Spanish-American cattle range, and since time immemorial rawhide has been the natural material of the Mexican.

Most of the cowboys employed on the Circle Arrow outfit are Mexicans, or " Greasers," as all Mexicans are called by the American inhabitants. Their high-peaked hats, tight trousers and red sashes make them picturesque objects. These men do not speak any English, being popularly supposed to be too lazy to learn it. The speech of the American cowpunchers, on the other hand, is nearly as much Mexican as English, and in common conversation many Spanish words are met, permanently engrafted upon the local tongue and used in preference to their English equivalents. For instance, one rarely hears the word " yes," it being usually given as the Spanish " *si*." The

small numerals, one, two, etc., are usually spoken in
Spanish, as *uno, dos*, etc. A horse is nearly always
called *caballo*, a man an *hombre*, a woman a " *moharrie* "
(*mujer*). Even cattle are sometimes called *vacas*,
though this is not usual. The cow man of any range
clings closely to the designation " cows " for all the
horned creatures in his possession. Every one says
agua when meaning " water." The Spanish diminu-
tives are in common use in the English speech of this
region, as *chico, chiquito*. The cowboy will speak of the
"cavvieyah" or "cavvieyard" (*caballado*) instead of the
" horse herd." One hears *poco tiempo* instead of " pretty soon "; and this expression as coming from a native
he will learn all too well, as also the expression *mañana*
(to-morrow), which really means " maybe sometime,
but probably never."

There are many common descriptive words used
in the ranch work which would be strange to the
Northern rancher, such as *rincon, salado, rio, mesa*,
etc.; and many of the proper names would seem unusual, as applied to the Mexican cow hands, slim, dark,
silent fellows, each with a very large hat and a very
small cigarette, who answer as José, Juan, Pablo, San-
chez, or Antone, and who when they are uncertain answer, as do all their American fellows, with the all-
convenient reply, " *Quien sabe!* " (" kin savvy," as the
cowpuncher says).

The Northern ranch country got most of its customs, with its cattle, from the Spanish-American cattle
country, and the latter has stamped upon the industry
not only its methods but some of its speech. The cowboy's " chaps " are the *chaparéjos* of the Spaniard, who
invented them. Such words as *latigo, aparéjo, broncho*
are current all through the Northern mountain and
plains region, and are firmly fixed in the vocabulary of

the cow country of the entire West. Indeed, widely sundered as they are in geographical respects, it is but an easy and natural subsequent step, in manners, speech, and customs, from the ranch of the South to its close neighbour, the ranch of the North.

CHAPTER III.

THE RANCH IN THE NORTH.

IT was in the North that there was first established what one would think an obvious principle, though it was one which the Texas rancher was slow to recognise— namely, that a fatted animal is worth more in the market than a lean one. On the range of the Southwest a cow was a cow, a " beef "—any animal over four years of age—was a beef, no matter what the individual differences. Far into the days of the cattle trade all Texas cattle were sold by the head and not by weight. The Northern rancher was the one to end this practice. He did not drive to market the sweepings of his range. Moreover, he saw that the beef-producing qualities of the old long-horned Texas breed could be much improved by the admixture of more approved blood. The cattle of England met the cattle of Spain, to the ultimate overcoming of the Southern type. In less than five years after the first Texas cattle came upon the territorial ranges, the latter were sending better cattle to Texas, over the very trail that had brought the first stock from the lower range. To-day the centre of the beef cattle trade is on the Northern range, and it is some portion of that range which the average Northern man has in mind when he speaks of the " cattle country."

Yet it is a vast country, this Northern cattle range.

28

The edge of the Dakota grass lands would make a little
state. The basin of the Big Horn alone is as large as
any two New England States. There are mountain
parks in Colorado which would hold a principality,
and the plains of Wyoming are wider than are many
European kingdoms. The ranch in the North may
be a dugout, well to the east in cold Dakota, where some
hardy soul has determined to try the experiment of
bringing at least a portion of his cattle through the
bitter winter. It may be a cabin in the wild region
of the Bad Lands, that Titanic playground of creative
evil spirits, where the red scoria buttes and banks, peak
after peak, and minaret and tower and high cathedral,
all in parti-coloured clays, are burned out of the earth to
endure and mock the dreams of man the architect. The
ranch may be a hut in some high mountain valley,
where the bold summits of the white-topped mountains sweep about in the wild beauty of the Snowy
Range. Again, it may be a sod house, built on some
wide bleak plain, where the wind never is still, and
where the white alkali cuts and sears the unseasoned
skin. It is somewhere upon that vast, high, hard, and
untilled table-land which runs from the Gulf coast to
the British possessions, upon the eastern slope of the
Rocky Mountains.

This is a land of little rain and of infrequent
water courses, but a land where cattle can live the
year through without the aid of man, summer and
winter, upon the short gray grass which grows in
abundance all over the former range of the buffalo.
This upper portion of the great plateau is dry enough
to be classified as belonging to the arid lands, but is
nevertheless watered much better than the southern
range. The streams are larger and more frequent, and
are not so apt to go entirely dry in the droughty season

of summer. The snows are heavier in winter, and the rainfall of the spring months is relatively more abundant, so that the grasses are much better nourished and are not burned out so cruelly as in the South. Under such conditions the cattle of the plains were found to grow far more bulky than in the Southern country. Moreover, the upper part of what is now the northern range was still open and unsettled at a time when a great body of population was pressing up to the edge of these plains, looking for new country and new grazing grounds, and only waiting for the Army to clear away the hostile Indians sufficiently to make the region safe for occupancy. Indeed, long before the Indians had been removed, and before the range was anything better than a dangerous Indian hunting ground, the adventurous ranchmen had been all over it, and were living there, scattered about here and there, and already engaged in the early and cruder stages of their calling.

After the years of 1868 and 1869 the Northern country was occupied, as if by magic, by the herds of the enterprising ranchers who saw the rapid wealth that was to be accumulated under the conditions of the trade in a new and favourable region. Cattle bought at a few dollars per head, delivered on the range free of freight charge, raised " on air," and free air at that, attended by a few men to many hundred head of cattle, and sold in a few years at prices four or five times the first cost per head—surely it was no wonder that at once an enormous industry sprang up, one that attracted the interest of conservative capital in this country, and invited floods of capital not so wise from other lands. Enthusiastic at the prospect of early wealth, and enamoured of the manly and independent life that offered, very many young men of the Eastern States, some with money and financial resources, some

with only hope and a branding iron, plunged into the
cattle business of the upper ranges. Many of these
made money, and all of them brought energy and a
certain amount of new intelligence to their chosen calling. The Southern rancher perhaps grew up in the
trade, knowing no other, whereas sometimes the Northern rancher was a new man, who learned the business
later in life. None the less the cattle industry received a tremendous impetus in a very brief time, old
men and new studying the requirements of the new
countries opened, and uniting in perfecting the operations of the range in every possible respect of system
and detail.

Already there was upon the range an instructor, a
guide, and a practical leader, waiting to take charge of
every phase of the cattle business. The cowpuncher
appeared upon the Northern plains as rapidly and mys-
teriously as the thousands of cattle. It were bootless
to ask whence he came. From the earlier Southern
regions originally, no doubt, but not in all his numbers. He drifted in upon these upper ranges from
every corner of the globe. There was always upon the
Western frontier a press of hardy young men, born and
inured to the rude conditions of the life beyond the
line of the towns, and the natural fitness and natural
longings of these led them readily into the free outdoor life of this peculiar calling. Some would-be ranch
owners, failing in their undertakings, settled back into
the occupation of the cowboy. Wild and hardy young
men from other countries came in, attracted by the
loadstone of freedom and adventure, ever potent upon
hot-headed youth.

The range riders had odd timber among them,
men rude and unlettered, and men of culture and
ability. Quite a noticeable feature of the new cattle

country was the influx of young men of good family who became infatuated with the cowboy's life and followed it for a time, perhaps never to forsake the plains again. In the late '70's and early '80's one might often see strange company in the great cattle yards at Kansas City, where the train loads of Western cattle came in charge of the men who had had them in care upon the range. Among groups of these men, often rough looking and roughly clad, and sitting sometimes on the ground in the shade of the cattle cars, one might perhaps hear in progress a conversation which he would rather have expected to hear in an Eastern drawing room. It was no unusual thing to see men clad in regulation cowpuncher garb reading a copy of the latest monthly magazine or a volume of the classics. This may have been reversion to early habit, and such men may or may not have remained in the calling.

Certainly the man aspiring to the title of cowboy needed to have stern stuff in him. He must be equal to the level of the rude conditions of the life, or he was soon forced out of the society of the craft. In one way or another the ranks of the cowpunchers were filled. Yet the type remained singularly fixed. The young man from Iowa or New York or Virginia who went on the range to learn the business, taught the hardy men who made his predecessors there very little of the ways of Iowa or New York or Virginia. It was he who experienced change. It was as though the model of the cowboy had been cast in bronze, in a heroic mould, to which all aspirants were compelled to conform in line and detail. The environment had produced its type. The cowboy had been born. America had gained another citizen, history another character. It was not for the type to change, but for others to conform to it.

He who sought to ride by the side of this new man, this American cowboy, needed to have courage and constitution, a heart and a stomach not easily daunted, and a love for the hard ground and the open sky. There were many who were fit so to ride. Of these the range asked no questions. If there had been trouble back in the " States," trouble with a man, a sweetheart, or a creditor, it was all one, for oblivion was the portion offered by the hard ground and the sky. Let us not ask whence the cowboy came, for that is a question immaterial and impossible of answer. Be sure, he came from among those who had strong within them that savagery and love of freedom which springs so swiftly into life among strong natures when offered a brief exemption from the slavery of civilization. The range claimed and held its own. The days of the range were the last ones of American free life. They preceded the time of commerical life, that stage of civilization when all men must settle down to wear, patiently or impatiently, the yoke that is imposed by the artificial compact of society.

It is probable, then, that we should see small difference between Jim, the foreman of the T Bar ranch in Wyoming or Montana, and the Jim who was foreman of the Bar Y, or of the Star D, or of the Circle Arrow in the Southwest country. It is still uncertain where Jim lived before he came on the ranch, and it is still immaterial, for it is certain that he is a good cowman.

In appearance Jim is a man of medium height, with good shoulders, none too square, but broad enough. He is thin in flank, lean and muscular, with the firm flesh of the man not only in perfect physical health but in perfect physical training. Life in the saddle, with long hours of exercise and a diet of plain food, has left not an ounce of fat to prevent the free play of the firm

muscles one above the other. His skin is darkened
and toughened by the wind and sun and alkali. His
hair is not worn long, as persons of a certain class
would have us believe was the correct thing for scout
or Westerner in the "old times." Jim's hair is hid
under his big hat, but very likely hangs in a rough mop
down from under his hat and upon his forehead, like the
forelock of a pony.

Jim's eye may be of the red hazel of the ready
fighter, or the gray of the cold-nerved man, or the
blue of the man who is always somewhere about
when there is fun or trouble afloat in whatever corner of the world. It is hard to see Jim's eyes, because
the bright sun causes him to hold them well covered
with the lids, with a half squint to them. His mustache may have been tawny or brown or nearly black
at first, but now it is sunburned and bleached to a
yellow, faded hue. Upon his feet Jim makes a very
poor figure. He is slouchy, awkward, and shambling
in his gait, for his feet, in the vernacular of the range,
do not "track," but cross each other weakly. His
legs are bowed, with the curve which constant horseback riding in early youth always gives. His toes turn
in distinctly as he walks. He does not stand erect,
but stoops. But in the saddle he sits erect, and every
action shows strength, every movement the grace of
muscles doing their work with unconscious ease
and sureness. The world can produce no horseman
more masterly. With the "rope" he can catch the
running steer by whichever foot you shall name. He
can "roll a gun" with either hand, or with both hands
at once. He has a perfect knowledge of the nature
of the steer, and knows the trade to the last detail. He
has all the hardihood and courage which come of long
familiarity with trouble, hardship, and peril; for what

is called courage is very much a matter of association and habit.

With his employer Jim is as honest and faithful as any man that ever breathed. In his conversation he is picturesque and upon occasion volcanic of speech. In his ways of thought he is simple, in his correspondence brief. It was perhaps this same Jim, foreman of the T Bar, who wrote to the Eastern ranch owner the quarterly report which constituted for him the most serious labour of the year, and which is said to have read as follows:

" Deer sur, we have brand 800 caves this roundup we have made sum hay potatoes is a fare crop. That Inglishman yu lef in charge at the other camp got to fresh an we had to kill the son of a ——. Nothing much has hapened sence yu lef. Yurs truely, Jim."

It was possibly Jim, the foreman, who licked the young cub whom everybody called " Kid " into the shape of a cowboy, and it may have been he who taught the wealthy cattle owner something of the essentials of the business as they have come down in the traditions of the range. Grim, taciturn, hard-working, faithful, it was this cowboy of the range who made the mainstay of the entire cattle industry. Without him there could never have been any cattle industry. He was its central figure and its reliance, at the same time that he was its creature and its product.

If it make small difference who the cow puncher was or whence he came, it will make little difference, either, at what exact portion of the vast empire of the Northern cattle range there was located the home ranch of the T Bar outfit. It might have been at any point within a circle of five hundred miles, and still have had the same general characteristics. Let us suppose the ranch building to be located upon the upper portion of some one of the great rivers of the Yellowstone system, in that region so long the range of the buffalo and the home of the red ranchers who never branded their cattle. This river debouches from the great and snowy mountains which are plainly visible beyond the foothills of the chain. The soil of the river valley, the detritus of ages carried down and spread out by the waters, is deep and rich. The river, subject as are all the streams of the region to sudden freshets or to seasons of low water, is well fed and regulated in its upper waters by the deep snows which each season fall upon the mountains and which hardly melt entirely away throughout the year. Into this larger stream flow other streams at intervals, these heading back into the high grounds of the plains. Along the stream in this upper valley the red willows grow densely. They form a heavy bank of shelter at the arm of the river where the ranch house is built. Below this point the valley spreads out into a wide natural meadow, and here the water has been led out in an irrigating ditch, so that a considerable extent of hay land has been established. All that this soil needs is water to make it fruitful as any in the world. The ranch owner has realized this, and at times a tiny, scraggy garden gives rich reward for all the care bestowed upon it, though here, as all over the cow country, the tin can is the main dooryard decoration. Wheat, oats, and corn could be raised here also, but the ranch man hopes that fact will be long in its discovery by others. His own concern is the raising of cattle.

Over all the high plains back from the river valley the sage brush and the bunch grass grow, as they do all over the " arid belt," and give no promise of the vegetation that needs water at its roots. Not far from the ranch there may be small green valleys, six or seven thousand feet above sea level, each with ten or twenty miles of grazing ground, where the grass grows tall and green as it does in the " States " ; but contrary to what the tenderfoot would expect, the cattle do not crowd in to feed upon this luxuriant and fresh-looking grass, but range far out upon the desolate bunch grass country where, to the eye of the novice, there is no food at all for them. The big flies go with the tall grass, and in these green valleys neither cow, horse, nor human being can endure their vicious and continuous assaults. The green grass is forsaken utterly. Early teamsters who crossed the plains, freighting to Denver in the days before the railroads, often struck such valleys where the greenhead flies made life for their horses or oxen almost unbearable. The valley of the Rawhide, in Nebraska, was such a spot. Here the flies were so bad that the horses had to be kept in darkened barns all day, and at night the mosquitoes swarmed upon the unprotected horses of the freighters in such numbers that the poor groaning creatures could not rest and were driven nearly frantic.

Below our ranch house the river marches on, broadening out and flowing more and more gently, until it in turn passes into some other affluent of the Yellowstone-Missouri system. At the point where the ranch house is located, or a little way above it, the waters have not yet lost the colour they bore in the mountains, a bright, bluish green. There are fine mountain trout within a day's journey that the cook sometimes catches when he is not too lazy to go out after them. But soon after leaving this elevation, and reaching the red soil of the lower plains, the river becomes tinged and discoloured, then red, roily, perhaps full of quick-

4

sands, and no longer beautiful to behold. Here the cottonwoods, those worthless yet indispensable trees of the plains, troop in along the water and spread out their brittle, crooked arms. They give a little shade, and serve for a sort of fuel. In the old freighting days the teamster of the plains always carried an extra axle and a spare wheel or two against accident on his long journeys, but it is related of one improvident wagoner that he at one time found himself with a broken axletree and no timber near except some cottonwoods. He tried a half dozen times to make an axle of the ill-grained soft wood, but finally gave it up, and history states that he finally turned out his team there, and stopped and located a farm, because he could not get away from the country.

In times past these cottonwoods along our river served another purpose. Here, in a sheltered valley, where the willows make a wide thicket extending back over the bottoms for half a mile or more, there are cottonwoods which bear strange burdens, long and shapeless bundles, wrapped in hides or rags. It is the burial place of the red men, with whom the cowpuncher is at war. For these rude graveyards the irreverent cowpuncher has no respect. He tears down the bundles and kicks them apart, hunting for beads and finger bones. Around the cow camp there is knocking about the skull of an Indian, a round hole in the temple. This came from the sandhills, where it had never been accorded even so rude a burial as the one described. Once the Cheyennes swooped down and the cowmen met them. Thirteen of the Cheyennes did not go back when the war party retreated to the villages to tell their people of the new fighting men who had come into the country.

The T Bar cattle roam over a million acres or so

of land, of which the rancher perhaps owns one hundred and sixty acres. Of course, at this date, no attempt is made at fencing the range, though a few rough stops of logs or trees may keep the cattle back from some creek valleys or cañons where it is not desired that they should go. It is still "free grass" on the range. The cattle are held on a certain part of the country, and prevented from drifting off to the range of another outfit by "outriding." Each day the cowpunchers "ride sign" around the edge of the agreed territory, turning back or looking up any cattle that seem to be wandering from their proper range. At points some miles away from the home ranch, perhaps fifteen or twenty miles or more, there are other and less pretentious quarters built for the outriders. For instance, Red, one of the hands, starts out in the morning and rides the eastern edge of the range to the Willow Spring cabin, where he meets Curly, who came down from above on the same side. They stop together over night at the cabin, if they are near it when dark comes, and in the morning separate and return the way they came. Or perhaps both may live at this camp most of the time. The range riders are continual sentinels and pickets, besides being courier, fighting force, and commander, each for himself.

Our ranch house stands upon a sightly spot, here in the bend of the blue river. This was a favourite camping place for hunters and trappers in the days before the beaver were gone. The old camps are gone now, and in their place stands the long and substantial cabin which makes the home ranch house. This is a building better than those seen on the southern range, for here the climate, though very hot in summer, is exceedingly cold in winter, and more care needs to be taken with the habitation. The house is built of logs, the logs perhaps hewn and squared. The roof is made of logs, boughs, hay, and dirt, or if very modern it may be covered with riven "shakes" or shingles, with perhaps an attempt made at a rude porch or veranda, this taking the place in some extent of the midway hall of other ranches we have seen. The doors and windows are well fitted, for the intense cold of winter will tap sharply every open joint. There is a huge fireplace, and moreover a big "cannon" stove. Rough bunks line the walls, as in the general scheme of the Western ranch house, and on these are beds of heavy blankets, underlaid with robes and skins. The matchless robe of the buffalo at one time played an important part in Northern ranch economy. Upon the floors are the skins of elk and deer, of the mountain lion, and of the bear. The ranchman is almost of necessity a hunter, and this range lies in the heart of one of the great game regions of the land. Upon the walls of the room there hang upon long wooden pegs some of the less used saddles, bridles, "chaps," ropes, and other gear of the men. The cow puncher may throw his hat upon the floor, but is very apt to hang up his spur. Or he may come in tired from a long ride, and rolling himself up in his blankets in the cocoon style of the Westerner, fall asleep with his clothes on, boots, spurs, and all. His life is one of camps and marches. Of a regular home life or settled habits he knows nothing. Civilization is still far off. He sees the railroad perhaps twice a year. Then he sleeps upon a mattress and has a "reg'lar goose-har piller," of which he tells his companions when he comes back to the ranch. He sleeps as well as he eats or rides. The fresh air of the mountains has blown every *malaise* from his system. He rises in the morning with his "fists full of strength," exulting in the sheer animal vigour of perfect health, the greatest blessing that can come to any man. The cowpuncher is a survival.

The harsh Northern country, stern as it is and unfriendly of aspect, is none the less in some of its phases kindly and beautiful. In the spring the wind blows soft, and many small flowers come out from under the snow. The willow buds swell and burst. The trout run, and the hordes of grouse in the willow thickets break up their packs and spread out over the country. The wild geese cross northward, bound still farther on toward the land of cold. Small birds twitter and flit about the ranch house, and little squirrels come, and the mountain rats appear from their nests. The wind blows steadily, but its bravado is understood and not dreaded. The spring floods of snow water boil down all the water ways, and presently the spring rains come and drench out all the frosts that lie in the ground. Then the prairies show a carpet of flowers dotting in their brief beauty the strips of green so soon to lose their colour. Deeper dashes of green spread out along the wet grounds bordering the smaller streams. The sagebrush blossoms and the trees of the little parks put out new buds and begin again the cycle of unfailing hope. Yet spring is not greeted here as a seedtime. No ploughs cut the soil of these iron plains. No wagon wheel marks the hard surface for the notice of the range rider going upon his long rounds. No figures of men setting forth to fields, of horses labouring at drill or harrow, meet his gaze fixed upon the far horizon. Just seen upon some distant ridge there may be the outline of a figure, but if so, it is that of another rider like himself, and bound upon a similar errand. Or it may be the shape of an Indian rider, perhaps several of them, off their reservation with or without permission, and hurrying under whip across

the country on some forbidden hunt or distant visit.
The Indian plies his whip and looks straight ahead,
but he has seen the cowboy. The cowboy sees him
too, and smiles contemptuously. He dreams not of
the day when he, too, shall be a flitting figure disappearing across the range.

In the spring the cattle straggle out from the
warmer and more sheltered portions of the range where
they have been huddled during the more biting times
of winter. They feed with eagerness and unceasing
industry upon the fresh-growing grasses. The little
calves begin to totter along awkwardly by the side of
their gaunt mothers, whose hips and ribs project
prominently in sign of the long season of cold and
scarcity with which they have been at war. Coyotes
sneak along the hillsides at the edges of the herds, in
the morning at sunrise sometimes sitting upon the tops
of the high ridges and joining in a keen tremulous
chorus, one of the familiar sounds of the range. At
times a circle of the great gray buffalo wolves—pests
of the cattle range—close in about a mother and her
calf, lying down, bounding about, playing and grin-
ning. The feeble cow fights as she can, perhaps getting to the circle where others stand and fight. The
snarling pack will in time pull down their prey. The
rider of the T Bar range reports many calves and
heifers killed by wolves. It is one of the factors of
loss to be figured upon regularly. He notes also
roughly as he makes his early trips over the range the
numbers of cattle that " did not winter." At these
red or tawny blotches which lie about over the landscape the coyotes are feeding, then the foxes and
swifts. Perhaps by some carcass the cowboy notes the
long footmark of the grizzly bear, which has awakened
from its sleep in the hills and begun a long series of

marches in search of food, always scarce for it in the early spring before the crickets and mice begin to move and before the berries ripen. The bear has torn apart with his rugged strength the ribs of the carcass and battened his fill upon the carrion. Ravens cross from side to side. Life and death are in evidence together upon the range in spring. These lean cattle, their rough hair blowing up in the wind, are the survivals. The range is no place for weaklings. The cowpuncher, who is no weakling, rides along over the range, guessing at the proportion of survival in the herd, estimating how many calves the outfit will brand at the round-up soon to begin, figuring on how many strange cattle have drifted in on this part of the range during the last storms of the winter. His eye catches with trained precision the brand of each animal he sees. He is observant of every detail connected with his calling as he rides along, unconscious of his horse, his arm high and loose, his legs straight to the big stirrups, his body from the hips up supple and swinging, his eye ranging over the wide expanse of plain and *coulee*, butte and valley that lies before him. This wide book is his, and he knows it well. The little larks twitter and flit from in front of him low along the ground as the pony trots ahead, and the prairie dogs chatter from their mounds. If the horse makes a shying bound from some lazy rattlesnake that has come out from winter quarters to stretch awhile in the sun, the thighs of the rider tighten, and the ready oath leaps to his lip as he strikes the spur to the horse's flank and asks it, in the picturesque language of the plains, what are its intentions as connected with a future life.

And then comes on the summer time, with its swift and withering heat. The range shrivels and sears.

The streams dwindle and shrink. The flowers are cut
down by the torrid winds. The sage brush is gray and
dismal. The grass is apparently burned to tinder. The
edges of the water holes are trampled and made miry
by the hoofs of the cattle which press in to water.
Out in the hot air the white alkali flats glimmer and
shift in the distance. Above them stalk the strange
figures of the mirage, cousins of the *Fata Morgana*
of the southern range. In this weird mirage the figures of the cattle appear large as houses, the mounted
man tall as a church spire. The surface of the earth
waves and trembles and throbs in the heat like an
unsteady sea. The sun blisters the skin of any but
the native, and the lips of the tenderfoot blacken and
shrivel and crack open in the white dust that arises.
In the soft mud which lies between the shore and the
water at the watering places lie the figures of cattle
which have perished there, but in this hot dry air they
dry up like mummies, the skin tightening in parchment over their bones. Though the nights are cold,
the day flames up into sudden heat. If there be a rain,
it is a tempest, a torrent, a cloud burst which makes
raging floods out of dried-up river beds, and turns
the alkali flats into seas of slimy, greasy mud. Through
it all, over it all, the cowpuncher rides, philosophical
and unfretted. With him it is unprofessional to complain.

In turn comes autumn, when the winds are keener.
The cattle are sleek and fat now, though by this time
the fattest have after the beef round-up found their
mission in the far-off markets. Now the leaves of the
quaking asp in the little mountain valley, which were
light green in spring, dark green in summer, begin to
pale into a faded yellow. The wild deer are running
in the foothills, and over the plains sweep in ghostly

flight the bands of the antelope. The bears have gone up higher into the table-lands to seek their food and look about for a sleeping place. The wild geese are again honking in the air, this time going toward the south. The mallards swim in the little eddies of the creeks, not to leave them till later in the winter when the ice closes up the water. The smaller birds seek warmer lands, except the mountain jays, the camp birds, and the ravens, which seem busy as with some burdening thought of winter. The rousing whistle of the challenging elk is heard by the cowboy whose duties take him up into the hills. The pause of Nature gathering her energies for the continuance of the war of life is visible and audible all about. The air is eager and stimulating. In the morning the cow-punchers race their plunging ponies as they start out from the ranch, and give vent in sheer exuberance to the shrill, wolf-keyed yell which from one end of the range to the other is their fraternal call.

The snows whitened long ago the tops of the mountains in the range. The foothills are white with snow every morning now, and the wind blows cold even down in the little valley where the willows break its force. Winter is coming. The wild deer press lower down from the mountains. The big bear long ago went to sleep up in the hills. With a rush and a whirl some night the winter breaks. In the morning the men look out from the cabin door and can see but a few feet into the blinding, whirling mass of falling snow. This is not the blizzard of midwinter, but the first soft falling of the season. Presently the storm ceases, the sun shining forth brilliantly as though to repent. The earth is a blinding mystery of white. The river has shrunken in its barriers of ice, and over the edges of the ice hang heavy masses of snow. The willows are heavy with snow, and the grouse that huddle in packs among them are helpless and apathetic.

Then the early snow settles and hardens, and is added to by other snows. The mallards in the little spring creek have but a narrow swimming place now left to them. Along the bank of the river appears the curious drag of a travelling otter, driven down by the too solid closing of the stream above. The great round track of the mountain lion has been seen at one or two places on the range, and that of the big gray wolf, the latter as large as the hoof mark of a horse. The cowpuncher at one of the out camps who steps to the door at midnight and looks out over the white plain, when the moon is cold and bright and the stars very large and beautiful, hears wafted upon the air the long, dreary, sobbing wail of the gray wolf, sweeping in its tireless gallop perhaps forty miles a night across the range in search of food. He will find food.

And now midwinter comes. The cold becomes intense. Horse and cow have now put on their longest coat of hair, all too thin to turn the edge of the icy air. Yet the wind is their friend. It sweeps constantly for them, moaning that it can do no better, the tops of the hills where the blessed bunch grass lies curled and cured for food. It sweeps at the hillsides, too, and makes the snow so thin that the horses can easily paw it away and get down to the grass, and the cattle find at least a little picking. From the hills the snow is blown away in masses that fill the ravines and gullies in deep drifts. It packs against the cut banks so hard that the cattle may cross upon it. The hand of the winter is heavy. It is appalling to the stranger in its relentless grasp at the throat of life. The iron range is striving bitterly with all its might to hold its own, te drive away these invaders who have intruded here. It is hopeless. These men are the creatures for the place and hour. They survive.

And the cattle. Ah! the cattle. They did not choose of their own volition this Northern country of cold and ice. They were driven here from a very different clime. Yet they retain the common desire of animate things, and seek to prevail over their surroundings. Gradually the creature shall adapt itself to the surroundings or perish. The cattle feed on the swept hillsides, losing flesh, but living. A thaw followed by a freeze is the worst thing that can befall them, for then the grass is sealed away from them, and upon their backs is formed a cake of ice, a blanket of cold continually freezing their very vitals and oppressing them with a chill which it is useless to attempt to escape. The cattle then soon cease in their struggle for life. They huddle together in little ragged groups in the lee of such shelter as they can find, their rough coats upright and staring. They no longer attempt to feed. One by one they lie down.

The Northern cattle range is not a hay country, and the early cowman counted naught on hay. Yet sometimes a little hay was made, and, in the case of a prolonged cold season such as that described, an attempt was made to feed the cattle. Of course, the thousands of the herds can not be fed, but some of the weaker of the cattle are rounded up and a rough effort is made at giving them a little care. The hay is thrown off the wagons to them in the corrals as they stand where they were driven, humped up, shivering in mortal rigours, many of them frozen. At times their legs, frozen to the bone, are too stiff to have feeling or to be capable of control. The animals stumble or fall or are jostled over, and are too feeble ever to rise. The croak of the raven is the requiem of the range.

It is winter on the northern range, but though it be winter the work of the cowboy is not yet done. At times he must ride the range, in a partial way at least, to keep track of the cattle, to see whether any are back in box cañons from which they should be driven, to see whether any are " drifting." Knowing the danger of a sudden storm upon such a ride, he goes well prepared for the work. Many men have gone out upon the range in winter who never came back again to the cabin. Their rough companions at the ranch do not say much if the cowpuncher does not return from out the sudden raging storm that may set in without an hour's warning. Each man would risk his own life to save that of his fellow, but each man knows how futile is the thought of help. The whole atmosphere is a whirling, seething, cutting drift of icy white, in which the breath is drawn but in gasps, and that only with face down wind. The heaviest of clothing does not suffice, and not even the buffalo coat can stop the icy chill that thickens the blood into sluggishness and makes drowsy every vital energy. The snow covers the trail of the wanderer, as it winds his burial sheet about him and hides him from hope even before death has come to stop his last feeble, insentient efforts to struggle on. But all the men know which way to look —down wind somewhere, for it could have been in no other direction. He may be lying a long, shapeless blot on the earth, his clinched hands over his head to shut out the snow and the thought of death, in some little *coulee* miles and miles from where the blizzard caught him. There have been seen riderless horses on the range, with parts of saddle still hanging to them. The round-up may perhaps find the place where the cowpuncher is sleeping through many sleeps.

But in winter the work of the cowman is much less. He has time to sit and spin a yarn and smoke a pipe indoors even in the daytime, and at night he adds disfigurement to the single deck of cards. In the ranch house it is warm no matter what the snows and winds are doing. Perhaps the employer of these men does not live upon the ranch; indeed, it is most unlikely that he is spending the winter there. Perhaps back in some city in the "States" the owner may be sitting in his comfortable home, possibly planning about his trip out to the ranch for the spring round-up. The owner may be rich, but he may be ill, and he may not be entirely happy here in his Eastern home. He may know the troubles incident to life in the complex fabric of highly organized society. In his heart he may long for that other fireside, the roaring fireplace in the house of the T Bar ranch. He can see the cowboys in their shirt sleeves sitting about the fire smoking after their evening meal, their knees in their hands or their elbows resting on their knees, their hair hanging down tangled. He can see the big shadows the fire is making on the rude tapestried wall of the T Bar house. He envies those wiry fellows who loll or sit about the fire.

CHAPTER IV.

THE COWBOY'S OUTFIT.

In the cowboy country the fashions of apparel do not change. The fashion plates of our own history show the extremes of customs based largely upon folly or caprice, or the plots of tradespeople. The cowboy has been above such change. He is clad to-day as he was when he first appeared upon the plains. His character has been strong enough to be above prettinesses and uselessnesses. His weapons and his dress show none of the idle ornamentation bestowed by those peoples who would rather carve and embroider than march and fight. The costume of the cowboy is permanent because it is harmonious with its surroundings. It is correct because it is appropriate. It will remain as it is so long as the cowboy himself remains what he has been and still is—a strong character, a self-poised individual, leaning on no other soul. We call his costume picturesque, but that is because it takes us into places to which we are unaccustomed. We call the absurdities of many European natives also picturesque, with their starched and frilled appendages, which can be of no possible use or advantage in any human garb. But when we come to note closely the costume of the cowboy, we shall find that it has been planned upon lines of such stern utility as to leave us no possible thing which we may call dispensable.

50

By the costume we may tell the man. We can not fail to recognise a nature vigorous far beyond those weak degenerates who study constantly upon changes in their own bedeckings.

The coat, trousers, and waistcoat of the cowboy are of the rough sort commonly obtained at the rude stores of the frontier. They are, of course, ready made, and of course they do not fit in the city acceptation of the term. They are sure to be of wool, and they are sure to be large and roomy enough. It is one of the odd things of the Southern country that the men largely affect black or dark-coloured clothing. The men of the Southern cities to-day nearly all wear black clothing as their business dress, and it is rarely that one sees anything but a black hat, though that would seem to be precisely the sort of wear most illy adapted to a land of blazing sun. The early cowboy ideas of perfect dress reverted somewhat to this predilection for dark clothing. In more recent times the mixed goods and lighter colours, which one would naturally consider far more sensible for such wear, have come into wider use, but this is mainly because the storekeepers of the frontier have had such goods for sale.

The typical cowboy costume can hardly be said to contain a coat and waistcoat. The heavy woollen shirt, loose and open at the neck, is the common wear at all seasons of the year excepting winter, and one has often seen cowboys in the winter time engaged in work about the yard or corral of the ranch wearing no cover for the upper part of the body excepting one or more of these heavy shirts. If the cowboy wears a coat, he will wear it open and loose as much as possible. If he wears a vest, you will see him wear it slouchily, hanging open or partly unbuttoned most of the time. There is reason in this slouchy Western habit. The cowboy will tell you that your vest closely buttoned about the body will cause you to perspire, so that you will quickly chill upon ceasing your exercise. His own waistcoat, loose and open, admits the air freely, so that the perspiration evaporates as rapidly as it forms. If the wind be blowing keenly when he dismounts to sit down upon the ground for dinner, he buttons up his waistcoat and is warm. If it be very cold, he buttons also his coat. Meantime you, who have followed the customs of the " States " in your wearing apparel, will be needing two overcoats to keep you warm. A tight coat, a " biled shirt," or a buttoned waistcoat are things not recognised in Cowboyland.

When we come to the boots of the cowboy we shall find apparent foundation for the charge of inutility. Very curious boots indeed they are, and it is an easy wager that one would be unable to buy a pair of them in the length and breadth of most large Eastern cities to-day. Of fine leather, with light, narrow soles, extremely small and high heels, and fitting so tightly as to bind the foot and cramp the toes in a most vicelike grasp, surely a more irrational foot covering never was invented. Yet the cowboy wears this sort of boot, and has worn it for a generation. His ideas of " style " oblige him to cling to these peculiar boots, and to be particular in the make of these as well as in the fabric of his hats and gloves. For the quality of his clothing he cares nothing whatever. Yet these tight, peaked, wretched cowboy boots have a great significance of their own, and may indeed be called insignia of a calling. There is no prouder soul on earth than the cowboy. He is proud that he is a horseman, and he has a contempt for all human beings who walk. He would prefer death to the following of a plough. A day's walk through the streets of the city which he infrequently visits leaves him worn out by evening, and longing for the saddle. It is a saying that he would rather walk half a mile to get a horse in order to cover a distance of a quarter of a mile than he would to walk the latter distance in the first place. The cowboy does not walk, and he is proud of the fact. On foot in his stumpy, tight-toed boots he is lost. But he wishes you to understand that he never is on foot. And if you ride beside him and watch his seat in the big cow saddle you will find that his high and narrow heels prevent the slipping forward of the foot in the stirrup, into which he jams his feet nearly full length. If there is a fall, the cowboy's foot never hangs in the stirrup. So he finds his little boots not so unserviceable, and retains them as a matter of pride. Boots made for the cowboy trade sometimes have fancy tops of bright-coloured leather. The Lone Star of Texas is not infrequent in their ornamentation.

The curious pride of the horseman nearly always extends also to his gloves. The cowboy is very careful in the selection of his gloves. The Ishmaelite clothier who sells him shoddy stuffs at outrageous prices in his clothing knows better than to offer the range rider sheepskin in his gloves. You will be unable also to find these gloves in the Eastern cities. The proper glove will be made of the finest buckskin, which will not be injured by wetting. It will probably be tanned white and cut with a deep cuff or gauntlet, from which will hang a little fringe. The fluttering of little bits and things in the wind when at full speed of horseback was always one of the curious Western notions which were slow of change.

The hat of the cowboy is one of the typical and striking features of his costume, and one upon which he always bestows the greatest of care. The tender-

5

foot is known upon the range by his hat. He thinks
it correct to wear a wide white hat, and so buys one for
a couple of dollars. He is pained and grieved to find
that at the ranch he is derided for wearing a " wool
hat," and he is still more discontented with his head
covering when he finds that the first heavy rain has
caused it to lop down and lose all its shape. The
cowboy riding by his side wears a heavy white felt
hat with a heavy leather band buckled about it, which
perhaps he bought five years before at a cost of fifteen
or twenty dollars; but he refers with pride to the fact
that it is a " genuwine Stetson, an' a shore good un."
There has been no head covering devised so suitable as
this for the uses of the plains. The heavy boardlike
felt is practically indestructible. The brim flaps a
little, and in time comes to be turned up, and possibly held fast to the crown by means of a thong. The
cowpuncher may stiffen the brim by passing a thong
through a series of holes pierced through the outer
edge. The heavy texture of this felt repels the blazing rays of the sun better than any helmet. There
are no recorded cases of sunstroke on the range. The
record might be different were straw hats or " derbys "
substituted for the rational headgear which for so long
has been the accepted thing in the cowboy country.
The cowboy can depend upon his hat at all seasons.
In the rain it is an umbrella. In the sun it is a shade
and a safeguard. At night, if he sleeps cold, he can
place it beneath his hips, and in the winter he can tie
it down about his ears with his handkerchief, thus
escaping the frostbite which sometimes assails tender-
feet who rely upon the best of caps with ear-flaps. A
derby hat is classed contemptuously under the general
term " hard hat." Once upon a time a ranch foreman
went to Kansas to get married, and report came back

from the town that he had been seen wearing a "hard hat." It required many and elaborate explanations on his part to restore confidence in him after his return to the ranch. There are many stories which recount the wild delight with which the cowboys greeted the appearance of a silk hat in a frontier town where they and the owner of such hat happened to be sojourning together, and it is literally true that in the earlier days of the frontier such hats were often shot "full of holes" by cowpunchers who did not wait for the removal of the hat from the owner's head. These stories date to the wilder days of the cattle towns, when one of the favourite amusements of the wild range men was to induce some tenderfoot to dance for them by means of the persuasive argument of shooting into the ground close to his feet. Such times passed away long ago. To-day there are many gray-headed cowboys on the range who solemnly deny that they ever did exist.

A starched collar was never seen on the cow range, and it is matter of doubt what might occur to it were it attempted by one of the cowboys of a ranch. The wearer would probably soon find himself the possessor of some nickname which would cling to him for the rest of his life with annoying adhesiveness. The neckwear of the cowboy is to-day what it was decades ago. The loose shirt collar has loosely thrown about it a silk kerchief, which may rest about the neck quite above the shirt collar. The kerchief is tied in a hard knot in front, and can hardly be said to be devoted to the uses of a neck scarf, yet it will be found a great comfort to the back of one's neck when riding in a hot wind. The cowboy very probably wears the kerchief in his peculiar fashion out of deference to the conventional style of the range. It is sure to be of

some bright colour, usually red, for these strong and
barbarous natures have learned no admiration for the
degenerate colours, such as pale green and the like.

A peculiar and distinctive feature of the cowboy's
costume is his "chaps" (*chaparéjos*). Here the inexperienced man might think he had found ground to
twit the cowpuncher with affectation, for the heavy,
wide-legged and deeply fringed leg covers certainly
do have rather a wild look. The "chaps" are simply
two very wide and full-length trouser-legs made of
heavy calfskin, and connected by a narrow belt or
strap. They are cut away entirely at front and back,
so that they cover only the thigh and lower legs, and
do not heat the body as a full leather garment would.
They are loose, roomy, and airy, and not in the least
binding or confining to the limb, for the cowboy wears
no tight thing about him except his boots. The usefulness of the "chaps" can be very quickly and thoroughly learned by any one who rides with a cowboy
for a single day over the ordinary country of the range.
They are not intended for warmth at all, but simply as
a protection against branches, thorns, briers, and the
like, being as serviceable among the willow switches
and sage brush of the North as against the mesquite
and cactus chaparral of the South. The invention, of
course, came from the old Spaniards, who gave us all
the essential ideas of the cattle trade. In the country
where *chaparéjos* were first worn the cactus, the Spanish bayonet, and all the steellike hooks and whips of
the chaparral make a continual menace to the horseman. The hunter in following the hounds in that
Southwestern country has perhaps at times found himself in the middle of a dense growth of cacti which
reached higher than his head as he sat in the saddle.
To turn in any direction seemed impossible, and every

movement of the horse brought fresh thorns against the unprotected legs of the rider. Well for him then had his legs been incased in the "chaps" he should have worn. Not even the best tanned calfskin always serves to turn the thorns and daggers of the cactus. Sometimes there is seen, more often upon the southern range, a cowboy wearing "chaps" made of skins tanned with the hair on. These appendages, with their long shaggy covering of black or white hair, would again tempt the inexperienced to twit the cowboy with affectation, but once more he would be wrong. The cowboy of the Southwest long ago learned that goatskin left with the hair on would turn the cactus thorns better than any other material.

The overcoat of the cowboy, or rather his overcoat and mackintosh combined, is the ever-present "slicker" which he is most pleased to wear tied behind him at the thongs of his saddle. This garment is an oilskin, similar to that used by fishermen on the seacoast. It is cheap, almost indestructible, and exactly suited to its uses.

At times in the winter time, and in a colder country, the cowboy slips on a blanket coat, a long garment of heavy brown canvas lined with flannel. These coats, in a better grade, however, than is usually found upon the cow range, are issued by the Government to the soldiers at the Northern army posts, and the teamsters there declare they are as warm as a buffalo overcoat. Of course, upon the range in a cold Northern country, where the thermometer at times reaches 45° below zero, the cowboy abandons distinctive type in clothing and dresses, as do all men in that climate, in the warmest clothing at hand. He will wear mittens then instead of gloves, and will have heavy overshoes upon his feet. Perhaps he will take to the heavy knit German socks or to the felt boots of the North. In such costume, however, we do not find the cowpuncher at his usual work, and so may dismiss it as not pertaining to his dress properly speaking.

The wearing of arms upon the person is in many of the Western territories now prohibited by law, and it is no longer customary to see the cowpuncher wearing the revolver or even carrying the Winchester which at a time not many years ago were part of his regular outfit. In some of the ruder parts of the range, and at some seasons of the dangerous cattle wars, it was a matter of personal safety that required such arms and a ready familiarity with them. For instance, the laws of New Mexico required the citizen to "lay aside his arms upon reaching the settlements," and said nothing against the wearing of arms in the country outside the towns. The law was made for the safety of organized society, for the arms bearers rarely came to town except upon times of hilarity and drunkenness, and more than ninety per cent of the "killings" of the West occurred among men where intoxicants had been in use or were near at hand. Thus the notorious Joel Fowler, who was eventually hung in Socorro, New Mexico, in 1883, had been required by the sheriff to "give up his gun" as soon as he came in town, his character when under the influence of liquor being well known. Fowler unbuckled his belt and gave the sheriff his revolver, but kept a knife concealed about him. Less than two hours later, when crazy drunk, he stabbed and killed his own ranch foreman and best friend, who had tried to persuade and quiet him. The young sentiment then just growing in favour of law and order allowed Fowler his trial for this, but his lawyers took appeal and got the final hanging postponed for too long a time; so the citizens, who had

only waited for the hanging as matter of form, concluded to save expense and keep on the safe side by
hanging Joel themselves, which they did, leaving him,
in spite of his loud objections thereto, suspended to
a telegraph pole. That was back in what might be
called the old times on the range, yet even then the
sentiment against bearing arms was beginning to be
felt, and some ranch owners would not allow their
men to carry the revolver at all. Later on, say in
1887, on some of the ranges not so wild as the far
Southwestern country, there was slowly growing a
sentiment against the wearing of a " gun." In 1894,
in one of the wildest parts of Texas, one heard a ranch
foreman say, with a noticeable personal pride, that he
" never did pack a gun." The candour of this statement is open to a shadow of doubt, for that same foreman had spent his life upon the cow range, and in the
old times the cowpuncher certainly did " pack a gun."
Indeed, he looked upon it as a part of his dress and one
of the necessities of life, and as such it should be mentioned here.

The cowboy never wore " galluses " (braces), and
he rarely wore a belt to support his trousers, depending upon buttoning them tightly enough for that
purpose; but he did wear a belt, this the wide, heavy
leather belt that carried his pistol holster. This belt
had loops for half a hundred cartridges, and the
total weight of the affair, gun and all, was several
pounds. No pistol of less than .44 calibre was tolerated on the range, the solid framed .45 being the one
almost universally used. The length of the barrel of
this arm was eight inches, and it shot a rifle cartridge
of forty grains of powder and a blunt-ended bullet that
made a terrible missile. In the shooting affairs of the
West some one nearly always got killed, because the

weapons used were really deadly ones. The tenderfoot who brought the little .32 pistol of the "States" to the range was laughed at till he threw it away. Thereupon the tenderfoot bought a .45, and was very wretched. He found the heavy thing almost unsupportable in its constant dragging down, and he could never get at it when he wished to practise on a prairie dog. He buckled the belt tightly about his waist, and perhaps decorated himself with one of the useless sharp-pointed knives which, for some inscrutable reason, have always had a place and a sale in the Eastern sporting-goods shops under the name of "hunting knives," though they are scorned by any man who really hunts or who has ever lived in the West. If our tenderfoot would study the belt of the cowpuncher he might learn something to his benefit. He would, of course, see no knife there. The foreman has a clasp knife at the branding corral for purposes connected with his work, but the cowboy has none at his belt. The belt itself is not buckled about his waist at all, but is worn loose, resting upon the point of the hip on the left side, and hanging low down upon the hip on the right side, none of the weight of the gun coming upon the soft parts of the abdomen at all. In riding, a cowpuncher's gun is no incumbrance to him, and he gives it no more thought than a well-dressed man does his necktie. Yet quicker than the latter citizen could jerk loose his tie the cowpuncher can jerk loose his gun. Knowing the value of time and the danger of overshooting in a little affair, he will begin to "set the gun agoing" as soon as it gets out of the holster, maybe cutting a little dust inside the distance of his man, but before the second or so of the time of the shooting is past something has usually happened.

Some of the bad men of the West tied back or removed altogether the triggers of their revolvers, thus simplifying the lock and making it more absolutely certain. The gun can be fired much more quickly by cocking and releasing the hammer with the thumb, all six of the shots being thus almost continuous in the hands of a trained gun fighter. The two horse thieves who were killed in lower Kansas by Three-finger Carter, after their long flight across the range from Nebraska in the early '80's, had their revolvers thus arranged. Though Carter was lucky enough to get in two shots with a Sharps rifle, which killed one and disabled the other before they had managed to hit him, he said that the " ar was plum full o' lead " while he was getting in his second cartridge. The well-founded respect which the cowpuncher had for simplicity and certainty in his arms caused him to generally reject the double-action revolver. His dependence was placed in the old-style single-action revolver, with the wooden handle. Some young and more modern cowboys sometimes " toted " guns with pearl or ivory handles, on which the head of a " longhorn " was sometimes engraved handsomely; but these works of art were not cherished in the holsters of the old-time men. The genuine cowboy of the times when some men needed guns and all men carried them, wanted a gun that would " shore go off " when it was wanted. It needed to be an arm which would stand rain and sun and sand, which could be dropped in a stampede and run over by a herd of cattle, but which when picked up would still be ready to go to shooting.

The cowpuncher wore his revolver on the right hip (if a right-handed man), and the butt of it pointed backward. The army man wears his revolver on the left side, with the butt pointing forward—about as poor a way as could be devised, though of course the saber is supposed to occupy the right hand of the cavalryman and most of his personal attention. The cavalryman who goes on many plains marches soon learns of the plainsman how to carry his belt without fatiguing himself to death with his own weapons.

An essential part of the cowpuncher's outfit is his "rope." This is carried in a coil at the left side of the saddle-horn, fastened by one of the many thongs which are scattered over the saddle. The rope in the Spanish country is called *reata* (*la reata*), and even to-day is often made of rawhide, with an eye re-enforced with that durable material. Such a hide rope is called a "lariat" in the South. The *reata* was softened and made pliable by dragging it for some days behind the ranch wagon or at the saddle, the trailing on the ground performing this function perfectly. The modern rope is merely a well-made three-quarter-inch hemp rope, about thirty feet in length, with a leather eye admitting a free play of the noose, the eye being sometimes well soaped to make the rope run freely. This implement is universally called on the range a "rope." The term "lasso," which we read about in books, is never heard, unless in California, nor is the common term of the Mexican, "*reata.*" The "lariat" is in the North used sometimes as another term, more especially to describe the picket rope by which the horse is tied out. In Texas this would be called a "stake rope." The common name gives the verb form, and the cowpuncher never speaks of "lassoing" an animal, but of "roping" it.

The "quirt" of the cowpuncher (possibly from the Spanish *cuerda*, a cord or thong) is a short and heavy whip, made with a short stock less than a foot in length, and carrying a lash made of three or four heavy and loose thongs. The handle is a wooden stick, or sometimes a short iron rod, covered with braided leather, and a thong attaches the quirt to the wrist. The quirt is now made as a regular article of saddlery, but in the early days the cowboys often made their own quirts. The cowpuncher took to leather and rawhide as a fish to water, and some of them, especially those from the Spanish Southwest, were exceedingly clever leather workers. But they never cared much for the fancy-coloured quirts so ingeniously braided of horsehair by the Mexicans, who are fonder of display than the American cowpuncher proper. The quirt was merely supplement to the spur which the cowpuncher wore on each foot. The spur in the old days was made with a very large rowel, the latter being a great wheel, with blunt teeth an inch long about its circumference. Often little bells or oblong pieces of metal ornamented this spur, the tinkling of which appealed to the childlike nature of the plains rider of the early days. The style of spur has come down without pronounced change.

The bridle used by the cowboy—for we may as well continue to speak also of the dress of the cowboy's horse—was noticeable for its tremendously heavy and cruel curbed bit. This bit was originated by the most cruel people in the world, the Spaniards, and it has in some form retained its hold in the most cruel occupation of the world, the cattle business of the plains. A long shank hung down from the bit on either side of the mouth, and low down on these shanks were fastened the reins, with a leverage sufficient fairly to tear the jaw off a pony. Inside the mouth there was a cross bar of iron, made with a U bend in the middle. The pull on the reins could sink this U deep into the horse's tongue, sometimes nearly cutting it off. Very severe was the "spade bit," which could be forced into a horse's mouth willy-nilly, and still more cruel was the "ring bit," with its circle slipped over the lower jaw of the horse. This savage Spanish bit went out of common use as the Anglo-Saxon cattle men came in. It was capable of breaking the jaw of a horse, and has been known to do so. More humane bits are used now than in the past, and probably horses are upon the average not so "broncho" as the original Spanish ponies. In the wild riding of the cowboy he sometimes mercilessly jerks the pony up with his terrible bit, so sharply as to throw it back upon its haunches. The horsemanship of the plains has absolutely no reference to the feelings of the horse. It is the part of the latter to obey, and that at once. Yet in the ordinary riding, and even in the arduous work of the round-up and in cutting out, the cowpuncher uses the bit very little, nor exerts any pressure on the reins. He lays the reins against the neck of the pony on the side opposite to the direction in which he wishes it to go, merely turning his hand in the direction, and inclining his body in the same way. He rides with the pressure of the knee and the inclination of the body, and the light side shifting of both reins equally tightened. A cow pony does not know what you want of it if you pull upon the rein on one side. They have been known to resent such liberties very promptly.

The saddle of the cowboy is the first, last, and most important part of his outfit. It is a curious thing, this saddle developed by the cattle trade, and the world has no other like it. It is not the production of fad or fancy, but of necessity. Its great weight—a regular cow saddle weighs from thirty to forty pounds—is readily excusable when one remembers that it is not only seat but workbench for the cowman.

A light saddle would be torn to pieces at the first rush of a maddened steer, but the sturdy frame of a cow saddle will throw the heaviest bull on the range. The saddle is made for riding upon a country essentially flat, and it is not intended for jumping—indeed, can not be used for high jumping, with its high cantle and pommel. Yet it is exactly right for the use for which it is designed. The high cantle gives a firmness to the seat of the cowboy when he snubs a steer with a sternness sufficient to send it rolling heels over head. The high pommel, or " horn," steel forged and covered with cross braids of honest leather, serves as anchor post for this same steer, a turn of the rope about it accomplishing that purpose at once. The tree of the saddle forks low down over the back of the pony, so that the saddle sits firmly and can not readily be pulled off. The great broad cinches—especially the hind cinch so much detested by the pony, and a frequent incentive to steady bucking—bind the big saddle fast to the pony until they are practically one fabric. The long and heavy wooden stirrups seem ungraceful till one has ridden in them, and then he would use no other sort. The strong wooden house of the stirrup protects the foot from being crushed when riding through timber or among cattle or other horses. The pony can not bite the foot—as he sometimes has a fashion of doing viciously—through the wood and the long cover or leather that sometimes further protects it, neither can the thorns scratch the foot or the limbs of trees drag the foot from its place.

The shape of the tree of the cow saddle is the best that can be made for its use, though it or any other tree is hard upon the pony's back, for the saddle is heavy of itself, and the rider is no mere stripling. The deep seat is a good chair for a man who is in it nearly all the year. In the saddle the cowpuncher stands nearly upright, his legs in a line from his shoulders and hips down. He rides partly with the balancing seat, and does not grip with his knees so much as one must in sitting a pad saddle, but his saddle is suited to his calling, and it is a bad horse and a big steer that shall shake him, no matter what the theories of it be. The question of the cowpuncher's saddle and his use of it can be covered with a little conversation once heard on the trail of a cow outfit. A gentleman of foreign birth, but of observing habits, was telling a cowpuncher what he thought about his riding and his saddle. "I say, you couldn't jump a fence in that thing, you know," said he.

"Stranger," said the cowpuncher, "this yer is God's country, an' they ain't no fences, but I shore think I could jump more fences than you could rope steers if you rid in that postage stamp thing of yourn."

The cowboy loves his own style of saddle, but he goes further than that. He is particular to a nicety in selecting his saddle, and, having once selected and approved of it, he can not be induced to part with it or exchange it for any other. He might sell his gun or his coat or his boots, and he cares nothing how many times he changes his horse, for which he has no affection whatever, but he will never part with his saddle. The cowboys who came up with the drive from the lower range in the early days took their saddles back home with them, no matter how long the journey. To sell one's saddle was a mark of poverty and degradation, and perhaps the cowpuncher felt about it much as the Spartan mother about the loss of her son's shield. No matter how dark it is when he saddles up, no cowpuncher ever gets any saddle

but his own, and should any one borrow or misplace
his there is apt to be explanation demanded.

In the early days of the "Texas saddle," or the
first type of the cow saddles, these articles were made
in the shops of the Southwest. Before long, however,
after the drive got into the Northern country, the
saddles of Cheyenne became the favourites of the range,
North and South, they being made of better leather.
The "California tree" was sometimes used.   There
was some local variety in manufacture, but the saddle
of the cowman remained constant in the main points
above mentioned. The old Spaniard who designed it
put forth many models which have endured practically
without change.

A good saddle would cost the cowboy from forty
to one hundred dollars. In his boyish notions of
economy to want a thing was to have it if he had the
money, and a saddle once seen and coveted was apt
to be bought. The embossing and ornamentation of
the saddle had most to do with its cost. The Spanish
saddles of the Southwest were often heavily decorated
with silver, as were the bits, spurs, and bridle reins,
as well as the clothing of the rider; but this sort of
foppery never prevailed to any extent among American
cow punchers. There was one rude and wild sort of
decoration sometimes in practise by the younger cowboys on the range. They often took the skins of rat-
tlesnakes, of which there were very many seen nearly
every day, and spread them while yet wet upon the
leather of their saddles. The natural glue of the skin
would hold it firmly in place when it dried. Some
saddles have been seen fairly covered with these lines
of diamond-marked skins. It was not uncommon to
see the skins of these snakes also used as hat bands.

Let us suppose that chance has brought us to some

one of the little frontier towns in or near the edge of
the cattle country, and that there is in the neighbourhood of the village a band of cattle in the care of the
usual outfit of cowboys. Perhaps the duties of these
are well over for the time, they having shipped their
cattle or turned them over to another owner. It is in
the evening, and the party of cowboys have concluded
to come to town for a little celebration. Far across
the open prairie country we may see them coming,
their way marked by the rapidly flitting cloud of white
dust. In a few moments they are near enough for one
to make out their figures. They sit straight up in the
saddle, their legs straight down, the body motionless
except through the action of the horse. They are
in their shirt sleeves, their hats blowing back, their
right hands occasionally wielding the quirts as they
race·headlong over the rough ground of the unbroken
prairies. Now and again their heels strike home the
spurs to push on the racing ponies, which come flying,
their heads low down, their legs gathered well under
them, their ears back, their nostrils wide. As the
wild range men come on one hears their shrill call, the
imitation of the coyote yelp. They dash into the main
street of the town, never drawing rein, but spurring
and whipping the harder, the hoofs of the horses making a louder beat upon the hard streets. On they ride,
yelling and spurring, their loose scarfs flying, but each
man upright and steady as a statue in his seat. They
arrive at the main portion of the town, perhaps at the
central "square," about which some of these towns
are built. Still at full speed, each man suddenly pulls
up his horse with a strong jerk upward of his hand.
The heavy bit does its work. The pony, with its head
tossed high by the sudden pull, which it has learned
instantly to obey, throws its weight back as it does

in the corral when the rope has flown. It falls back upon its hind legs, sliding upon its fetlocks, and coming to a stop from full speed within a few feet. Before it has fully paused the rider is off and has thrown the reins down over its head. Then, while the pony rolls its eye in resentment, you will have opportunity to see the cowboy on his feet and dressed in his working clothes.

CHAPTER V.

THE COWBOY'S HORSE.

THE earliest written records of mankind show that man was first a warrior and next a cattle man, and that most of his wars were over cows. We are told that the Aryans were cowmen by universal occupation, and it is pointed out to us that the Sanskrit word for king means nothing more than chief of cowboys, or otherwise foreman of the ranch. Our word " pecuniary " is directly derived from the Latin *pecus,* thus pointing back sharply to the time when the cow was the unit of all values. The ancient warrior of Europe paid so many cows for his wife, as the warrior of the red peoples of America pays so many ponies, or as the head men of the pale faces to-day pay so many dollars, by a slight modification of standards and customs. It needs but the most casual glance back over the history of the race to see how primitive, how strong and steadfast, have been the customs of the cattle men from the time of the Aryans to the time of the beef barons of a decade ago. Until within a very short time a cow was a cow on the cattle range, and one cow was as good as another. Surely it was a radical and ominous change which broke down so old and strong a custom. It means that the days of our Sanskrit and Roman and Western heroes, men " who fought about cows," are gone forever, and that a new time has set on in history, wherein the money changer and the merchant shall take their place forever. Woe is that time in the history of any people.

In the ancient days of the cattle industry the same problems must have presented themselves which were offered to the earliest cattle men upon this continent. These cows, which constituted the wealth of the individual, were four-legged creatures, which could run far away from man, the two-legged creature. Man as Nature made him cut a sorry figure as a cowboy. But Nature had given to man another creature as strong as the cow, more fleet, and more courageous. This creature man took into his plans, and upon the back of the horse he at once became the physical superior of the cow. With the horse he is master of his herds. Without it he must ever have remained the hunter, and could never have been the cattle man. He could never have organized his means of increasing his own wealth or of commanding it. Most intimately blended, then, is the horse of the cowman with every movement of his calling.

It is impossible to tell beyond the stage of guesswork just at what time the first cowman rode into view upon the hot and desert plains of the vast Southwest—that lean and bronzed fighting Spaniard who had set his stubborn foot upon the virgin soil of a new continent sometime in the early and glorious day at the opening of American history. It is sure that as a military man the Spaniard knew the value of a beef herd with the marching column or at the base of his operations. He brought over cattle almost as soon as he did horses, and the one grew with the other. There is a tradition that the Spanish Government, toward the close of the sixteenth century, turned loose upon the plains of the Southwest some numbers of horses in order to stock the country with that animal. The common supposition is that the wild stock of America began in the stray and runaway horses which were lost by the Spaniards. Be that as it may, the horse of the Spaniards soon had a better hold on American soil than the Spaniard himself. By the year 1700 the Northern Indians had not yet become generally possessed of horses, and many of them used dogs as beasts of burden, while their hunting was all done on foot. Yet at this time the Southern Indians had horses, and had learned to use them extremely well. The natural course of horse trading and horse stealing soon spread the animal all over the vast country of the West. The advent of the horse upon this continent changed the entire manner of life of the native tribes. It only perpetuated the manners and customs of the people that had brought the horse. So strong, so virile were these customs that the type of the horse itself has changed more in three centuries than that wild industry of which it has always been and must always be a central figure.

If we should have a look at the continent of Europe at the time of the wars of the Moors and Spaniards, we should see there a state of matters much as we may see upon our own cattle range. In the north of Europe the cattle and the horses, as well as the men, were bulky, powerful, and large of frame. In the south of Europe the cattle, the men, and the horses, reared in a hot and dry country, were smaller, and were lean, sinewy, and active rather than big and bulky. The Moors were always horsemen, and they brought from northern Africa with them into Spain the horse of a hot, dry land, a waterless land, where the horse was alike a necessity and a treasure. The Moor prized his horse, and so developed of him a creature of worth and serviceableness, one which could carry an armed man all day under a tropic sun and subsist upon such food as the desert offered.

The horse of the Moor became the horse of the Spaniard, and the horse of the Spaniard became the horse of the Spanish-Indian or Mexican, which in turn became the horse of the cattle trade which was handed down along with it. The animal certainly found an environment to its liking, one indeed similar to that which had produced its type in northern Africa. The suns of the great Southwest were burning, the lands were parched and dry, and small shade ever offered. Water was rare and precious, and to be reached only by long journeys. These journeys, this dry and unfattening food of the short grasses of the hot plains, took off every particle of useless flesh from the frame of the horse. It needs moisture to furnish fat to a people, and a fat person must always be drinking water. The Spanish pony had no more water than would keep it alive, and soon came to learn how to do without it in great measure. For generation after generation it lost flesh and gained angles, lost beauty and gained " wind " and stomach and bottom and speed, until at the time of the first American cowboy's meeting with it it was a small, hardy, wiry, untamed brute, as wild as a hawk, as fleet as a deer, as strong as an ox. It had not the first line of beauty. Its outline of neck was gone forever, merged into a hopeless ewe neck which looked weak, though it was not. Its head was devoid of beauty of outline, often Roman nosed, but still showing fineness and quality in the front and the muzzle. Its head was very poorly let on. Its ribs seemed a bit flat and its hips weak. Its back was roached up forward of the " coupling " in a pathetic way, as though the arch were in sympathy with a stomach perpetually tucked up from hunger or from cold. Its eye was not good to look upon, and its fore legs not always what one would ask of his favourite saddler. But suppose the stripping of Nature had been followed out until the bony framework of this plains horse had been laid quite bare, and the skeleton alone left in evidence, this skeleton would be worth a study. The quality of the bone of this forearm would be found dense and ivorylike, not spongy as the bone of a big dray horse. The hoofs and feet would be found durable and sound. The cat-hammed hips would be seen to supplement that despised roach in the back, and we should have offered that grayhound configuration which is seen in all the speedy animals where the arch of the back is marked and the hind legs set under and forward easily in running. Such an animal " reaches from behind " well in running, and turns quickly. Moreover, these flat-bladed shoulders would be seen to be set on oblique- ly, which again one asks of his speedy dog or racing horse, if he knows the anatomy of speed. The shoul- ders play easily and freely, and the hind legs reach well forward, and the chest, though deep enough to give the lungs and heart plenty of room, is not too deep to interfere with a full extension of the animal and a free and pliant play of the limbs. In short, the pony of the range as first seen by the American cowboy was not a bad sort of running machine. It had, moreover, the lungs built upon generations of rare pure air, the heart of long years of freedom, and the stomach of centuries of dry feed. It stood less than fourteen hands high, and weighed not more than six hundred pounds, but it could run all day and then kick off the hat of his rider at night. In form it was not what we call a thorough- bred, but in disposition it was as truly a thorough- bred as ever stood on two or four feet. Jim, the fore-

man of the Circle Arrow outfit, down near the line
of old Mexico, would have told you long ago that such
a horse had "plenty sand." It was very well it did
have.

This was the cow horse of the Southwest, and the
type remained constant in that region until the middle
of this century. All the horses of the North and the
East on the plains came up from Mexico and Texas
on the eastern side of the Rockies, where much the
same sort of climatic conditions prevailed. Meanwhile
there had been another line of migration of the horse,
also from Mexico, but up along the California coast
west of the Rockies. There was heat and dry air and
little water for a long way to the North, but at length
the wet climate of Oregon was reached. Here the way
of Nature went on again, and the type began to change.
The horse became a trifle stockier and heavier, not
quite so lean and rangy in build. The cow horses of
the early trade in Montana came in part from Oregon
across the upper mountain passes by the route over
which the Northern horse Indians who lived close to
the Rockies first got their horses. On the northern
range the cow horse was called a "cayuse," a name, of
course, unknown upon the southern range, where the
horse was simply a "cow horse," or, if a very wild and
bad horse, was called a "broncho," that being the
Spanish word for "wild." The term "broncho" has
spread all over the cattle country and all over the country until its original and accurate meaning is quite
lost. There never was any very great difference between the horses of the North and those of the South,
for they came of the same stock, bred in the same unregulated way, and lived the same sort of life. Either
cayuse or broncho would buck in the most crazy and
pyrotechnic style when first ridden, plunging, biting,

bawling, and squealing in an ecstasy of rage, and either would rear and throw itself over backward with its rider if it got a chance, or would lie down and roll over on him. The colour of either was as it happened, perhaps with a bit greater tendency to solid colours in the Northern horse. Bay, sorrel, black, gray, " buckskin," roan, or " calico " were the usual colours of the cow horses. In the South a piebald horse was always called a " pinto," from the Spanish word meaning " paint." In the upper parts of Texas one often hears such a horse called a " paint horse." In the South a horse does not buck, but " pitches," which comes to the same thing with a tenderfoot. A " wall-eyed pinto that pitches " is an adjunct to be found upon almost any Southern ranch even to-day. Both in the South and in the North the horses are now generally bred up by crosses of " American horses," though this is much a misnomer, for the cow horse is the American horse *per se* and *par excellence*.

In the " States " we pen our cattle and house our horses, and have both horse and cow always at hand and under control. Not so fortunate is the cowboy with his mount. The latter is a wild animal loose upon the range. From year's end to year's end it has no care but the hand of mastery and no food but that afforded by Nature. This we shall say for the cow horse proper, and as applying to the days of ranching in the old times, before modern methods had come in. On the upper ranges, where the snows of winter are on the ground for long months and the weather is often very cold, it has long been the custom to make all the hay possible and to keep a little feed on hand for use in winter. Even in the country of the middle range, as in the Indian Nations, baled hay and oats are used in the winter for the saddle band. This, how-

ever, is not that typical ranching of the old times
which will offer us most of picturesqueness and of interest. In those loose, wild times the cow horse was
treated the same as the cow, with only such differences
in the handling as a different nature required or necessity of the business made desirable. Both were wild,
there is not any doubt of that. Jim, the cowboy who
handled both, was as wild as they. Upon that time
let us rather linger than upon a more degenerate day.

There is no more interesting time in which to study
the business of horse ranching than just at the beginning of the great drives to the North which marked the
sudden expansion of the cattle business. Such study
will take us to the plains of upper Texas, for here the
day of the well-conducted horse ranch began. At a
time before the middle of this century, before the civil
war and before the railroads, the great State of Texas
began to fill up with settlers from States above it.
These travelled in colonies at times, the journey being
made in a long cavalcade which was sometimes upon
the road for months. From the old State of Mississippi a great many families went to Texas in that
strange and restless American fashion, absolutely leaving their former homes and pulling up root and
branch. These families took with them their horses,
their cattle, and their household goods, and the entire
family of each emigrant went with him in his wagons,
accompanied by all his slaves, for this was in the slavery
times. One of these great parties settled at a lovely
spot near the head of a clear spring-fed river and
founded the town of San Marcos, which even to-day
bears all the character of that earlier settlement in the
names and families of its citizens. Here began some
of the first experiments in grading up the native Spanish horses with the better blood of the Northern States,

more than a quarter of a century before the great and well-conducted horse ranches of the North commenced their systematic work.

One of the first horse ranches was established on the Rio Blanco about 1849 by Jim Patton, an eccentric recluse who was born in Pennsylvania and wandered down into that country and fenced a few hundred acres which surrounded a deep spring of live water. Patton began slowly, and at the time of the civil war had only a few hundred head of horses. The foundation of his herd was the native Mexican pony, which could then be bought at two to five dollars a head. Patton had a very fine black stallion, for which he always evinced the greatest regard. The horse was fed at the house, and followed his master about like a dog, and his owner made of it almost his only companion. In the rude times just previous to the civil war, when all things were much unsettled, a band of raiders—scouts, pillagers, or whatever they might be called—came in upon Patton's ranch and said they wanted horses for the Southern army. Patton told them to go to the horse herd and help themselves; but they demanded the favourite horse, and this he told them they could not have. They insisted, and Patton made some temporizing excuse, though he had resolved they should not have the horse. He called up a negro servant, and told him to get the animal and lead it to the spring back in the timber, for that he intended to kill it himself rather than allow it to be taken by the raiders. The negro did as he was told, and Patton started to follow, having his gun ready to shoot his own favourite; but as he stepped into the path to follow after it the raiders shot him in the back and killed him. They then took the horse, but did not take any others of the herd. Patton's brother came down from the

North later to clear up his estate, but the ranch was allowed to go to pieces. This ended what was probably one of the very first of the attempts at horse ranching east of the Rockies on the cow range. Another early and well-known horse ranch was the Key brand ranch of Joe Brown, and yet another and more extensive one was the C. O. X. ranch, both of these near San Marcos, and both established in the early part of the decade which began at 1850. The trail horses of these outfits were known from the Rio Grande to Abilene in the days of the drive.

In these different ranches there were several sires—fine-bred Kentucky horses of proved blood and excellence—and it was soon discovered that the progeny of these made better cow horses than the native horses. The grade horse would weigh perhaps eight hundred pounds instead of six hundred, and would have a better turn of speed and more strength, though retaining the hardiness and staying quality of the native stock. One of the famous horses taken from Kentucky to that region was known as Buckskin, and grading of that strain began about 1856. By the time the days of the cattle drives began there was well established in northern Texas a strain of cow horses which must have had superior qualities, for they came to be sought far and near by outfits going "up the trail."

Life in those early days was very free and wild and picturesque. It was long before the day of fences, and all the country belonged to the settlers who had discovered it. The neighbours were very far away. The horses ranged quite free and unfenced, as wild as the cattle. Horses naturally band up more closely than the cattle, and this trait was strengthened by the habits of the stallions, which would drive off, each for himself, a band of forty to seventy-five (known as his "*menatha,*" this being the native pronunciation of the Spanish word "*manada,*" a band or drove), endeavouring always to steal more mares from other bands. These bands would come to feed more or less apart, and each would localize itself, establishing a range upon which it could nearly always be found. The climate of that country did not offer such extremes as that of the northern range, and this in a manner simplified the work of ranging the animals. A horse never liked to leave its native range, and if stolen and taken away would often come back, sometimes over a distance of more than two hundred miles. A band of thirty-five horses has been known to break back from the drive and return home over two hundred miles in about twenty days. Much was left to this home instinct of the horses, and it was considered sure that they would range over a country not much more than twenty-five or forty miles from where they were born, if the feed remained good. Fences were therefore not needed, for fifty miles on the range is but a little way.

The men of the horse ranches joined in the spring round-up just as the cattle men join in their round-ups. The start was usually made about the first week in March in that country, and the early search was made among the hills and broken ground along the water courses. Each ranch sent a proper proportion of men, and these travelled very light. Each man had for his own saddle band only about three extra horses. The camp baggage was all carried on pack horses. The round-up party went very free and independent, as it needed to be, for it should be remembered that the animals to be gathered were very much swifter than cattle, and at times harder to control or bring to a given point at a given time. It was usually the inten-

tion to drive the entire gathering of the horse range
to some conveniently located ranch where there was
plenty of corral room, but sometimes the horses made
these plans difficult of carrying out. The horse round-
up required very much faster horses than the cattle
round-up, as the saddle horse had to carry the weight
of the rider and was forced to head off the bands of
fleeing horses, which at times would start back exactly opposite to the direction desired. This wild
trait of the horses was offset by the trait above mentioned, of keeping together in bands and not scattering when pursued, as cattle are more apt to do. A
cowboy would see a little band of horses on a ridge
and would start to head them around to the central
body which was gathering near by. The horses would
make off at full speed, and all he could do was to follow
and endeavour to turn them. Sometimes he would
need to run his horse eight or ten miles before he could
head them and get them to " rounding up " (not " milling," as this is termed with cattle). In such a race the
top speed of his own mount was tried, and no attention could be paid to the character of the ground. It
is common to speak of " giving a horse his head " on
such a race, but the rider who gave his horse his head
in such going might not succeed in his purpose. He
had to hold up his horse with a good stiff rein, keep
it from running its wind out the first mile, and so
growing weak and apt to stumble on the rough ground
over which the run was made. It needed the best and
" longest " of his own stock for this work, and of
course there were favourite horses on each ranch for
this work. The horse round-up was much harder work
for men and horses than the cattle round-up. There
were some bands of especially fleet horses which gave
the utmost trouble, and perhaps several days of run-

ning would ensue before such a band would finally be surrounded and gotten under control. Only the superior bottom of the Kentucky strain would at length succeed in wearing out these fugitives, though sooner or later the perseverance of the riders got them all in. It was a singular fact that the little colts, some not more that a week or two old, were the swiftest of the band, and these always were in the lead, the colt usually running ahead of its mother.

As the horses were picked up on the round-up here and there over the country they were driven toward some convenient corral or meantime held under herd. It was the custom in that country to corral the herd at night and to herd it during the daytime, three or four men being set apart for that work. The herd thus grew for some weeks, being shifted as seemed necessary until in perhaps a month all the horses of the range were thought to be gathered, these, of course, belonging to various owners. Then the whole herd was rounded up at some favourable place, and the process of cutting out began, this being much as it is in a cow round-up. The owner's brand determined ownership, and the colts went with their mothers. Each man helped with the entire herd until finally each owner had his own horses all separated from the main herd. Then the round-up party broke up, and each owner drove his own horses back to his own home ranch. It might be toward the close of April when the horses reached their home ranch, a date about equivalent to the first of June on the northern range. The herd was held here as it had been on the round-up in the big ranch corrals, feeding under guard during the day and confined in the corrals at night.

Upon the arrival at the ranch of the season's product of horses, the horse rancher at once went about branding his young stock. The branding was all done in the "round pen," as a circular corral was called in the South. This was an inclosure with fence walls ten or twelve feet in height, strongly built, and, as the name indicated, of circular form. A horse when frightened is far worse than a steer, and if any angles were left in the corral it might result in injury to the horses, which when pursued by the ropers were sometimes very wild in their attempts at escape. A little bunch of fifteen or twenty horses were driven into the round pen at once, and then the ropers went to work. These, of course, were cowboys of the same sort as those of the cattle ranches. It may have been upon a horse ranch that our foreman Jim had his first education as a roper, under the tutelage of some swarthy Mexican of high straw hat and kerchief bound about his forehead, who perhaps made a prominent figure in the round pen at the horse ranch when the spring branding was in progress. It was Jim, or Manuel, or José who dashed after the flying horses as they sped about the smooth walls, his hide lariat hissing about his head with the turn of his wrist as he rode. With the swoop of the rope and its louder hiss as it cut through the air even against the sharpest wind, some luckless little colt was sure to get its first lesson in the domination of mankind. The roper caught the colt by the fore feet, not by the hind feet as the calves are usually roped, and of course at the instant the rope tightened the colt went head over heels on the ground: lesson No. 1 of the cow pony, which is not to "run against rope."

At once the colt was dragged to the gate of the round pen, where just outside a fire was burning and an iron glowing for his tender hide. A hissing of hair and a plaintive scream from the colt and it was all over, and another animal had become the property of the ranch. Perhaps a dozen and a half of colts would be branded and marked in an hour, and then another bunch was brought in from the big corral. Cattle were not customarily branded in the corral but upon the range, while horses were always taken to the corrals for this work. After the branding the colts had little attention except now and then a rude examination to see that worms had not gotten into the burned spot on the shoulder or hip. The brand mark was sore for a week or so, but in about fifteen days it would heal and peel off and give ho further inconvenience. At the same time as the branding of colts progressed the yearlings and two-year-olds received such attention as seemed necessary, and the herd was looked over for any stock which for any reason it was desired to hold out. By the end of April or middle of May the horse rancher could tell what had been his year's profits or losses in stock.

The loss of horses on the Southern ranges was mainly from scarcity of water or through drought that cut down the feed too closely. Some animals would be bogged down and lost in that way. The " brand blotters " and horse thieves would get a few, and the wolves and cougars would get a few colts. Lastly, the wild mustangs might run off a number of the herd. A great many persons think that all Texas ponies were " mustangs," and so call them, but the rancher made a sharp distinction between his stock and these wild horses of the plains. For years they made one of the menaces of his industry, and did not all disappear from the range until as late as 1878 or 1880. Indeed, even in 1896 a few bands of mustangs were still running in the Panhandle country of Texas. These are the increase of a few individuals left from the old horse-hunting days. The Southern rancher believed these horses to be of a stock distinct from his own, and thought they were descendants of the wild horses which sprang from the horses turned loose upon the plains by the Spanish Government. It is certain that these were swifter and warier than the range horses, for no cowboy could ever round up a band of mustangs, no matter how hard he rode. The leader of a band of these wild horses was always a stallion of great cunning and speed, often of great size and beauty. It was useless to try to trap the mustangs in any way, and they seemed to have a preternatural shrewdness at suspecting and foiling any effort made for their inveiglement into the toils. Once a party of cowmen worked all night to lay a corral fence back in a mountain pass through which a band of these wild horses were accustomed to run whenever they were pursued. The next day they were started again, and took their usual course till they came opposite the mouth of the narrow pass, when without hesitation they ran on by and did not enter the pass, thus breaking a custom which they had invariably followed up to that day, though the new corral was built far back from their sight in the narrowest part of the pass.

These wild horses could not be run down by any horses ever brought upon the range. They were sometimes " walked down " by parties of horse hunters—a wild, half-civilized breed of individuals, the fascination of whose singular calling was something never shaken off. These men would take turns in following a herd of mustangs day and night for perhaps six or eight days, allowing them not a moment's rest, until the animals would become entirely worn out and could be readily approached closely enough for roping. A few of them were at times taken by the singular method

7

known as "creasing," which killed a dozen horses to every one ever taken alive. The hunter who wished to crease a wild horse stalked it as he would game until close enough for a sure shot. He then sought to plant a rifle ball through the cartilage of the top of the neck, just above the spinal processes. Such a shot could sometimes be made in such way that the horse would fall to the earth stunned, but would afterward recover and be uninjured; but in the great majority of cases the horse was missed or killed outright.

At one time there was a celebrated white stallion in charge of a band of mustangs which ranged near the Big Thicket of the Blanco, and on this horse a certain famous mustang hunter, a Mexican by name of Soyez, had long set his heart. He sought many times to snare or trap the creature, but could not do so, and at length tried to crease it. Secreting himself in a tree near a water hole where the band watered, Soyez waited until his quarry came down to water, himself not scented because he was above the ground and at a little distance from the water. He aimed to strike the stallion just upon the crest, but, with Mexican skill, shot it instead square through the head. Years afterward Soyez would nearly weep when telling of his chagrin and sorrow at this unfortunate ending of his quest. This stallion was milk-white, except for a black forehead and black ears. In the year 1856 there was another one of these famous wild stallions which ranged in somewhat the same country. This horse was a pacer, and could never be urged into a gallop by any means. When pursued, he would always forsake the main herd and strike off by himself, taking up a gait which soon shook off pursuit. He was a grand black horse, and was much coveted by all the ranch men and their cowboys, and very often these would make up hunts for him, taking stands along his known runways. But though this horse was chased for over ten miles by six mounted men in turn, he was never turned and never reached within roping distance by any rider. At length he was chased so much that he forsook his range and went over to a spot lower down on the Blanco. For two years word came from that country that he was being pursued by the cowmen of that country, but he was never taken and at length seems to have disappeared from the country altogether, perhaps at the hand of another ambitious creaser. These wild mustangs often ran off the stock of the ranch men, and even mules sometimes joined these wild bands. The ranch men hated the mustangs on this account, and were not averse to the work of the horse hunters. At times choleric cowboys who had pursued such a wild band of plains horses dismounted and in wrath opened fire from their rifles upon the fleeing herd, sometimes killing several of the mustangs from no motive except that of wantonness or anger.

These several perils of the horse range having been evaded or overcome, the horse rancher finds himself, let us say, at the middle of the month of May with several hundreds of horses on his hands. These are not " mustangs," and not all " bronchos," and not all pure-bred Texas stock. Some of them are pure Texas or Spanish, and some are grades. All are wild as deer, and every one of them will " pitch " as sure as that he will breathe, for it is said that no horse was ever born on Texas soil which would not buck at some time or other of his career. The rancher sometimes sold his saddle stock as it stood, untrained and untamed, but the regular horse ranchers usually sold nothing but broken horses, as they got a better price for that class of stock. The process of breaking the young

horses for the saddle occupied the great part of the
entire summer after the round-up and the branding,
and this branch of the work was one of the most picturesque and exciting phases of life on the cattle range.
No better riders were ever turned out than those who
were raised on or near the horse ranches, for there the
business of riding wild horses went on for nearly half
the year.

The differentiation of the cattle trade has made
horse breaking a trade of itself in much of the cow
country, but at first the cowboys of each ranch usually
did the breaking for the ranch, with such help as
might come through the services of some neighbouring
rider of exceptional gifts at horse breaking. Such
specially gifted men gradually became a class of themselves, known all over the range as " broncho busters,"
and they took to the hazardous trade of horse breaking
as a steady business, usually working under contract,
and " busting " horses at so much a head for all the
big ranches having unbroken stock on hand. The
name given this process of breaking is suggestive and
not inaccurate. A horse was considered " busted " after
he had been ridden two or three times under the hand
of iron and the heel of steel. Out of such an ordeal
the horse came with a temper perhaps ruined for life,
and with a permanent grudge against all things human.
It would really never be cured entirely of the habit of
bucking, and was never absolutely safe unless ridden
to the point of fatigue. Some of the best cow horses
on a ranch will always buck when first mounted after
a long rest, and some need a little preliminary training every time they are mounted. These animals probably had their first touch of the saddle at the gentle
hands of the " buster," who got four or five dollars a
head for proving ocularly that such and such a horse

could actually be mounted and ridden without death to either horse or man. Sometimes the event was not thus for either the horse or the man. Horses were at times killed in the process of " busting," and very often the " buster " himself was the victim. The most successful of these men, who came of the hardiest and most daring of the range riders, rarely lasted more than a few years in the business. Sometimes their lungs were torn loose by the violent jolting of the stiff-legged bounds of the wild beasts they rode, and many busters would spit blood after a few months at their calling. Injury in the saddle at some stage of this wild riding was almost a certainty, and falls were a matter of course. A broken leg or arm was a light calamity, accepted philosophically with the feeling that it might have been much worse. The life of the soldier engaged in actual war is far safer than that of the broncho buster. There is no wilder or more exciting scene than the first riding of one of these wild range horses. It is a battle of man against brute, and of a quality to make the heart of a novice stand still in terror. Yet upon the range this is one of the necessities, and those who engage in this business go about it methodically and steadily, probably with no thought that they are doing anything extraordinary, because they have never done anything else.

Between the more modern methods, such as one may see practised on Northern ranches to-day, and the methods of the earlier Southern ranches there is something of a distinction. On a Northern horse ranch, for instance, which sells sixty or eighty horses a year, the breaking is commonly done by a " contract buster." Perhaps thirty or forty horses are gathered in the big corral and are turned one by one into the small round corral, which has a snubbing post in the middle. Two or three men rope the horse by the fore feet and throw him, using the snubbing post if necessary. He is then quickly tied up and the "hackamore," which is provided with a blind already fastened to it, is put on his head. The blind is now slipped down over the horse's eyes, and he is allowed to stand up. The reins of the hackamore are led back, and the saddle is put on and cinched up. Sometimes the stirrups are tied together, but usually not, the buster perhaps being too proud to take advantage of this aid to easy riding, though it would perhaps save him some fatigue or danger. The blind is now lifted a little and the horse is led out, the blind then being slipped down again. Now the buster comes to the horse and mounts him, the beast usually standing quietly and cowering in its supposed helpless blindness. Two other men, sometimes known in these days of modern ranching as "hazers," now mount and ride up with their quirts in hand ready to drive on the horse that is to be broken. When all is ready the buster leans forward from his seat, lifts the blind, and sets whip and spur to the horse, the assistants meantime yelling, waving their hats, and pounding with their quirts. The horse so beset is apt to be "bad" for a time, but is likely to start away from sheer fright, and as soon as he leads off the assistants leave him, and the buster "rides it out," perhaps making a run of two or three miles, and then gradually getting back to the corral again. Here the horse is again blinded, and his saddle and hackamore are taken off. He is then turned into a separate corral, as a horse that has been "ridden." Another horse is then prepared for the buster. The latter may ride five or six horses in a day, all of these operations of course being repeated until each animal has been reduced to what seems near enough to the Western idea of docility.

In the early days of ranching in the Southwest the main ideas of horse breaking were much the same as above described, but the methods employed varied in some particulars. As those were the earliest days, they are perhaps the most interesting, and offer the best field for the examination of this essential phase of ranch work.

Some of the early Southern busters were negroes, and very good breakers they made. Many were Mexicans, whose cruelty and roughness were practically certain to ruin the disposition of any horse, and who soon came into disrepute with American ranchers. Others were rough riders from the cowboy ranks, who had been riders from their youth and feared no horse that ever stood on earth. Many of them were graduated from the horse ranches where cow horses were bred and broken as a business. It is perhaps in such a school that our foreman Jim learned his splendid horsemanship, away back in the early days. In no calling known to man shall we find more of rugged, stern, and masterly quality demanded than was asked in this original school of the cowboy. In no scene of civilized life shall we find more vivid and animated interest and action than made common features about the home ranch at the time horse breaking was going on.

A horse ranch of average size would employ from six to ten men for the summer breaking season, and these would be busy from the middle of May till the end of summer. It took about a week to break a horse, and each breaker would usually handle two horses at the same time, riding them a part of the day each. After the first work was done, others might continue the handling of the horse through several weeks more, but about six days would usually fit a horse for the saddle so that a good rider could ride it; and none but good riders had any business about the cow country. For this sort of work the cowboys were usually paid about twenty to forty dollars a month, according to their value. Some Mexicans were employed, but they were not so much valued. Of course, there were always some of the young men about the ranch who were breaking their own saddle horses for themselves. Such horses were not run with the band, but usually kept up about the house. It was a notorious fact that one of the "pet horses" was sure to be about the worst case of the lot when it came to riding it, especially if it had been allowed to go late in life before it was ridden.

Any visitor to a cow ranch has seen the men at work among the horse herd, and has noticed how quickly a horse will stop as soon as it feels the rope touch it, even though it may perhaps not be caught by the noose at all. This submission to the magic of the rope is a cardinal principle in that horse's ideas of common sense. He bears deep within his mind the early lessons of his youth. The wildest broncho is very apt to cool down when he feels the iron grip of the rope. The first lesson of the rope he receives, as above mentioned, when a brawny cow puncher circles both his fore legs with a noose of this dreaded rope, throws him flat with a turn of the wrist, and hales him on his side through the dust away from his mother's side to the spot where the fiery iron is waiting. From that instant the colt hates man and all his doing. He hates the rope. He resolves that if ever he gets a fair chance he will break that rope into a thousand fragments. He is a couple of seasons older and bigger and stronger when he is at length driven into the round pen some fresh spring morning, so strong, he is sure, that he can rend any rope. He breaks into a run about the wall of the corral, but Jim, the lean and sinewy rider on the older cow horse, follows, about his head curling always that unpleasant snakelike thing the pony remembers and has hated from his babyhood. The rope comes at him with a wide curling sweep, and, in spite of his tossing and plunging, settles fair about his neck or fore feet. It tightens with a jerk. The old horse which Jim is riding stops in his stride and falls back, bracing his fore legs firmly. The young wild horse which was determined to break the rope finds himself upside down, the rope perhaps choking the life out of him. He has had lesson No. 2.

Jim, the cowpuncher and horse breaker, calmly waits till the young horse's eyes nearly start out of his head, and then signs to his assistants, who loosen the rope just in time to save the pony's life. The latter is furious at the indignity he has suffered, and as soon as he can breathe begins to plunge and kick and rear, throwing himself quite over in his struggles. Yet quietly he is pulled up, pulled down, pulled along, until he is ready for another lesson.

Upon the head of the horse now ready for breaking there is slipped a curious bitless bridle, or halter, of strands of rope, very strong and capable of being so arranged that too much pulling on it will close it fast upon a pony's nose and make the act of breathing difficult. This halter is called a "hackamore," and of course it was the invention of the Spaniard. The pony when put on the hackamore is staked out on the open ground on a long "stake rope." He is left alone for awhile here, and soon learns his next lesson. Resolved again in his heart to break this hated rope, he runs full speed to the end of it, and there comes to a halt with his heels high in the air and his neck perhaps doubled under him. If his neck happens to be broken it makes no difference, for there are other ponies just as good, plenty of them. If his neck is not broken, he gets up and does it over again, and perhaps again. Then he shakes his head and thinks it over. His next act will be to get himself tied up thoroughly in the coils of the rope, tripping himself, throwing himself, and burning his heels terribly on the harsh fibre of the rope. In this he is allowed to fcllow his own sweet will, because he is not intended to be used on Broadway, and a little skin missing here or there constitutes no drawback for the purposes of the range. The pony cuts and bruises himself and falls down, and no doubt reviles and swears in Spanish, but it does no good, except that ever there grows in his mind a vast and vaster respect for this relentless thing, this rope which has him fast.

And then Jim comes along after a while, with a rope or blanket or something of the sort, and begins to whip it over the back of the pony, driving the latter half crazy with fright, for never has he had such a thing near him before. The pony cringes and plunges, but Jim lays a hard hand upon the hackamore and draws him into submission and into a personal contact resented with all the soul of the fiery little creature thus robbed of his loved liberty. A second man comes up on the other side of the pony and lays hands upon him. In a twinkling a red kerchief is slipped across his face and tied fast to the side strands of the hackamore. Smitten with blindness, the pony cowers and is motionless and dumb. The end of the world for him has come, for never in all his wild life did he ere this fail to see the light of day or the half light of night, which served him full as well. Surely, thinks the pony, all now is over, and the end has come. He shrinks and does not resist the hand laid upon his muzzle, the other hand laid upon his ear, the twist given to his head,

the whipping of the blanket over and on his back,
touching him where never any object has touched before. But with a jerk he may perhaps throw off the
blinder of the handkerchief and begin instinctively
the wild stiff-legged bucking of his breed. "He's
shore bronch'," says Jim. "You'll have to hold his
head closter." Then the hackamore tightens again,
and the hands lay hold of the ears and the trembling
muzzle again, and—and then, before the frightened
and frenzied pony has had time to dread or suspect
anything further, there comes a rattle and a creak, and
there falls with an awful thud and crash upon his
back a vast thing the like of which he had never
dreamed for himself, though he has seen it upon the
tamed slaves which aided in his own undoing. The
saddle has been thrown upon him. Unless closely
blindfolded, he promptly bucks it off again, wildly
kicking into the bargain, his head tossed high with
terror and hatred, his legs straining back from the
iron hands that hold him.

But the iron hands do not relax. They hold like
the hands of fate. The saddle is bucked off time and
again, a dozen times, but it comes back again with the
thud and crash, and someway it does not actually kill,
after all. The pony stops to think about it. Jim, who
has been waiting for this moment of thought, cau-
tiously reaches under the pony with a long crooked stick
to the girth that hangs upon the farther side. Slowly
and quietly he pulls this girth to him, talking to the
pony the while. Slowly and quietly he puts the end of
the girth through the iron ring or buckle. Then, quietly, slowly, Jim gets out to the end of the "cinch"
as far as he can, because he knows what is going
to happen. Commonly the girth of the breaking
saddle has a big buckle with a tongue which will

quickly engage in the holes punched through the girth. Taking the cinch strap firmly in his hands, Jim gives a sudden jerk backward and upward, and the pony feels an awful grip of something tightened about his body where never such a thing had been felt before. At once, wild and demonlike in his rage and terror at such indignities, he falls wildly to bucking again; but now Jim is close up at his side, pulling the harder at the cinch, which does not slip but holds its own. The men at the pony's head swing down and twist his head askew. The hackamore tightens, the saddle holds. Tighter and tighter the girth goes, and at length the trembling beast feels he must endure this also. Panting and red-eyed, courageous and full of fight still, he braces his feet apart and stands so, trembling with anger and shame. And Jim quietly pokes another stick under and gets hold of another girth, the hind cinch (" flank girth," it is called in the South), and soon the pony feels upon his stomach the grip of this hairy, hateful thing, which all his life he never ceases to resent, because it cuts off his lung room and makes him feel uncomfortable with its sinking into the soft part of a pony's anatomy, which ought to be respected even by a cowpuncher, but isn't. The pony rebels again and viciously at this flank girth, but it does no good. The great saddle stays with him.

And now Jim, with his eyes gleaming a little and his jaws set hard together, slips up to the side of the panting pony, who stands with his head down, his legs apart, his eyes bloodshot, flinging his head from side to side now and again in a wild effort to break away and win back that freedom for which his heart is sobbing. Jim puts a cautious foot against the stirrup. The pony whirls away and glares at him. He realizes now what is the purpose of these enemies. Jim

speaks in low and soothing tones to him, but calls him
perhaps by some such name as, " You d—d black devil,
you hol' on a minute, kain't ye? Whoa, bronch'! "
Again and again Jim seeks a place with his left foot.
He has now gathered up into a coil the long stake
rope, and this he holds in his left hand or ties with
a half turn at the saddle horn. He knows there may
be a severance of the personal relations of himself
and the pony, and if so the rope will be needed to re-
establish them. At last Jim makes a swift run, a bound
and a spring all in one. Before the pony knows how
it has happened he feels upon his back a horrible
crushing weight. He feels his side half crushed in
by the grip of a long pair of human legs. He feels his
head " turned loose." He hears a long keen yell from
a dozen throats about him, answered by a similar shrill
yell, not of fear but of confidence, above him from
this creature which is crushing down his back, breaking in his sides. All the hate, the terror, the rage, the
fear, the viciousness, the courage of this undaunted
wild beast now become blended into a mad, unreasoning rage. He has fought the wolves, this pony, and
is afraid of nothing. He will unseat this demon above
him, he will kill him as he did the wolves; he will
trample him into the dirt of the plains. Down goes
the pony's head and into the air he goes in a wild,
serio-comic series of spectacular stiff-legged antics.
His nose between his knees, he bounds from the ground
with all four feet, and comes down again with all legs
set and braced, only to go into the air again and again.
He " pitches a-plungin' "—that is, jumping forward as
he bucks, perhaps going six hundred yards before he
stops for lack of wind. Or he may stand his ground
and pitch. He may go up and down, fore and aft, in
turn, or he may pitch first on one side and then the

other, letting his shoulders alternately jerk up and droop down almost to the ground—a very nasty sort of thing to sit through. He may spring clear up into the air and come down headed in the direction opposite to that he originally occupied, or he may " pitch fence cornered," or in a zigzag line as he goes on, bounding like a great ball from corner to corner of his rail-fence course of flight. The face of Jim may grow a little pale, his hand that pulls upon the hackamore may tremble a bit, and the arm that lashes the pony with the quirt may be a little weary, but still his legs hold their place, and his body, apparently loose and swaying easily from the waist up, keeps upright above the saddle. Jim knows this must be ridden out.

The pony soon exhausts himself with his rage. His breath comes short. He stops. The legs of the rider relax a trifle, but the eye does not. With a renewal of the wild screams or " bawling " with which he has punctuated his previous bucking performance the pony springs forward again at speed. He stops short with head down, expecting to throw the rider forward from the saddle. The rider remains seated, perhaps jarred and hurt, but still in the saddle. Then the pony rears up on his hind feet. The cowpuncher steps off with one foot, keenly watching to see whether the broncho is going over backward or going to " come down in front," and go on with his performance again. If he goes on, the rider is in the saddle as soon as the horse's feet are on the ground. If the pony throws himself over backward, as very likely he will, the rider does not get caught—at least, not always caught—but slips from the saddle, jerking up the pony's head sharply from the ground. He quickly puts his foot on the horn of the saddle, and there is the wild horse flat on the ground and absolutely helpless, trussed up by the bridle and held down by the foot at the saddle horn. If the horse could get his head to the ground he would have a leverage, and could break away and get up, but Jim is careful that he shall not get his head down. Meantime he " quirts him a-plenty." He does not talk soothingly now. He wants this pony to know that it is better to keep his feet on the ground than to acquire the habit of travelling on his back or on his hind feet. At last Jim lets the pony up, and, much to the surprise of the latter, the rider is someway again in the saddle.

Now the pony stands quiet, stubborn, with his head down, grunting at the stroke of the long rowelled spurs which strike his sides. At once he bounds forward again wildly, repeating his former devices at accomplishing the undoing of the rider, whom he now begins to fear and dread as well as hate. The latter is immovable in purpose, relentless of hand and limb. All this time he is riding without a bridle bit, depending only on the hackamore, which allows the horse much more freedom to show his repertory of feats than does the savage Spanish bit. The pony in time grows weary, and determines to vary its campaign by a Fabian policy. Again he stops still, " sulling," his ears back, but his legs braced stiffly. Jim is talking soothingly to him now, for Jim is no cruel Greaser horse breaker, after all, and has no vindictiveness for his mount, whose breaking is purely an impersonal business matter to him. The pony at length slowly turns his head around and bites with all his force straight into the leg that grips him. The heavy " chaps " protect the leg, and the spur strikes him upon the other side. He turns his head to that side also and bites that leg, but the same process occurs again. With a sullen fear eating at his heart, the pony tries yet another trick. Deliberately he drops to his knees and lies down quietly upon his side, perhaps holding the rider a willing prisoner fast by the leg which lies under his body. The rider need not be so caught unless he likes, but it is a superstition with Jim that the pony should never unseat the rider nor loosen the grip of the legs on his sides. Jim thinks that should he do this the matter of breaking would be longer and less effective, so he takes chances and holds his grip. Were the pony a big " States " horse, his manœuvre would be effective, and the rider would be in a sad predicament; but this horse weighs scarcely more than six hundred pounds, and the big stirrup, perhaps tied to its fellow on the opposite side, is under him, protecting the foot of the rider, who is now stretched out at full length upon the ground beside the horse. Moreover, the grass is up a few inches in height perhaps, and all in all the leg is able to stand the weight of the horse without being crushed, there being no stone or stub to offer injury, and so long as that is true the cowpuncher does not worry about it. He lies and talks to the pony kindly, and asks it how long it intends to stay there in that way, suggests that it is about time for him to go home for dinner, and that he has other work to do before the day is over. If the pony be very stubborn, he may lie so for several minutes, and Jim may take off his hat and put it under his own head to make the ground feel more comfortable. Both these wild creatures are watchful and determined. It is a battle of waiting. The pony is first to tire of it, for he does not clearly know how much damage he is doing the cowpuncher's leg, and would himself prefer to act rather than to wait. With a snort and a swift bound he is up on his feet and off, his spring jerking the rider's foot clear of the stirrup. At last he has won! He has unseated this clinging monster! He is free!

But almost as swift as the leap of the pony was that of the rider. He has tight in his hand the long stake rope, and with a flirt of the hand this unrolls. With a quick spring Jim gets to one side of the horse, for he knows that an " end pull " on the rope along the line of the horse's back will be hard to stop, whereas the matter is simpler if the rope makes an angle with the horse's course. His gloved hand grasps the rope and holds the end of it close against his right hip. His left hand runs out along the rope. His left leg is extended and braced firmly on the ground, and with all his weight he leans back on the rope until it is nearly taut. Then, just at the instant when the rope is about to tighten, he gives a swift rolling motion to it with his whole strength, sending a coiling wave along it as a boy does sometimes to a rope tied fast to a tree. This indescribable and effective motion is magical. The roll of the rope runs to the head of the pony just as the cowpuncher settles back firmly on his heels. The head of the horse comes down as though drawn by a band of iron. His heels go into the air, and over he comes, a very much surprised and chagrined cow pony. He awakes and arises to find the iron hand again at his head, the legs of steel again sitting him firmly. The pony has not known that, by this skilled handling of the stake rope at a time when a tenderfoot would be jerked clean from his feet, the cowpuncher can " bust wide open," as he calls it, the strongest pony on the range, the twist giving five times the power of a straight pull.

The heart of the pony fails at the shock of this sudden fall. His head droops. His ears relax from the side of his head where they have been tight tucked.

8

Through his red, bloodshot eyes the landscape swims dully. He looks with a sob of regret at the wide sweep of the prairie lying out beyond, at the shade of the timber mottes on the horizon, at the companions of his kind, who look toward him now with heads uplifted. At last he begins to realize that he is a captive, that freedom is for him no more, that he has met his master in a creature stronger in will and in resource than himself. The cowpuncher urges him gently with his knee, talking to him softly. "Come, bronch'," he says. "It's 'bout dinner time. Let's go back to the ranch." And the broncho, turning his head clear around at the pull on the hackamore—for he is not yet bridlewise—turns and goes back to the ranch, his head hanging down.

The next day the pony has regained something of his old wildness and self-confidence, but is not so bad as he was at first, and the result is the same. Meantime he has been learning yet more about the lesson of not "running against rope," and has cut his heels so much that he is beginning to be more careful how he plunges at the stake. The cowpuncher rides him at times in this way for four days or so on the hackamore, and then puts on a light bridle bit, riding him then a couple of days longer, gradually teaching the use of the bit and bridle. Then the hackamore is taken off, and the pony begins to learn that the best thing he can do is to turn at the touch of the rein on the neck and to stop at the instant the reins come up sharply. In two weeks the pony is quite a saddle horse, though it is well to watch him all the time, for he has a lightning estimation of the man about to ride him, will know if the latter is afraid, and will take advantage of his trepidation. All his life the pony will remember how to pitch a bit at times, perhaps just for fun, be-

cause he "feels good," perhaps for ugliness. All his
life he will hate a hind cinch, but all his life he will
remember the lesson about "going against rope," and
will stop still when the rope touches him. Even if
very late in life he resumes a bit of friskiness and
evades the rope a little in the corral, the sight of another horse jerked end over end is apt to bring him to
a sudden sense of what may happen, and he sobers
down very quickly. The writer recalls a big black
Spanish pony which was very bad on the stake, and had
learned some way of getting up his picket pin and running off, contriving to loosen the pin by side pulls first
on one side and then the other. One day he ran off in
this way with rope and pin dangling, and started at full
speed through a bit of timber. The jumping picket
pin, whipped about at the end of the rope, caught
about a tree with a sudden twist, and the horse got
one of the worst falls it was ever the fortune of cow
pony to experience, going into the air clear and coming down on his back with all four feet up. He was a
dazed and repentant horse, and from that time on, in
the words of the cowpunchers, he was "plum tender
about rope."

In the breaking season on a horse ranch the education of several ponies would be going at once, and
thus a half dozen breakers would in the course of the
summer break in a good number of horses. Sometimes
a few additional "busters" would be hired, these sometimes paid by the head—say five dollars or so a head,
according to the time and locality. The close of the
season would see the horse ranch ready to sell off quite
a band of broken horses. These might go into the
"cavvieyard" (*caballada;* sometimes corrupted also into
"*cávayer*" or "*cáv-a-yah*") of some outfit bound up
the trail, or they might go to some other part of the

cow range. Some of the breakers would be apt to go
up the trail—a great ambition among cowpunchers in
the early days. Thus Jim was something of a traveller.
He saw many parts of the range, and became as ready
to settle in Wyoming as in New Mexico, in Montana
as the "Nations." But wherever Jim went, no matter
upon what part of the range, his mount was some one
of these sturdy little wild horses of the range. This
horse would stick with the herd when the day herder
came out to drive in the bunch for the day's work. It
would pause in its bound and throw itself back on its
haunches when the rope tightened on the leg of a steer.
It would stand still as though tied if the cowpuncher
threw the reins down over its head and left them hanging. It would stay in a flimsy rope corral made by
stretching a single rope from a wagon wheel to the
pommel of a saddle. It would comport itself with
some effort at common sense in a storm, though sometimes breaking out into the wildest and most uncontrollable of panics. A stampede of the horse herd was
far worse and harder to handle than a stampede of
cattle, and the very worst of all stampedes was that
of a band of old saddle horses. But gradually the
pony learned its trade, and forgot its former complete
freedom in the half freedom of the ranch work. It
learned to follow the herds of cattle with a vast touch
of superiority in its tone. It would plunge into the
mill of a round-up and follow like a bird each turn
of a running steer, cheerfully biting its thick hide at
every jump, and enjoying the fun as much as the rider.
It would travel hour after hour across the wavering
and superheated sands of the desert country, not complaining about water, and willing to make its living
at night by picking at the short grass of the hard
ground in the summer, sometimes living on browse in

winter, and never, in the early days, even knowing a
taste of grain. (The Texas herds that came up in the
early days would at first nearly starve before they
would eat corn or oats). This cow horse never had a
grooming in all its life, and if touched by a curry-
comb would have kicked the groom to death in a moment and then broken down the corral. Its back was
sure to be sore, and its temper accordingly a trifle uncertain, but it would go its journey and do its stint
and take what Nature gave it. Its rough rider had small
apparent love for it, but would occasionally slap its
side with a rough gesture of half regard after some
long ride when it stood, tucked up and steaming, panting with the fatigue of the work. No blanket ever
covered it after the hardest ride, and in winter it had
no shelter but what it could find for itself. Hardier
than a steer, and with more intelligence, it would live
where cattle would starve to death, pawing down
through the snow and getting food while the horned
herds were dropping of starvation all about it.

No cow horse ever attained to the dignity of a name
of its own, though it might for purposes of identification be mentioned in some descriptive term, as the
" wall-eyed cayuse," the " star-face sorrel," the " white-
eyed claybank," the " O Bar horse from Texas," etc.
Yet each cowpuncher of the ranch force would know
almost every horse belonging to the outfit, and if one
strayed could describe it to any one he met, and in
such fashion as would enable the other, if he were a
cowman himself, to identify it at once. This keen
observation was matter of habit on the range, and its
development was greatest among the old-time men of
the open ranges.

Without the American cow pony there could have
been no cattle industry, there could have been no cow-

boy. Thus the horse was the most essential and valuable property of the cowman—indeed, of any man who faced the great distances of the plains. The cow range was a horseback country. Men had few items of property, and could carry little with them. What they had they needed, and most of all they needed their means of transportation. The horse thief was the criminal most hated and despised in such a country, and his punishment was always summary and swift. The horse thief asked no mercy, for none was ever given. The justice of the plains was stern. The hunting parties who went out after a horse thief rarely came back with him. Commonly there would be a grave report made to the authorities that the prisoner had been taken, but had unfortunately escaped. Mexicans at times were enterprising horse thieves on the lower ranges. One ranch party pursued and shot four such thieves on one occasion, and threw their bodies up on top of the chaparral; yet the report at the settlement was that the prisoners had " escaped in the night from their guards." One other party came in empty-handed, and said their prisoner had " jumped over a bluff and received fatal injuries." So he had, though two bullet holes were found in his body by the coroner. A negro horse thief was pursued at another time, and it was declared that he had been " found drowned." This also appeared to be true, but he was later discovered to have stones tied about his neck and several bullet holes through his body. Nothing but extreme youth could serve as a defense for the man found guilty of stealing horses. It was of no avail for him to attempt to palliate or deny. It took the early cowmen a long time to become patient enough to wait for legal conviction of such a criminal, and the delays of the law seemed to them wasteful and wrong. An old-time cowpuncher, speak-

ing of this feeling, voiced the general sentiment.
" Why, h—l," said he, " a horse thief ain't folks! " In
these summary trials of the plains it was very rare that
mistakes were made. The same cowpuncher, for the
time more confidential than his kind on such topics,
where reticence was usually permanent, admitted that
he was out on one round-up of a horse-thieving band
when fifteen men were hung. " An'," said he, with
conscious virtue in his tone, " we never did make but
one or two mistakes, an' them fellers ought to a-been
hung anyhow."

There comes to mind one such hunt for a horse
thief, though in this case the youth of the offender
saved his life. The writer was riding alone over
a part of the cattle range in the extreme West, some
thirty miles from a settlement, when he saw the dust
of an approaching vehicle. In those times and in that
country any such coming traveller was regarded with
interest, for it was never known what he might prove
to be. In this case it turned out to be nothing more
formidable than a fourteen-year-old boy, who was driving a jaded team hitched to a buckboard. The boy was
anxious and alert-looking, and held between his knees
as he drove a Winchester rifle, on which he kept one
hand in a manner familiar enough for one so young.
He drove steadily on, and of course was not suspected
of being anything more than a chance traveller in a
country where nothing that one did ever attracted
much attention. Some miles farther along, however,
at a point where the trail turned into the rough volcanic country known as the Mal Pais, there came gal-
loping into view a band of eight dusty and determined-
looking cowpunchers, who pulled up short and stopped
the traveller, asking what had been seen back farther on
the trail. The description of the outfit passed fitted

their case exactly, and they said that the boy had stolen the team from a ranch fifty miles away. The men dismounted, loosened their saddle girths for a moment, and gave their animals chance to breathe, but soon were in the saddle again, and sweeping on over the hot flats on a long gallop. They caught the boy about twelve miles farther on, where he had stopped for food and water. He made a show of fight, but was disarmed. Some were for hanging him, but the majority thought it was wrong to hang a "kid," so he was set free. The cowpunchers brought back the buckboard and team, leaving the ambitious youth at last accounts on foot in the middle of the plains. His youth had been a blessing to him.

CHAPTER VI.

MARKS AND BRANDS.

LET us suppose that we have, so to speak, discovered our cowboy, and have traced rudely the beginnings of his occupation, that we have noted something of his equipment and his adjuncts, and gained some partial idea of his environments. It would seem, then, very fit to inquire somewhat of the motives and methods of the cowboy and his calling. If we have been in the least just to this rude character, we shall have seen that the foundation of his whole sense of morality is a love of justice. In that one thought we have the key alike to the motives of the cowboy and the methods of his trade. Crude and loose as were those methods, their central idea was the purpose of substantial justice, their animating and innate intent a firm respect for the property rights of one's fellow-man. Those rights, large as they were and as indefinite, were held merely on the tenure of a sign.

The sign of ownership on the cow range was as potent as the iron bars of hoarded wealth in the settlements. The respect for this sign was the whole creed of the cattle trade. Without a fence, without a bar, without an atom of actual control, the cattle man held his property absolutely. It mingled with the property of others, but it was never confused therewith. It wandered a hundred miles from him, and he knew not where it was, yet it was surely his and sure to find him. To touch it was crime. To appropriate it meant punishment. Common necessity made common custom, which became common law, which in time became statutory law. But with each and every step of this was mingled the first and abiding principle of the American cattle man—the love of justice.

For the salient features of the cow trade we must go far back into the past, and as usual search among its beginnings in the Spanish Southwest. What, then, must have been the problem which presented itself to that old Spaniard, the first cowman of the West, as he sat a half-wild horse in a country almost wild, and looked out over herds of cattle wholly wild? He could not feed these cattle, and he could not fence them. They roamed free and uncontrolled, mingled with herds from other parts of the country which were supposed to belong to some other owner. How should he establish the extent of his just claims as against the just claims of his neighbour? Surely it must have taken even the slow mind of the old Spaniard but a moment to realize that he must find some means of pinning upon each separate animal of all the thousands his own sign of ownership, so that it should not be confused with the animals belonging to other men. But how should this be done? This sign must be something which would endure always, which neither wind nor water would erase. How could such a thing be compassed? Surely, reasoned this distant and mist-enwrapped old Spaniard, this sign must be burned deep into the hide of the creature itself! For the creature did not shed its hide. The mark burned there would always remain. Had not the galleys of Europe shown that? Had not the Inquisition taught it, and the Incas proved it in their persons? Truly the question was solved. On each animal there must be seared this sign!

This was an idea which grounded itself upon justice—that justice in this case perhaps tempered with a respect for the knife and *escopeta* of one's neighbour. At least, our early ranchman talked this over with his neighbour, and thus they formed the first cattle men's association of the range, and registered the first brands. No doubt these primitive cowmen went at their business in a loose and inefficient way. They drove into the nearest corral all the cattle they could find, irrespective of age or sex, and, each agreeing upon what should be called his own, they began tracing upon the shrinking hides of the animals the first rude imagery of ownership. No regular stamp for the branding implement had been formulated. The only branding iron was a straight bar of iron, whose end was heated red hot in the fire and then used as a glowing pencil with which to inscribe on the living flesh the agreed emblem of title. It is not likely that the initials of the owners were the first signs used, for the old dons had so many initials and titles that the hide of an ordinary steer would hardly have served to show them writ large as their owners liked to see them. But that was a day of crests and coronets and heraldic signs, as well as a day of much religious fervour. The cross, the sword, the lance—these were things much in view in that time, and perhaps they contributed of their significance to these first totems of the trade. The circle, the square, the triangle, the bar, the parallel lines—all these, too, were things simple and not easily to be confused. Some of the old Spanish brands have hints of some such origin. They were executed upon a large scale, the expanse of hide seeming to invite large patterns for their tracery. When imagination failed a

ranchero in those days, he varied matters by a series of
unique cuttings of portions of the animal's anatomy.
Perhaps he cut off half an ear from each of his calves,
or cut an ear off on one side and made a deep V in
the other ear. Or he undercut one ear, or slit both
ears, or did many other ingenious embroideries in such
portions of the animal as offered him the best field for
operation. He might cut a wattle on a jaw, or slit the
dewlap so it hung down, etc. These marks were as
constant as the brands, and of course needed to be
done in the same regular fashion. They continue in
use upon the range to-day. Of course, as the country
grew older and more cattle came upon the range—the
property of an increasing number of owners—there
arose necessity for increasing variety in marks and
brands, each of which needed to be different from all
others, and yet simple and readily recognised under
the conditions of ranch life. To-day there are thousands and thousands of such different brands.

For many generations the cattle of the prolific
Southwest ran free, each bearing on its hide the sign
of the man who owned it. That is to say, a part of the
cattle did, for in the loose methods of the early days
the *rodeo* was shiftless and imperfect, and many cattle
got through year after year unbranded. Such cattle
ran wild over the range, and belonged to nobody or
to anybody. There was no system of dividing them
out among owners. They were not enumerated or
estimated or taken into account. Each *ranchero*
branded cattle until he felt too weary to continue in
the work, and so left it to the saints to finish, or until
he had all the cattle he cared for. A cow was worth
no actual price, and such a thing as a market there
was not. The unbranded cattle increased in numbers for
many years. Of course, every one has heard of the enter-

prising Texan of the second quarter of this century,
by the name of Maverick, who made a business of
searching the range for such unbranded cattle and
putting his own brand on all such he found. Thus in
a few seasons he got together an enormous herd, and so
laid the foundation for a vast fortune. His example
was followed by many, and until a time long after the
civil war the "Maverick" supply was a prominent
source of profit in the cattle trade. Many a young
man owed his start in life and subsequent independence to this custom, which at the time was an allowable
and legitimate one; and there were large herds in
Texas and New Mexico which had their beginnings in
such operations. At the time of the opening of the
Northern ranges the Maverick industry was less profitable, but the question of unbranded cattle still remained; for, of course, in the nature of things it was
impossible to collect every animal born upon the
plains, and so there ran at large the unestablished title
to a vast amount of wealth, whose consideration was
one demanding serious thought.

Yet another question came into the early problems
of the cattle trade. At times a man might wish to sell
some or all of his cattle. His son might wish to marry
and move away, or his son's wife might wish to bring
as dowry a few cows, or he might wish to pay his wife's
father a few cows for his daughter. How could such
change of ownership be indicated? Naturally, by the
addition of the receiver's personal brand. But then
some suspicious soul asked, How shall we know whence
such and such cows came, and how tell whether or not
this man did not steal them outright from his neighbour's herd and put his own brand on them? Here
was the origin of the bill of sale, and also of the coun-
terbrand, or the "vent brand," as it is known on the

upper ranges (probably through the corruption of the word " vendor " or " vend "). The owner used his own brand on another part of the animal, and this, in the sign language of the range, meant, " I, owner of the recorded brand of, say, Triple Cross, have sold this animal, as see his hide, to the owner of the recorded brand of, say, J. Bar A." The bill of sale corroborated this unchanging record. It was a trifle unfortunate for the animal if it chanced to be conveyed a great many times. Some animals from the Spanish ranges in the early cattle days were covered with a medley of composite marks with which the fabled lawyer from Philadelphia would certainly have been quite helpless.

Yet another use of the idea of marks and brands came up at the time of the transfers of the great herds from the South to the North at the time of the trails. As it was very likely that such herds would suffer much loss on the way from straying or stampeding or theft, it was customary to "road brand" each animal of such a herd, this brand being the sign of ownership *en route*. This brand saved many cattle to the drovers, as there were certain men who made a business of looking up missing cattle and returning them for a *per capita* consideration to their owners.

Such were some of the more obvious and simple forms of the necessities and uses of marks and brands. Almost without further investigation one could predict the method and the system of the trade, and see how efficient though rude must be such methods, how just the results obtained by them under the wild surroundings of an unsettled region. One could predict also something of the character of the cowboy. Of all the methods of the cattle industry and of its dominating intention of justice the cowboy was the active agent. He lived his life in a high and not ignoble atmosphere, and he learned a creed whose first tenet was the rugged spirit of fair play. The natural offspring of such surroundings was a normal and manly nature, too bold for craft, too strong for a thing dishonourable. Popular opinion, formed upon impressions entirely erroneous in the first place, clings to the belief that the chief characteristics of the cowboy were his "toughness" and lawlessness. Those who knew him were aware that his chief trait was his honesty.

But if we set so high a standard for our cowpuncher—one which is certainly not too high—let us not be deluded into the belief that the calling transmuted into metal of equal value all the material that came under it. At the very hour that the American cowboy first rode upon the stage of history there rode behind him a man almost his counterpart in the rugged qualities of the physical man, and like to him in every way except in moral manhood. As the cowboy was the guardian of herds, so was this slinking shadow their menace and their enemy. The advent of the cattle thief was simultaneous with that of the cowboy. We shall need to see how the system of marks and brands was concerned with the operations of this dishonest man.

It is very easy to see how temptation was offered to the cow thief and "brand blotter." Here were all these wild cattle running loose over the country. The imprint of a hot iron on a hide made the creature the property of the brander, provided no one else had branded it before. The time of priority was matter of proof. With the handy "running iron," or straight rod, which was always attached to his saddle when he rode out, could not the cow thief erase a former brand and put over it one of his own? Could he not, for instance, change a U into an O, or a V into a diamond,

or a half circle into a circle? Could he not, moreover,
kill and skin an animal and sell the beef as his own?
Between him and the owner was only this little mark.
Between him and changing this mark was nothing
but his own moral principles. The range was very
wide. Hardly a figure would show on that unwinking
horizon all day long. And what was a heifer here or
there?

The cow thief was a danger to the interests of all
cattle men, and the existence of a common danger suggested the idea of mutual organization against it. The
cattle men's associations were a necessity, and so came
early into life. To-day every State and Territory where
there are considerable cattle interests has such an
association, and all these are again united in a national
association. These organizations are a power in the
land, and have had very much to do with the development and expansion of the cattle trade. They enforce
the laws bearing upon this industry, and they have
secured the enactment of many salutary measures
which stand upon the statute books of a dozen different States. Thus a State may make it compulsory for
any butcher to produce upon demand the hide of any
animal he has butchered, and this hide must show the
brand mark, and he must be able to explain how he
came in possession of the animal. Always this little
mark of ownership is held the " best possible evidence "
that the law demands in any case at bar. Altering
brands was early made a very serious offence, and the
occupation of a brand blotter was a risky one.

Early in the history of the complexity of range
brands it became customary for each ranch to have its
branding irons made of a fixed stamp or pattern, the
brand being a stencil or stamp rather than a pencil
or pen for writing upon the hide. This was at first

a matter of convenience, but in time became in some States a matter of law. Texas in the '70's passed an act forbidding the use of the " running iron " in branding. The ranchman who had acquired by purchase several brands beside his own original registered brand, and who was in the habit of writing his brands with the single iron as occasion required, was forced to carry with him to his work a separate iron for each brand. This, of course, was a blow aimed at the brand blotter, whose innocent single iron would tell no tales if he were caught out riding across the range. The law made an object of suspicion the man found with the single running iron. He was obliged to explain, and that sometimes before a very urgent jury. To protect their brands and regulate the handling of the increase, the ranchers of the different portions of the range very early saw the necessity for the organization of their protective associations. The by-laws of one of these great bodies (the Montana Stock Growers' Association) will serve to show the purposes of all. Section 2 of the by-laws reads:

" The object of this association is to advance the interests of the stock growers in Montana and adjoining States and Territories, and for the protection of the same against frauds and swindlers, and to prevent the stealing, taking, and driving away of cattle, horses, mules, and asses from the rightful owners thereof, and to enforce the Stock Laws of the State of Montana."

Reference to the Brand Book of this association shows that the State board of stock commissioners numbers sixteen men; that the State association has, besides its regular officers, an executive committee of forty-two men; that its membership numbers nearly two hundred; that the different brands registered by owners of the association run fairly into the thousands;

9

for hardly any ranch exists which does not own cattle bearing marks and brands very dissimilar in their nature. A range covered by a given rancher's cattle may have upon it a great many cattle strayed in from other ranges, which mingle their brands with those owned by the ranch through purchase. Very curious and interesting indeed are the pages of such a " brand book " of a cattle association. A page taken at random from the book of the Montana association shows thirty-five different brands besides the home brand of the owner and his " vent " or selling brand. Each of these brands is registered, and each must come into account in the cattle trade along with those of the many other cattle men of the State. Is it not easy to see to what extent has run the idea of the old Spaniard who first conceived the notion of writing his totem on the hide of his cows? Moreover—for we are concerned not so much with the cattle trade as with the cowboy who conducts that trade—is it not easy to see what intelligence and skill such a calling demands of any man? The brands of a single ranch would confuse utterly the eye of a tenderfoot; but the foreman Jim, or nearly any man under him, will in his riding over the range unconsciously record upon his mind the brand of almost every animal within his vision, and that at a distance which to the unpractised eye would be impossible. He will note the presence of a strange brand upon some animal, and will note that yet another is carrying no brand at all.

This last animal which Jim finds in the category of those met in his daily review, this Maverick of the range, still remains an interesting element in the cow industry. At an earlier day on all the ranges it was customary for any man who liked to rope and brand such animals found wild and unmarked on the open

range. Then it became customary to brand only such
as were found on that country so circumscribed as to
be called the individual range of such certain owner.
For instance, in the waterless Southwest, the cattle
were limited in their feeding habits by the necessity
of going to water. The water of one ranch held its
own cattle pretty well distinguished from those of another. At times the round-up in such a country was
a very loose affair, perhaps only one or two owners par-
ticipating in it. In such a country, if in the spring
or summer after the round-up a calf was found carrying no brand, it was branded forthwith by the man
finding it on his range. The question of drifts and
strays was not then so important as it has since become, and the sharp-eyed cowboy who saw an unbranded animal on the range of his ranch took it for
granted without investigation that it was the descend-
ant of one of his employer's cows. This might or
might not be just, but it was the nearest approach
to justice under the obtaining conditions. As the
conditions changed with the advent of additional numbers of cattle owners upon the range, so also the demands of abstract justice changed. Thus it is to-day
the custom in a round-up district—say, of the State of
Montana—to offer at sale in public auction all the
Mavericks that may be found in the round-up. These
are bid upon and sold at so much a head before the
round-up, no one, of course, knowing how many head
there will be. The amount of money thus obtained is
distributed *pro rata* among the cattle owners, the sole
idea being, as we have above suggested, the intention
to be just to all. This is thought to be fairer than
to allow each man to hunt up his own Mavericks. Diligence in the Maverick industry is no longer a desirable
trait in the cattle country. On the contrary, it is some-

thing regarded with much suspicion and watchfulness, and has led to the stretching of many necks as well as many pocketbooks. The "rustler" may brand upon the range, but in many parts of the cattle country to-day the associations ask every one else to do his branding in the presence of his associates in business; this rule subject to local variations.

Thus we see that the old Spaniard's idea has travelled very far in its widened applications and its extension of usefulness. Indeed, it goes yet further in its bearings upon the trade. As the brand is lifelong in its nature, so is it lifelong in its usefulness. The beginning of an animal's life is upon the range; its end is in the markets of the East, in the stock yards of the great cities. At each great live-stock market—such as Chicago, Kansas City, Omaha, etc.—each cattle association of the States and Territories where range cattle are shipped now has a special officer, known as a brand inspector, who has such help as he needs in his work. Whenever a car load of ranch cattle comes into the market, it is viewed by the proper inspector, who examines the cattle to see if they are branded in uniform manner. Suppose the brand of the shipper is IXL, and that among these IXL cattle there are found two steers branded AXL. The inspector at once asks where the latter came from, and if the shipper can not explain at once how they came to be with his cattle, he is subjected to rigid examination, which may lead to his prompt arrest by the inspector. Unless satisfactory answers can be made to such questions, the suspected animals are taken away from the rest of the shipment and sold by the inspectors. The money from such sale is sent at once, not to the owner of the IXL cattle, but in due routine to the owner of the AXL brand. The whereabouts of the latter is very

likely easily discovered by reference to the State Brand
Book; but if he can not be found, and no representative secured to accept this money sent him from the
inspector, the proceeds are finally given to the treas-
urer of the State association, to be applied to the good
of the whole cattle industry of the State.   Here again
is a very powerful example of the idea of justice, and a
very good instance of the fact that the old Spaniard
builded far better than he knew.

The cattle trade with all its ramifications has never
gone, and can never get any further than the possibilities
of the old Spaniard's marks and brands.   These tokens
of ownership remain to-day the expression of a sentiment of integrity and of a wish for common justice.
The outdwellers of the plains have as high a standard
of commercial honour as obtains in the most intricate
banking system of the cities.   Not Wall Street nor
the Board of Trade ever inculcated principles more
rigid or of more worth.   But, as a house is no better
than its servants, and as no law is stronger than its
executive measures, so is the cattle trade no better
than the cowboy.   He is its head executive and its
working manager, and upon his personal qualities of
hardihood and honourableness depends the success of
every venture in the wild unfettered business of the
range.   It is the cowpuncher who first brands the calf
when it becomes the property of his ranch.   He is
perhaps foreman of the ranch which raises it.   He may
pull it out of the bog hole where it would perish.   He
may protect it against theft.   He may drive it to a
range where it can better live.   He is perhaps captain
of the round-up which " throws it over " to its proper
range if it has strayed.   He may assist on the drive
which takes it to the market after the beef round-up,
or he may even go with it to the distant city.   The

very brand inspector who examines it there as the rules
of justice require is certainly no man who got his place
through political preferment, but is some old cowboy,
trained by long years of experience to catch quickly
the brand upon any living creature. He practises
his trade here in the cattle pens of the city, but he
learned it out there on the range, where the earth was
very wide and gray, and where the sky was very wide
and blue, bending over him with even arch on each
hand alike, as wide and as blue for one man as for
another.

CHAPTER VII.

FREE GRASS AND WATER FRONTS.

FORTUNATE indeed must have been our ancient *ranchero*, the first cowman of the West. Before him lay an untouched world, vast, vague, and inviting. What must have been to him the whispers that came across the plains? Did the spirits say nothing to him of the mysterious, the unexplored? Did no wild bird, winging high over this calm and smiling country, carry to him some hint of that which lay beyond? Was there not some voice whispering in the grasses telling him of things yet to be? Did there not come to him out of that vague, alluring, compelling Unknown some unseen, shadowy, irresistible beckoning? We know of the tasks of those first travellers, but what do we know of their impulses? Perhaps they dared go forward because they dared not do otherwise.

To the imagination of the old Spaniard this unknown country was not a land of cattle, but a land of gold. His thought was always upon gold, and all else was incidental. He looked out over the range of these "cattle of deformed aspect," as Coronado called the buffalo, and he figured to himself that somewhere out in that vast wind-swept solitude there must lie the fabled Seven Cities of Cibola, whose streets were of solid gold, and whose edifices were all builded in that same precious metal. Coronado—bold soul!—had this thought ever in his mind as he pressed on in his march from Mexico to the Missouri River, the first man to cross the American cattle plains. Always he thought to see the towers arise beyond, out there in the blue and gray horizon. Nay, in his dreams by night he must have seen these cities. In his dreams by day he must have seen them, rising, beckoning, eluding, evading, the wraith of his cherished hope. On and on, far across the red *mesas* of New Mexico, across the white flats of Texas, the gray plains of Kansas, he pressed, until he stood at the banks of the great Missouri, boundary to-day of the cattle range, a disappointed but still believing man. He turned back—he and all his men on foot—and crossed the great range again on his return to Mexico, seeing many thousands of these cattle of "deformed aspect," but not finding the cities of Cibola. Yet behind him, as they had been before him, there arose and danced on the air, waving, beckoning, these cities of gold. To their beckoning have come since then the thousands of the world. The gold that built their structures lay under Coronado's feet as he walked those many weary leagues, this glorious and still remembered soldier of another day.

All the gold of the cattle range lay before the first *ranchero*, all the untouched resources of an empire. All the range was "free grass" then, and the Spaniard grumbled because it was not all free gold. Alas! for those days, and ah! for one more country anywhere upon this globe which shall for one moment compare with that West which lay before the first cowman on the range!

For a century or two it was still free grass. Since all the earth lay open to everybody, what need to fence a portion of it? If a neighbour came from a hundred miles away, was he not welcome? His cattle would not come so far, but would stay nearer to the range where they were born. But after a time there began to be more people and more cattle. Some strong-legged *hidalgo*, who had walked a thousand leagues or so and made some hundreds of Indian converts by the simple process of cutting off their heads, had for this high service to the Crown and Church gift made to him of some great grant of land. The sovereign granting this land to his beloved subject had no idea where it was, and neither had the subject. He came to America with a parchment entitling him to enter into possession of so many miles of land, beginning at a stone and running to a tree, and this was description good enough so long as no one cared. The *hidalgo* was pretty sure to locate his grant upon the best water he could find, for in that dry and desert country water was something of the most constant concern. The man who went on a journey took with him certain skins of water, lest he should find none on the way. A little *rio*, a living spring, a tank that never failed—these were the things which determined the locations of *haciendas* and of towns. The families which were later to be the great and wealthy ones were those lucky enough to get in upon the shores of some large river such as the Rio Grande. Less fortunate was he who had but a tiny spring which flowed a feeble rivulet over the thirsty soil.

There came a time when the cattle of some adjoining *rancho* trampled the spring of some old *ranchero*, who in wrath laid down a few crooked cedar boughs about the spring, and thus built the first fence upon the range. As this old *ranchero* had his sheepskin grant, and as he, moreover, perhaps had a body of men trained and paid to fight for him, he was no doubt allowed to leave his fence as he had placed it, and the cattle went elsewhere to drink. Their owner in turn fenced off for himself a bit of water, building a fine large fence of cedar limbs, bound well together with strips of rawhide. And so this went on, generation after generation, each generation needing more range and more water, though still the generous West had enough for all.

There was abundance of grass for all, but the water was startlingly and disproportionately scanty. Yet if a man kept his title legally or by force of arms to the water he had fenced, what was to be done? The cattle could go only so far to drink, and if the owner of a water front wanted all the water for himself, there was no way to settle it but to buy him out, kill him, or marry into his family—all of which methods were popular, and each of which had especial merits of its own. Water front thus came to be the one desired thing in the cattle trade of the dry Southwest. In brief, the grass was free, but the water was not free. The result was that the man who owned the water had all outdoors for his range, and needed to pay not a dollar for any land outside that along the water. No one wanted this outside land. Any one could settle upon it who liked, but it was very sure no one would like.

Perhaps there was a daughter of some *ranchero's* family who owned a mile of water front and a heart susceptible to the charms of the robust *Americano*. Some wandering teamster, perhaps a deserter from one army or other in the civil war, drifted in across this country, met and wooed and married the *señorita*, and so after a fashion got control of the water front. Perhaps the teamster sold out after a while to some ranch agent, giving at least a quit-claim deed to his shadowy rights, and moved off across the country again, probably to marry some other *señorita* at some other place. Then perhaps the ranch agent hired some cowboy or some one else who was not very busy just then to " file on a quarter " on some other water at another place, he making his claim under the Desert Lands Act, or the Mineral Lands Act, or the Homestead Act, or any other act upon which there could be hung a lawsuit or a fight. Since the only opposing title was perhaps one dating back into the impenetrable haze of some Spanish land grant, and since it was very far to the city of Washington, and since, moreover, it was a weary country, where no one cared very much what any one else was doing, the affair was probably concluded pleasantly all around, with not more funerals than seemed absolutely necessary. Thus the land agent got control of several " pieces of water," no one knowing or caring who owned the land. Then, if this were in the palmy days of the trade, the agent very likely went to Europe and sold out all the land lying between these pieces of water which he owned and which he did not own, Government land and all, fraudulent homestead or desert or mineral land entries included, to whatsoever customer he could find. It was not difficult to find a buyer in those days, for Europeans had no knowledge of this country, and were wild at the stories of the profits of the cattle trade, than which nothing ever did figure out more handsomely upon paper. Sometimes the land agent had a map of his country nicely executed. It is of record that one of the most successful of these ranch agents took over to Holland with him a finely drawn map of a tract of land in New Mexico, showing many rivers no one else had ever found, and displaying steamboats, with pretty clouds of smoke rolling from their smokestacks, navigating the waters of the upper Pecos, where really a

man could wade comfortably for mountain trout. Yet
this map did its work, and made the man his fortune.
Some time after he had departed, the Holland syndicate bethought itself to send over a representative to
look into this land of steamboats. This representative
assured them that they ought certainly to have their
money back, for no steamboats could be found. It
was too late then, however. The jovial inhabitants
laughed merrily at the protests of the foreign customers for a cattle ranch, nor has explanation ever been
forthcoming for the absence of the steamboats on the
Pecos. A wealthy Englishman or English syndicate
was a favourite customer for such a tract of land, and
history hath not yet recorded all the frauds that were
perpetrated upon foreigners under the name of ranch
property in the sunny and calm Southwest. In these
operations there were so many crimes committed
against the United States land laws that early in the
'80's inspectors were sent down by the Government,
who looked into matters and uncovered a very pretty
kettle of fish.

In other portions of the Southern country where
also the soil was dry and valueless, vast bodies of land
held under various individual or State titles were upon
the market at a price of not more than a few cents an
acre. Fifteen cents an acre was long thought to be
an exorbitant price for land which has since then sold
for many dollars an acre. Many men thus got control
of large bodies of land by actual purchase. Many
leased or bought large tracts of school lands or railroad lands, perhaps leasing every alternate section of
the land. This latter tenure usually seemed sufficient
to warrant fencing in the entire tract upon which the
alternate sections lay, this keeping out other parties
who did not know just what was the description of

the land. Limits and bounds were more elastic in those days than they are now, for the country seemed unspeakably large and inexhaustible. Numbers of alien landholders went into the State of Texas under ranch titles such as the above. In time there came to be trouble over ranch titles in that State, just as there has been trouble in every State where the loose nature of such titles has finally been discovered. Meantime the farming element came steadily on in Texas, and now that State is free grass no more, and the rancher must there control his holdings under some process of law.

In the Indian Nations, to follow the course of the ranch to the North, the cattle men did not have free grass, but made very desirable leases of large tracts of land of the Indians, often gaining extremely valuable privileges at a nominal cost. Later these privileges were much curtailed by the Government. The Kiowas and Comanches leased their own land direct to the cattle men. In the case of the Cherokees and Creeks the leases had to run to the United States Government, the usual form being a *per capita* tax upon all cattle pastured upon the tribal lands. But as this tax was sometimes estimated upon the cattle actually shipped, and not upon those actually ranged, the sophisticated ranchmen were able to stand the hardship. The " ten-mile strip " on the upper part of these lands, adjoining the State of Kansas, was parceled out into lots of perhaps ten by twenty miles, and leased to cattle men, who fenced it, charging up the cost of the fencing against their lease payments, and leaving the Indians owners of the fences, as they desired to be; for they did not want their own cattle running over the farms of the Kansas grangers. All the moneys of the ten-mile strip leases were applied to the joint revenue of the tribes. The cattle men of the Nations have their ranges under fence, so that the old forms of cattle growing are there much changed, the business being more like a vast farming operation. Under such conditions all the features of round-ups, the question of Mavericks, etc., are much simplified. Yet the tenure of the ranch holdings in the Nations is a more or less uncertain thing, held in some sections only from year to year, and subject to the watchfulness of the authorities at Washington. There is no free grass in that country now.

In Kansas there is a herd law, under which the farmer does not fence his land, but which compels the cattle man to pay for any damage done by his cattle to the crops of the farmer. Naturally the cowman does not love a State where they "turn out their farms and fence up their cows," as the cattle man expresses it. This State is now largely given up to farming, though at the time of the great drives it had large tracts of free grass. Ten years after the drives the settlers had flooded all over the Government lands and left little open ground. Since that time many of the homesteads of the dry southwestern parts of the State have been abandoned, and there are some cattle ranging there without objection, though there is little left to appeal to a large operator.

In Nebraska the same herd law exists. This State was also long ago tested as a farming region, yet there remain some tracts of wild land in the western part of the State, where a great many cattle are ranged. Some ranchers there hold large bodies of school lands under lease. These are fenced, and it is very possible that there may be included in these fences some lands not included in the leases. The Western cowman has always had a naïve way of believing that everybody wished to give him the benefit of all the doubts in the matter of range limits.

In Colorado we come again upon the dry country similar to that of New Mexico, where the question of water fronts first came up. There is free grass in Colorado, but much of it is free upon country which is of no use without water, and the best of the water was taken up long ago. Here, as also to a great extent in Texas, the cattle depend upon water raised from artesian or other wells by windmills. The best of the natural water of Colorado is fenced and used for irrigating purposes. In this we meet still another factor of great moment in the cattle questions of the day. The tendency of a country where crops can be raised by irrigation is toward small holdings, and this is, of course, contrary to the spirit of the cow trade. Yet there are many large tracts of land in Colorado which are leased or owned by cattle men.

Both North and South Dakota have herd laws similar to those of Kansas and Nebraska. Yet there are vast tracts of "bad lands" in the Dakotas which will never be farmed, and where the hopes of the cattle man for undisturbed range may flourish, subject only to the constant fear of the depasturage of the range from too great numbers of the cattle. There are bodies of Government and railroad lands in these States which are leased by cattle men, and in the wilder parts of the country the grass is free or practically free for the small rancher, though technically under the herd law. The herd law, of course, has no terrors for the man who has no neighbours.

Wyoming is now the greatest or second greatest of the cattle States. There is free grass in Wyoming and no herd law, and much of the land is so high, dry, and broken in its nature that the farmer will never trouble the cowman, who will continue to be as he is now—the controlling citizen of the commonwealth, the enormous cattle industry overruling all others. It is forbidden by State law to fence in any of the public lands of Wyoming, though certain descriptions of lands may be bought or leased of the State and then fenced. Of course the homesteader may fence his little holding if he likes. The small farmer has made his appearance in Wyoming, and will be more and more of a figure there from year to year. Millions of acres of the lands of the State are really fertile as any in the world when only they have water brought upon them, and for some time both large and small irrigating interests have been at work seeking to increase the wealth of the State in agricultural regards. The future of the cowmen in Wyoming lies in the exceedingly uncompromising nature of much the greater portion of the land, which is too broken or too high for farming. In the Dakotas and in Wyoming the natural water is for the most part abundant enough to obviate all question of water-front rights.

Montana has also free grass for all men, and one man has as good a right as another to let his cattle run free over the unoccupied Government lands. Here the cowman has the best of the farmer, who must fence his crops if he would sustain action against a cowman for damage done by his cattle. Great bodies of land lie wild here which can never be farmed, though all the little flats and valleys over which the water can be led are now pretty well taken up by the man who irrigates and farms. (Properly speaking, the rancher is himself a farmer, though the meaning of the word has been changed by popular usage. The rancher himself is more generous or perhaps more accurate in his own use of the term. He speaks of a " hay ranch," a

" fruit ranch," a " hen ranch," etc.) In Montana the
question of water front is of little consequence, for
there is natural water enough to balance the natural
grass.

In the free-grass country, such as that of Wyoming
or Montana, there may be seen again proof of the
cattle man's custom of respecting the rights of others.
Although the country is as much one man's as another's, the man who has possession of a certain portion of the range has his rights roughly regarded,
even though he be smaller in importance than his
neighbour. The latter will be affected by a depasturage
as much as the former, though sometimes a body of
cattle is driven in and must take its chances. The
new man on the range respects the lines commonly
accepted by the local men as the limits of the respective
ranges, and hunts about for the best place left open
for himself. Of course, the future will see more and
more curtailment of the free-grass privilege, especially
in such parts of the country as are well watered, and all
things point to the day when the rancher must control
his land in such way that he can legally fence it and
shut out all others.

A great enemy to the cattle trade has for years
been growing up upon the same country with it and
under the same conditions. At this writing this danger has assumed such proportions as to threaten the
permanence of profitableness of cow ranching even
upon that portion of the open range which may still be
called free grass. This menace is no less than the
sheep industry, itself a great one, albeit cordially detested by your genuine cowman, who has a deep-seated
contempt for any one who will look at a sheep. The
great flocks of sheep differ in a singular and important respect from the herds of the cowman. They can

10

not live unless they move. Confined on close pasture, they contract disease and die by thousands. Allowed to "walk," or range and feed forward over a great extent of country during the season, they increase and thrive. A flock of sheep starting, say, in Colorado or the Green River country, may range over five hundred miles in a year, entirely leaving their original range. Of course, these sheep can only be driven over a "free-grass" country, and on such a country they have as good right as the cattle have, though often their owners fail to enforce that right upon the range. One of these great flocks of sheep coming over the native range of a local band of cattle will eat off the grass so closely that the cattle will leave the range or starve to death upon it. This year sheep are coming in from the West in such numbers over some of the Wyoming free-grass country that many cattle men have shipped their cattle out of the country, giving up their interests and seeking other range. Yet others have sold out entirely and relinquished the business. The farmer, the irrigator, the sheep herder have been fatal to the old order of things which obtained in the days when all the range was free grass, or even the days when the key of the water unlocked the wealth of the range. More and more the cowman himself will become a farmer, as indeed many are now. More and more the cowboy will become a farm labourer. Even to-day, in a round-up on the Wyoming plains, you may see as many overalls and jumpers as chaps and shirt sleeves. Thus, it seems, and not in garb of silk or steel or gold, are to be clad the builders of the cities of Cibola.

CHAPTER VIII.

THE DRIVE.

EARLY in the history of the cowboy, as that history is popularly known, there came from the crowded ranges of the South the urgent cry for a market and the demand for additional territory out of the empire of free grass. It was in the stars that the cattle must go North. To get them North was a problem in transportation to which there could not then be summoned the aid of the railroads. The cattle must walk these hundreds of miles. Hence arose one of the most picturesque phases of the cowboy's occupation. He became a wanderer, an explorer, as well as a guide and a protector. The days of '67 in the cattle drive were as the days of '49 in the history of gold, inaugurative of an era full of rude and vivid life. Those were epoch-making times, and swift and startling were the changes which they brought. All the West was then in turmoil. The inhabitants of the Eastern and Middle States were just beginning to learn definitely of the great unsettled region into which the railroads were moving. To meet the railroads there came rolling up from the South the great herds of longhorns over the trail. With them came the cowboys, a news *gens*, reported a *gens horribilis*. In a trice the trail became one of the institutions of the West, and the cowboy became a character. Prior to the days of the drive he had existed, but he had not

been differentiated. His calling had not been specialized, he had not become a type. The trail was the
college of the cowboy. In all the lusty life of the
West in the old days there was no wilder and no
rougher school. Out of it came a man whose rugged
and insistent individuality has for a triple decade excited alike popular admiration and popular misunder-
standing.

To-day the cattle drive is one of the occasional
necessities of the trade all over the cow country, but it
exists only in modified form. The cowman drives
to his shipping point the beef he has "gathered" in
his fall round-up, or perhaps he drives some grown
cattle from one range to another a hundred miles or
so distant. At times one cowman purchases young
stock cattle from another, and these may be driven to
the new range. In one way or another a drive nowadays may perhaps occupy at most a month or so. Perhaps, again, a cowman of some upper country—say
Wyoming—has also a ranch down in the lower country,
such as the Nations, where he raises his own stock
cattle, which he wishes to put on his upper range. He
is situated perhaps well up in Wyoming, and a hundred
miles or so from the nearest railroad point. He ships
his cattle by rail from the Nations to this railroad
station, and then drives across country as in the old
days. No such operations as these, however, compare
in extent or interest with the old drives of the early
days, when things were booming in the cow towns.

Let us suppose it to be in those early days when
the herds of the South were just beginning to break
from their confines and push on in their strange and
irresistible migration to the North. Some rancher
has learned that he can command at the railroad to
the north of him a price far in advance of any obtain-

able in his own country. Perhaps he has a contract
for so many head to be delivered at some Northern
point, or perhaps he drives on general speculation and
in search of a buyer. Perhaps he drives his own cattle,
or his own and some of his neighbours', or perhaps he
purchases additional numbers and thus embarks in a
still greater mercantile venture. In any case the chief
problem of his venture is that of transportation. The
herds are to cross a wild and unsettled region, un-
mapped lands, with floods to swallow them up, with
deserts in which they may be lost irretrievably. There
is continual risk and danger of great loss in such transportation, for everything depends upon the control
a few human beings may be able to maintain over thousands of powerful and untamed animals.

These wild cattle are sold, let us say, upon the
hoof as they run, uninspected, at so much per head.
They of course do not reach the dignity of being
weighed, but are only counted. The seller may very
likely see to it that his men bring in many of the poor-
est specimens to be counted in such a transaction, but
the etiquette of the trade prevents the buyer from
taking any notice of such a fact. On the range a cow
is a cow, and may be worth two or three dollars. A
" beef " (any animal over four years of age) is a beef,
and may be worth three to six dollars. A " dogy " or
" dobe " yearling (a scrubby calf that has not wintered
well) is such a yearling, and nothing less nor more, and
may be worth one or two dollars. It is a day of large
methods, and haggling is unknown. It is jubilee for
the man of the depastured range who thus finds offered
him a price for cattle which have been bringing scarce
enough to pay for branding them.

The riders go out over the range and round up
the cattle by tens and hundreds, holding them must

of the time in the big corrals until the herd is made up and until the "road branding" is done. Then, after they are counted and sorted, the bill of sale gives the buyer his right and title and his permission to take these cattle off the range. Perhaps the great herd will number four, five, or even ten thousand head when it pulls out North bound over the trail. Another herd of this or another buyer may follow close behind it, and indeed in the height of the driving season there will be many herds strung out all along the trail.

To handle one of these great bodies of cattle the drover establishes his outfit well in advance of the start. His horses he may buy on the spot or at some horse ranch not far distant. His foreman, or " boss " for the drive he has secured, and been careful in his choice in doing so. The foreman's name may as well be Jim as any other, and it is certain that in his skill and judgment and faithfulness the owner has absolute confidence, for he is putting into his hands a great many thousand of dollars' worth of property. Besides the foreman there are a dozen other cowboys, most of them Americans, for Mexicans are not fancied for this work. In addition to these is the cook, who has nothing to do with the handling of the cattle. The cook may be a negro or a Spaniard or a " Portugee," but it is almost a certainty that he is hard-featured and unlovely, with a bad temper and perhaps a few notches on his knife handle. If he were not " hard up " he would not hire out to cook. The cowpunchers very likely call the cook the " old woman " or the " old lady," but really the language of a drive cook is something no lady would think of using. It is good times on the range, and the cook may receive fifty dollars a month and all of his own cookery he can eat. The cowpunchers will have wages of forty-five to sixty-five dollars per month,

according to their age and skill. The "cavvieyard"
or horse herd will have fifty to one hundred head of
horses in it, and will be under the charge of the day
herder and night herder (known as "horse wranglers"
in the North). The cook has a wagon or cart, which
carries himself, his supplies, the bedding, and a few of
the scant necessaries of the men. The latter travel
light as did ever any cavalry of the world. A tent is
something unknown to these men. A scant blanket
and the useful slicker, a flip of the roll, and the cowpuncher's bed is made. The saddle is his pillow. He
may look freely at the stars. The wolf is not more
wild, the broadhorn more hardy than he, nor either
more truly a creature of the open air.

When the great herd of "coasters" moves out on
its Northern journey its outset is attended with confusion. The cattle are unruly and attempt to break
back to their native feeding grounds. The drive outfit
is riding day and night, and even then its numbers
and its efforts may not be sufficient. A second outfit perhaps assists the first, pushing the cattle as rapidly
as possible over the first hundred miles of the trail,
tiring them so that they will be willing to lie down and
rest when nightfall comes. After these few days the
second outfit returns to start out the next herd in a
similar way. Ordinarily it may take a week or ten days
to break in the herd to the trail, but when fairly started
the cattle will travel ten to fifteen miles a day easily
and without much urging, and in the second month of
the drive will have so well learned what is required of
them as to march with something like military regularity, following certain recognised leaders of tacit
election. The order of march is in a loosely strung-
out body, the herd in motion covering a strip of country
perhaps only a few hundred yards in width, but a mile

or two miles in length from front to rear of the herd.
The stronger animals, or those least footsore, march
in advance, the weaker falling to the rear. When it
is seen that an animal can not stand the march, it is
cut out from the herd and abandoned. There are no
close figures in the cattle drive.

While the herd is on the march the cowpunchers
ride at intervals along its flanks, keeping the stragglers
up and in as much as possible, and controlling the
cattle by that strange mastery the mounted man has
always had over the horned creatures of the range.
Why the cowboy should be called a " cowpuncher " is
one of the mysteries. The whip of the States' drover
is unknown to him. He guides the cattle simply by
the presence of himself and horse, riding at them when
he wishes them to turn, heading them back when he
wishes them to stop. Each man on the drive knows
what to do, and the duties are for the most part rather
monotonous than urgent. The march each day is in
much the same order, the dusty herd strung out ahead,
the cook wagon and horse herd following on behind.
For hours and days the herd may work along stolidly
and quietly, with no sound but the monotonous crack!
crack! of thousands of hoofs and ankle joints or the
rattle of the long horns swung together now and then
in the crowd of travel. Or there may arise even in
daytime that thunderous unison of the clacking feet
and the continuous, confused, and awful rattling of
the horns which tells of the horrors of a stampede.

By nightfall the cattle are usually weary enough
to be willing to stop, and need little instruction when
they arrive on the bedding ground which has been
selected by some forerunner. Water they have probably had more than once during the day.* In the

* The cattle trail moved westward in Texas as the plains

evening they graze a little, and shortly after dusk begin
to lie down, so that by eight or nine o'clock they may
all be "bedded down" by the cowpuncher's art into
a fairly compact body capable of being watched. After
the cook has served his supper of bacon, beans, camp
bread, and coffee, with perhaps a very few items of
tinned vegetables and of course no fresh vegetables
except the inevitable El Paso onion, the foreman ar-
ranges the hours for the night herding. Two to four
men are put out at the same time, and these are out
for two to four hours, all of these details depending on
the condition of the cattle and the state of the weather.

Before lying down for his share of sleep at night,
the cowpuncher takes care of his horses. This is not
the act of feeding and grooming, be sure, but has

---

were cleared of the Indians and as the country settled up. The
first trail ran to southeastern Kansas and northwestern Missouri.
The so-called Shawnee trail ran east from the Red River, thence
north across the Arkansas and west along that stream. The
"Chisholm trail" was farther to the west, over the Neutral Strip.
The "Pecos trail" was still farther to the west, in New Mexico,
following the Pecos River north into Colorado, and crossing the
Arkansas River in that Territory. The latter trail was used only
in the territorial or stock cattle drive. There was an attempt
made at one time to set apart a strip of country north and south,
near the sixth principal meridian, for the exclusive purposes of
the cattle trail, though this was never done. The "Chisholm
trail" was laid out by a half-breed Indian bearing the name of
Jesse Chisholm, who drove horses and cattle to the western parts
of the Nations as early as 1840, before any one else dared go in
that country. He did a good business in horses, which he
bought of the lower plains Indians, the latter being able to sell
to him at low prices, since they stole all their horses themselves. He often had long trains of horses, cattle, and goods,
which he brought up over the best country for grass and water.
—E. H.

reference to that possession in hand which is the only concern the cowpuncher gives himself in the matter. He usually pickets the horse he intends to ride during the night, and hobbles out the one he has been using, the custom of hobbling being one brought down from the ancient plains days. His picket pin the cowpuncher carries with him, for much of the time he is in a woodless country. His horse hobbles he either ties at his saddle or flings into the cook wagon while on the march. These hobbles, as used in the early days, before buckle and chains were heard of on the range, were made of rawhide, that staple of the cow country. A wide band of rawhide was passed around the fore leg of the horse, and the ends twisted together loosely over and over, one end being left a little longer than the other. The shorter end was slit, and upon the longer end there was fastened a long wooden button. This longer end was passed about the other fore leg of the horse, and the loop for this leg secured by passing the wooden button through the slit in the shorter end of the hobble and turning it crosswise of the slit.

To guard against the restless condition of the cattle, so fatal to the success of a drive, there was put in practice one of the most curious customs of the range, and one in regard to which there exists even to-day something of diversity of opinion. The herd was rarely if ever left out of the hearing of the human voice, and it was considered a necessity at night to " sing to the cattle," as the peculiar process of vocalization was termed. The cattle when bedded down were timid and suspicious to a degree, and the sudden appearance of any strange object might set them off in a run. They might take fright at the dim form of one of the herders coming up in the night, though if they knew it was the herder they would not be frightened but reassured, through that vague and ill-understood feeling of dependence these half-wild creatures certainly had for their human masters. The night herder in riding about the bedding ground always kept up a low humming or singing, to let the cattle know of his presence, and the cowboy who could not or would not sing was inadequate in his profession. The " hymns " were sometimes of sacred air and profane words, and sometimes of compounds of both, but it was certain that some sort of this music was in course of rendition throughout the night. When one watch went in to sleep and another set of men came on duty the new men in riding up to the cattle always prefaced their approach with this odd psalmody of the plains.

Let us suppose that our friend the cowpuncher is called from his slumbers at midnight to take his turn at watching the cattle on a bedding ground along the trail. He arouses himself from his hard couch on the ground and goes after the horse which he has kept picketed as close at hand as practicable. If the weather has been threatening, he has perhaps, in common with every other man of the outfit, kept his best horse saddled ready for sudden call. If the weather is mild, he cinches up his unwilling and sulky steed and at once starts for the edge of the herd. The air of the high plains is chilly, and a tenderfoot would need an overcoat, but the cowboy probably does not even button his loose coat at the neck, and his flannel shirt is hardly caught the tighter at the throat when he rolls out of his blankets to take the saddle. His slicker is tied at the cantle of his saddle. Sleepily but methodically he takes up his round, calling to the cattle as he comes up to the herd. He rides slowly around them, sometimes stopping as he moves about the edge of the herd. Each gully and grassy swale, each bit of broken ground or ragged hillside is scanned closely as he moves about in the dim light. This may be country where there are men quite willing to run off a few head of cattle or to create a stampede. There may be Indians about, whose demands for toll have not been satisfactorily settled, and who are not averse to making a little trouble, even to the extent of a quiet arrow or so. Or there may be wild animals, whose presence will frighten the herd. The sudden appearance of a wolf on the outline of a hill may bring a hundred steers to their feet with snorts of terror. The sharp cracking of a twig may cause a sudden fright. It is of record that the appearance of the full moon, rising between the two peaks of a cleft hill and shining red and large over into a little valley that had been quite dark till then, once caused one of the most uncontrollable of stampedes. The aim of the cowboy is to prevent any cause of fright which can be prevented, and to give what courage and comfort he can of his own store in case any unusual or terrifying circumstances arise. Timidity relies on courage always. That thing does not walk the plains which shall terrify this bold soul, born and bred upon the range. The night has no secrets for him, nor the day any terrors. He is not afraid, and the cattle know it. He is the guard and protector, and they know it, even though they may fear him. So on and around he rides slowly, humming his little song, now a sweet one, let us hope, often not a good one, we may fear, and all the time he keeps his eyes open for anything and everything going on about him. Under the moon or the stars or the black sky, he fulfills the requirements of his wild calling, patiently and faithfully, shirking nothing and fearing nothing, doing his duty not more because he is paid to do it than because he would not feel himself a man up to the standards of his calling if he failed to do his duty in every detail.

At daybreak the camp is astir, the men rolling out of their blankets to the cook's cry of " Grub pi-i-i-le! " The hot coffee is gulped down and the rude fare goes into stomachs well able to withstand it. Ten minutes later the outfit is in the saddle. The blanket rolls, loose hobbles or such odds and ends are tossed into the cook's wagon; the hobbled horses, which have not wandered far during the night, are caught up, and each rider saddles the horse whose turn he thinks it is to carry him, the others going into the horse herd for the day. The sun is barely up when the long line of cattle is again on the move, slowly working to the northward, grazing, walking spasmodically, stopping, or plodding steadily along, according to the conditions of grass and water. Sometimes it is necessary to push the herd sharply along to reach water, for on the trail the cattle need water more regularly and more often than on their feeding range, where the cactus may give them some liquid, and where their blood is not heated by continuous exercise. If water is found often, the cattle will drink with something of regularity of order and in safety, but if there has been a long and thirsty march there may be a horrible crowding stampede to the stream or water hole, and many of the weaker animals may be crushed to death.

There were no bridges on the trail of the old drives, and all streams had to be crossed by wading or swimming, as the case might be. Often it happened that the cattle would not take to the water, and sometimes it was hours or days before a herd could be got across a swollen river. The most difficult thing in such an emergency was to get the leaders of the herd started into the water. Once that was done, the rest would follow without further trouble. The line of march for this indomitable cavalcade was the same in the water as upon the land. As upon the land, the cowboys in the river remained at intervals along the flanks of the herd, their hardy ponies swimming strongly under them. Sometimes in the water, as upon the land, a sudden panic would seize the herd, and they would fall to " milling " in the water, swimming round and round helplessly, to drown in scores if no remedy were found. Then again the hardihood of the range rider was called upon. Without a moment of thought or hesitation the cowboy spurred his swimming horse into the thick of the tossing heads, and by shouts and blows did all he could to break the " mill " and get the cattle headed properly. Often unhorsed and threatened with death among the plunging animals in the water, he was forced to swim out as best he could, sometimes scrambling upon the backs of swimming cattle, sometimes catching a floating tail and impressing it into service for a temporary tow. The rope of the cowboy came into full play in these exciting and perilous episodes. With it he pulled cattle out of the water or the quicksands or the mud, whether they wanted to come or not, the fierce little ponies seeming to know as well as their riders what was needed, and exerting a power which, thanks to the heavy and well-cinched saddle, was something remarkable to witness. Both horse and man had enough asked of them at such seasons of stress, and it was with great relief that the trail outfit saw the last of their herd, or at least the last of those left alive and under possession, across the stream and ready for the further march. Sometimes, at such a river as the Platte, on the north drive to the Territories, there would be a dozen herds piled up on the river shore in a distressing confusion, from which the heart of a States drover could see no possible extrication; yet patience and courage of the cowpuncher sort certainly brought each herd out in order, with only such loss as the river inflicted. The eye of the cowboy was keen to detect the brand of his herd, and his pony was swift and the rider was tireless. So the great herd worked on, always to the North, over obstacles of every sort. In course of time the herd, dusty, footsore, perhaps thin of flesh and reduced in numbers, arrived at its destination. This might be far up on the northern range, in Wyoming or Montana, or it might be at some of the lurid little cow towns along the new railroad. Perhaps in the latter case the owner of the herd found no buyer to suit him, and very likely he lost money after all his weary effort. Sometimes it was necessary to hold the cattle on the Kansas range over winter, and indeed at the time of the feeling against Southern cattle on account of the dreaded Spanish fever which they brought with them, there was a law forbidding the importing into many of the Northern States any Texas cattle which had not been " wintered " on a Northern range, this wintering seeming to destroy the germs of that disease, which was so fatal to Northern cattle. All these problems were new ones for the Southern drover, but he and his cowpunchers rapidly adjusted themselves to the new conditions, and thus the stocking of the great open ranges of the North went on, the herds bringing with them the guardians who were to become inhabitants and citizens of the widening range.

It was a curious, colossal, tremendous movement, this migration of the cowmen and their herds, undoubtedly the greatest pastoral movement in the history of the world. It came with a rush and a surge, and in ten years it had subsided. That decade was an epoch in the West. The cities of Cibola began. The strong men of the plains met and clashed and warred and united and pushed on. What a decade that was! What must have been the men who made it what it was! It was an iron country, and upon it came men of iron. Dauntless, indomitable, each time they took a herd North they saw enough of life to fill in vivid pages far more than a single book. They met the ruffians and robbers of the Missouri border, and overcame them. They met the Indians who sought to extort toll from them, and fought and beat them. Worse than all these, they met the desert and the flood, and overcame them also. Worse yet than those, they met the repelling forces of an entire climatic change, the silent enemies of other latitudes. These, too, they overcame. The kings of the range divided the kingdom of free grass.

It was natural enough that these wild fighting men who now made the great part of the population of the West, coming as they did from all quarters of the land, living in camps or in the saddle, living in a land wherein there had not yet been lit the first fire of a real home, and where the hand of a real woman was not yet known, should make commotion when they came to the end of the trail. It is no wonder there were wild times on the border in the days of the drive. Never were times wilder anywhere else on earth than they were in the ragged, vicious little cow town of the railroad markets and the upper ranges. There, indeed, it behooved the timid man to hie him elsewhere swiftly as that might be. Trouble came often enough when not sought for, and any one in search of trouble could find it with surprising ease. On the trail the men of an outfit usually got along fairly well together, being

held together with the friendship of common motives
and mutual interests; nor did different outfits often
go to war, unless there had been infringement upon
rights bound to carry respect. Of course, sometimes
there would be sudden affrays, and many are the unmarked graves the cattle have trodden flat along the
trail. Thus, it is reported that one cowpuncher, who
was spoken of as being "too particular to punch cows,
anyhow," had trouble with the cook, who was a surly
fellow and apt to resent any imputation upon his skill
in cookery, though there seemed a general consensus
of belief that he could not cook. The cowpuncher
made some objection to some trifle at the table, and the
cook caught up his gun to kill him for criticising his
bread or beans. The cowpuncher then killed the cook
promptly, and, standing over him as he lay prone,
remarked, "There, d—n you, I *knowed* you couldn't
cook!" In this rash act he found soon that he had
committed a crime of serious nature and likely to bring
serious consequences. It was pointed out to him that
had he killed any other man of the outfit it would not
have been so bad, but to kill the cook, even though he
could not cook, was to strand the entire party out in
the middle of the desert. There was a strong disposition to lynch the offender for this; but the foreman,
who was a generous-hearted man, overruled the sen-
tence of the outfit, and condemned the cowpuncher
to cook for the party for the rest of the way up the
drive—a punishment which is said to have brought
remorse not only to the offender but all the rest of the
party.

It was not often that such quarrels arose on the
cattle drive among men who should have been friends,
and if there was a hidden grudge it was usually
kept smouldering for the time. In the railroad town,

11

on the other hand, a quarrel offered was a quarrel begun, and once begun it was not far to its ending. Many and many are the border tales one may hear even to-day in the flourishing little Western cities which once had the vivid honour of being cattle towns. Abilene, Kansas, was one of the most famous of these markets of the early days, and at that point alone a whole fund of yellowback literature of a too truthful sort might even now be collected. One story will serve to illustrate the conditions of those times, taken as it is from actual life at the height of the cow trails. It seems that there was a Texas cowpuncher, whose name we need not mention, who had conceived himself injured in honour by another of his profession, and who had spent the day in an ineffectual attempt to find the latter in order to call him to account. Failing in this, he at length concluded to retire for the night, and went to his room in a certain hotel once famous as a cattle men's resort. This hotel was a long building, of pine boards, constructed in the most flimsy manner, the bedrooms being built on each side of a long hall, with partitions between them of thin and ill-fitted lumber, which therefore afforded but little privacy. Everything said in one room was heard in the other rooms. As the aggrieved cowpuncher sat upon the side of his bed, he having disrobed and prepared to go to sleep, he heard voices farther down the hall, in the third room from his, and recognised the voice of his enemy, who may or may not have made some slighting allusion to himself. The offended one at any rate did not pause to consider consequences to others than his enemy. He seems to have remembered that the shape of the little bedrooms was the same throughout the series along the hall, and that the position of the bed was the same in each. He presumed that his enemy was at that moment sitting upon his bed, as he himself was in his own room. Without further thought, he picked up his six-shooter and carefully aimed along what he considered to be the proper line to strike the man whose voice he heard. He fired, and the bullet, after passing through three of the thin partitions, struck the man in the body and killed him instantly. The shooter fled from the building in sudden fear and remorse, and appeared upon the street clad in nothing but his undergarments. He at once struck to the southward, headed for Texas in his blind impulse of seeking safety. He travelled on foot nearly all night clad as he was and barefoot, hardship unspeakable for a native rider. In the morning he met a man who was riding toward him on the trail. This man he covered with his pistol and forced to dismount and strip. Taking his clothing and his horse from him, the Texan dressed himself, mounted and rode away. From that day to this, so far as known, he has never been heard from again. In some distant corner of the cattle country there may perhaps have been a morose cowpuncher, who never spoke about his past, and whom the etiquette of the range forbade questioning as to his earlier history.

CHAPTER IX.

THE ROUND-UP.

SINCE the beginning of mankind's struggle with Nature the harvest season has been a time of victory and rejoicing. At that time man unbends his back and gives thanks for the reaping. Then come the days of final activity, of supreme exertion, the climax of all that has a material, an allegorical, or spectacular interest in the yearly war for existence. The round-up is the harvest of the range. Therefore it is natural that its customs should offer more of interest than those of any other part of the year. It were matter of course, also, that features so singular and stirring in their intense action as those of the cowman's harvest should be known and blazoned about for the knowledge of those living elsewhere than upon the cattle fields. Writers and artists have seized upon this phase of the cattle man's life, and given it so wide a showing that the public might well have at least a general idea of the subject. Yet perhaps this general idea would be a more partial and less accurate notion than is deserved by the complicated and varied business system of the cattle harvest. If we would have a just idea of the life and character of the man who makes the round-up, we should approach the subject rather with a wish to find its fundamental principles than a desire to see its superficial pictures.

The system of the round-up, while it retains the same general features over the whole of the cow country, and has done so for years, is none the less subject to considerable local modifications, and it has in many respects changed with the years as other customs of the industry have changed; for not even the ancient and enduring calling of the cowman could be free from the law of progress. The Western traveller who first saw a round-up twenty years ago would not be in position to describe one of to-day. Sectional differences make still other changes which should be regarded. Yet all these round-ups, of the past and of the present, of the North and of the South, ground themselves upon a common principle—namely, upon that desire for absolute justice which has been earlier mentioned as a distinguishing trait of the cowman and the trade he follows.

Reverting, as we must continually do, to the early times of the cattle industry, we shall find ourselves back in the days of water fronts in the dry Southwest. Here the round-up depended upon local conditions, just as it has ever since. If the *ranchero* had practically all the water near him, he had also practically all the cattle, and the harvest of the calves was merely a large going forth on his part and marking his own increase without being troubled with that of others. This feature would be apt to continue more in a wide and sparsely pastured country than in one where the cattle of many owners were mingled together on the range. Again, if we follow up the history of the range until we come upon the time of large individual holdings of land under fence, we must see how similar was the round-up then to that of the dry country; for here man had done what Nature had done in the other case, and had separated the owner's cattle from those of his neighbours. It remained, therefore, much a matter of an individual and not a community harvest; whereas the community harvest is the one which the average man has in mind when speaking of a round-up. The free-grass round-up is the one where the ingenuity, the energy, and the resources of the cowman are best to be seen, his way of carrying out his fundamental purpose of justice to all men on the vast, unfenced, and undefined farm of the range, where the thousands of cattle, belonging to dozens of owners, each animal wild as a deer and half as fleet, are all gathered, counted, separated, and identified with a system and an accuracy little short of the marvellous. Until one has seen such a round-up on the open plains he has neither seen the cowboy at his best nor seen the fruition of the system that he represents.

The time of the calf round-up is in the spring, after the grass has become good and after the calves have grown large enough for the branding, this time being later in the North than in the South by perhaps thirty days. Naturally, upon a country where the open range is common property there can not be a round-up for each man who owns cattle running at large. Naturally, also, there must be more than one round-up to gather all the cattle over the vast extent of a cattle region. Here the system of the cowman is at once in evidence. The State cattle association divides the entire State range into a number of round-up districts—let us say into a dozen or two dozen districts. Each district conducts its own round-up, this under the working supervision of some experienced man who goes by the name of the round-up captain or round-up boss, and who is elected by vote of the cowmen of his district. Under this general officer are all the bosses in charge of the different ranch outfits

sent by men having cattle in the round-up. In the
very outset of the levy for these troops of the range the
idea of justice is apparent. Not all men own equal
numbers of the cattle, so it would be obviously unfair
to ask all to furnish an equal amount of the expense
and labour in the total of the round-up duties. The
small outfits send a few men, the large ones more, the
aim being that of fairness to all and hardship to none.
The whole force of a small modern round-up may not
exceed thirty men. In one of the large Southern
round-ups there once met at the Double Forks of the
Brazos nearly three hundred men. All these men
met at one ranch, and it is proof of the largeness of
the cattle life and its methods that they were all well
fed and entertained by the owner of the ranch. Nowadays perhaps a ranch of ordinary size will send two
messes of men of half a dozen or more men each as its
pro rata in the round-up, each mess with its own cook,
and perhaps with two wagons to each mess to carry
along the tents and supplies. In the old days no tents
were taken, and the life was rougher than it is now,
but of late years the cowboy has grown sybaritic. With
each ranch outfit there must of course be the proper
horse herd, " cavoy," or " cavvieyah. Each man
will have eight or ten horses for his own use, for he
has now before him the hardest riding of the year.
All these horses, some of them a bit gay and frisky
in the air of spring, are driven along with the ranch
outfit as its own horse herd, the total usually split
into two herds, each under the charge of one or more
herders, known as " horse wranglers "—an expression
confined to the Northern ranges, and bearing a certain collegiate waggishness of flavour, though the origin of the term is now untraceable. There are, of
course, night wranglers and day wranglers, it being the

duty of these men to see to it that the horse herd is kept together and at hand when wanted for the work.

Sometime toward the middle of May, let us say, all these different outfits leave their home ranches and head for the rendezvous of the round-up. The opening date of the round-up is known, and the different outfits, big and little, move in so as to be on hand a few days before the beginning of the work. It may be imagined what a scene must be this general gathering of the cow clans, how picturesque this assemblage of hardy, rugged men fresh from their wild life and ready for the still wilder scenes of activity which are before them! There may be fifty men, perhaps five hundred horses at the main camp, and of the total there is not one animal which does not boil over with the energy of full-blooded life. The men rejoice as those should rejoice who go forth to the harvest, the horses exult because spring has come, with its mysterious stirring airs. The preliminary days are passed in romp and frolic, perhaps at cards and games. Each man, however, has his own work outlined, and makes his preparations for it. His personal outfit is overhauled and put in repair. His rope has a touch to " limber it up," his straps are softened, his clothing put in order. If he has a wild horse in his string, he takes the opportunity of giving it a few lessons of the sort which make up the cow pony's education. Swiftly the grand camp of the round-up settles into the system of veterans, and all is rapidly made ready for the exacting duties which are to follow.

The total country to be covered by the round-up is perhaps a strip forty by one hundred miles in extent. The direction in which the round-up will work will depend upon the habits and the ranging of the cattle at that time, there being no hard and fast rules possible. Local conditions determine also the location of the several round-up camps, which of course must be where grass and water are abundant and where there is room to handle the herds. At times there may perhaps be five thousand or more head of cattle in one body, though the numbers are more likely to run not over fifteen hundred or two thousand at a time. The tendency nowadays is all in favour of smaller round-ups, other herds being gathered after the first is worked, and the size of each assembling depending of course upon local circumstances. It may be better to drive in all the cattle from a large strip of country to a good working ground, or it may be more convenient to make several herds and frequent changes of camp.

The round-up captain knows the men who are to work under him, and from among these he appoints lieutenants who shall have each a certain band of men under him while covering the country. Advice is given to each party as to what direction it shall take after the start is made, all these arrangements being made so as not to give special inconvenience to the men of the respective ranch outfits, who will naturally wish to camp with their own mess wagon. On the day before the start the little army of the plains has its campaign all planned and lying out before it, and each man knows about what he is to do. On the night before the opening day the cowpuncher, if he be wise, goes to bed early and gets a full night's sleep, for not another will he have now for many a night to come. The flickerings of the cooks' fires, confined in their trenches so that they may not spread and so that their heat may be well utilized, rise and fall, casting great shadows upon the tent walls where the cowboys unroll their blankets and prepare for rest. The wind sighs and sings in the way the wind has upon the plains.

The far-off neigh of a restless pony, the stamp of a horse picketed near by, the shrilling yell of the coyote, and all those further vague and nameless noises which pass in the air at night over the wild range come to the cowboy as unneeded and unnoted lullaby. His sleep is deep and untroubled, and to him it seems scarce begun when it is suddenly ended amid the chorus of calls, groans, and shoutings of his companions answering at the gray of dawn the call of the uneasy round-up boss, who sings out his long cry of "Roll out! roll out!" followed by the shrill call of the cook, "Grub pi-i-i-le!" The cook has been up for an hour, and has made his fire perhaps of cottonwood limbs, perhaps of the *bois des vaches*—natural fuel, of the buffalo on the cattle range. This early morning summons the cowpuncher dare not disobey, for the etiquette of the round-up is strict enough in its way. It is but dim daylight at best when the camp has kicked off its blankets and risen up shoutingly. In a few moments it has broken into a scene of wild but methodical activity. In much less than an hour after the first call for boots and saddles the whole strange cavalcade is under way, and behind it the cooks are breaking camp and pitching the plunder into the wagons for the move.

Through the wet grass at break of dawn come the rush and pounding of many hoofs, and ahead of the swinging ropes of the wranglers gallops the horse herd as it is brought in for the morning saddling. To receive it a hasty corral is made, after the rude but efficient ways of the range. This corral is but a single rope stretched about the sides of an irregular parallelogram, or rather it is made of several single ropes united end to end. Sometimes the corral runs out from the wheels of two wagons, the ropes being supported at their outer ends by two men, who swing out and act as living gateposts, leaving open a gap into which the horses are driven. The latter will not attempt to break over this single strand, though they might well do so had they not learned the lesson of not running against rope. Sometimes this strange corral is made by stringing the rope from the saddle horns of several of the laziest and solemnest of the old saddle horses, which thus serve as the fence posts, this way being more common at midday or out in the open country, where a short pause is made by the outfit. Sometimes a wagon wheel, a horse, and a man or two may all be doing duty as posts for the corral, it being the peculiarity of the cowman to use what means are best and nearest to his hand in all his operations. The handling of the horse herd offers some of the most picturesque features of the round-up, and the first morning of the round-up is apt to furnish some thrilling bits of action at the horse corrals when the men are roping their mounts, pulling them unwilling forth and cinching the great saddles firmly upon their bulging and protesting sides. In the early times the cow horse was a wilder animal than he is to-day, but in these degenerate days a wild horse is not thought desirable, and indeed many or most of the cow horses are not roped at all for their saddling. The cowboy simply goes into the corral, picks out his horse, and throws his bridle over its neck with a most civilized disregard for the spectacular.

After the handling of the horse herd and the saddling up, the little army swiftly gets into motion and wings out widely over the plains, the men sometimes shouting and running their horses in prodigal waste of energy, for all is exuberance and abounding vigour on these opening days in spring. Each little party

spreads out under its commander until each man becomes a commander for himself, imposing upon himself the duty of driving before him to the agreed meeting place ahead all the cattle that may come in his
line of march. As the cowpuncher thus rides out into
his great gray harvest field he sees no great wealth
of horned herds about him or before him. It is a big
country, and the many thousands of cattle make but a
small showing upon it. Did they seem numerous as in
an Eastern pasture, the range must surely be a depastured and impoverished one. Here and there, scattered about, out beyond where the horse herds have
been feeding, there may be a few little groups of cattle.
Out farther, upon some hogback or along the side of
some *coulee*, a horned head is lifted high, gazing in
astonishment at this strange invasion of the range.
The animal may be a grade longhorn, though now the
old Texas stock has practically vanished from the range.
The shorthorn is valued, the white-faced Hereford
still more popular, since it is hardy and quick to mature. All these, one by one, by twos and threes, and
finally in fifties and hundreds, the keen-eyed and hard-
riding cowpuncher starts out and away from their feeding ground and drives on ahead of him toward the
meeting place. The string of other animals running
ahead, perhaps half a mile to one side, where some
other cowpuncher is driving, is sure to be noted by the
cattle near to him. He gives a shout and starts toward them, and, true to their gregarious habits, they
start on the run for their companions on ahead, this
being just what it is wished they should do. This
herding habit of the range cattle is the basis of many
of the operations of handling them. Thus each little
coulee and draw, each ridge and little flat is swept of
its inhabitants, which all go on forward toward where

the long lines of dust are beginning to converge and mingle. As a matter of course, all the cattle, big and little, cows, calves, and steers, are included in the assembling, and are driven in together. The driving is not the work of a novice, but yet is not so difficult, for most of the cattle are so wild that they run at the sight of a horseman, more especially if they be of the old longhorn breed, and all the cowboy needs to do is to ride hard to one side and so direct their flight. Other cattle join those running, so that the whole horned populace goes in and along, but a small per cent being missed in the round-up, though of course it is not possible to gather up every individual that may be ranging wild and unobserved in the vast expanses of the open plains.

Thus, later in the day, the gatherings of the individuals and of the separate parties meet in a vast, commingling multitude of cattle. The place is in some valley or upon some plain offering room for handling the herd. Clouds of dust arise. The sun shines hot. Above the immediate shuffle and clacking of the nearby cattle comes a confused and tremendous tumult, the lowing of cows, the bawling of calves, the rumbling bellows of other animals protesting at this unusual situation. The whirling flight of the cowboys on their many different quests, the neighing of horses, the shouts of command or of exultation—all these wild sounds beat upon the air in a medley apparently arising out of bedlam, and all these sights arise from what seems to the unskilled observer a hopeless and irremediable disorder. Yet as matter of fact each rider of all this little army knows exactly what he is about. Each is working for a definite and common purpose, and the whole is progressing under a system of singular perfection. This confusion is that of chaos falling into order. The guiding and controlling mind of man will subject all this mighty disorder to his own ends. These great horned creatures, outnumbering a hundred to one their human guards, are helpless to escape from the living cordon of fearless horse and daring rider. Out of the dust and heat and turmoil one gathers a single definite thought, evolves a single character. The yearly climax of his calling has brought into vivid view the cowboy in that position which shows himself and his profession in their most unique and striking form.

Perhaps a couple of thousand of cattle are gathered in this herd here upon a little flat valley a mile or so across. On the other side of the valley are lines of willows and low trees, and on beyond, in the direction of the sun, runs the shining thread of a river. Toward the shelter of the trees the thin blue smoke of the camp fires is arising. Possibly some of the cowpunchers run over to the camp to snatch a bite to eat, for the work of the cutting out has not yet begun. The milling of the cattle has thrown them into confusion, and the calves are separated from their mothers, so that a little time must be allowed. A calf does not always know its own mother, but no mother mistakes her own offspring. This is the second basis of the cunning handling of the wild herds. The cowman has the cattle of the range all together now, and knows they will tend to hang together for a time and not separate. He knows also that the calves will run with their mothers, so that the brand of the mother will prove the ownership of the calf. Presently the intense, trying work of the cutting out will begin, in which all these calves will be sorted out and labelled in the great joint inventory of the range.

At this stage of the round-up operations there

again comes into play the question of local conditions.
It is all a matter of locality what shall be the description of the cattle to be separated, and this again is
a matter which has been subject to change of custom
in the trade.   If this round-up be, for instance, in one
of the thickly settled districts of Montana, no attention is paid to any but the calves and unbranded cattle.   There is no attempt to sort or separate the different herds of branded cattle belonging to different
owners, or to drive back a given owner's cattle toward
his range.   All the cows and calves are cut out from
the general herd, and are held in a separate body,
the rest of the entire herd being allowed to scatter and
depart at will over the common range.   The calves
are then taken indiscriminately from this cow herd and
branded duly according to their mothers' brands.

On yet other portions of the range the ranchmen
may not be so numerous or the ranges may be larger.
Perhaps there are a few owners whose interests are
practically the same, by reason of the ranging habits
of their cattle.   They know that their cattle are not
apt to go off a certain range, and therefore they do
not trouble themselves to keep track of them.   But
they would not like these cattle to wander, say, one
hundred miles from home.   If in a round-up there
should be found cattle, say, of five or six different
brands, all pretty well within the country where they
belonged, no effort would be made to separate these.
But if on the same country there should be found a
number of cattle of some outfit, known to be perhaps a
hundred miles from the range where they belonged,
it would be part of the duty of the round-up to cut out
these cattle and "throw them over" to the proper
range.   In all things the common sense of the cowman governs.   Thus it may happen that the entire

herd of a certain outfit is thus cut out and thrown over without a single calf being branded, because the cowman knows it would not be good for these calves to be driven perhaps fifty miles or so immediately after the branding and other operations of the round-up. All the time there are numbers of these round-ups and subround-ups going on, as the necessities of the situation demand. Sometimes the big corrals of a convenient ranch are used. It is a singular fact that corral work was once more common, for instance, in certain parts of Wyoming than it is to-day. It was known that organized bands of cattle thieves, characterized by the cowmen as "some boys who were a little on the rustle," had a habit of using these corrals at night to hold together the bunches of calves they were running out of the country, the rustlers being shrewd enough to know that they could in no better way render tractable a bunch of calves than by keeping them a few nights away from their mothers, who would surely run them off during the night if all were left out in the open together. It thus seeming that the ranch corrals were being used in the robbery of the men who built them, the latter tore them down and after that relied upon the open round-up. The latter form of the round-up work is, of course, the more interesting, and we shall suppose that the herd is made out on the open range and held together simply by the force of horsemanship.

It having been agreed, then, what sort of cattle are to be cut out, the work of separation begins, perhaps two or three different "cuts" being in progress at the same time, each of these "cuts" being held at a distance from the main herd. As it is difficult to overcome the disposition of an animal to break back and join its fellows in the main herd when it is singled out and driven, it is customary to start the "cut" with some sober-minded old cattle which are willing to stand where they are placed, and so serve as a nucleus for the growing band, the cowboy here again calling to his aid the habit of gregariousness among the cattle.

The calf branding is the chief work of the round-up, and it would be difficult to find work more exacting and exhausting. The cowpuncher prepares for this deliberately. When he goes into the herd to cut out calves he mounts a fresh horse, and every few hours he again changes horses, for, though some horses are better than others in cutting out, there is no horse which can long endure the fatigue of the rapid and intense work of cutting. Before the rider stretches a sea of interwoven horns, waving and whirling as the densely packed ranks of cattle close in or sway apart. It is no prospect for a weakling, but into it goes the cowpuncher on his determined little horse, heeding not the plunging and crushing and thrusting of the excited cattle. Down under the heels of the herd, half hid in the whirl of dust, he spies a little curly calf running, dodging, and twisting, always at the heels of its mother. The cowpuncher darts in and after, following the two through the thick of surging and plunging beasts. The sharp-eyed pony sees almost as soon as his rider which cow is wanted, and he needs small guidance from that time on. He follows hard at her heels, edging her constantly toward the flank of the herd, at times nipping her hide as a reminder of his own superiority. In spite of herself the cow gradually turns out toward the edge, and at last is rushed clear of the crush, the calf following close behind her. Very often two cowpunchers work together in the operation of cutting out, this facilitating matters somewhat.

12

Already preparations have been made for the animals cut out. The branding men have fire and fuel, and irons are heated to a cherry red. All the irons of the outfits represented are on hand at the fire, a great many of them, and easily to be confused withal. A "tally man," to keep record of the calves branded to each outfit, has been appointed by the captain to serve as general clerk of the round-up. This man, of course, has opportunity to favour one outfit or another by falsifying his scores, but this contingency is never considered in the rude ethics of the range, where civilized suspicion, known as conservatism, has not yet fully entered. The tally man is usually chosen for his fitness to keep these accounts, or perhaps for his unfitness to do other work at the time. Perhaps there is some oldish cowman, or some one who has been sick, or who has been hurt in the riding of the previous day, and who, though not fit for the saddle, will do for the book. This man acts as the agent of all the outfits, and upon his count depends each owner's estimate of his season's profits.

As the cowpuncher rushes his first cow and calf clear of the herd, the tally man stands near the fire, sharpening his pencil with a knife disproportionately large. Even as he looks over toward the herd there is a swirl of the long loop which has hung just clear of the ground as the cowpuncher rode out into the open after his quarry. The loop spreads and hisses out into a circle as it flickers and curves about the cowpuncher's head, and then it darts out and down like the stoop of a hawk. The unfortunate calf is laid by the heels. The pony stops and squats, flaring back upon its haunches, its mane falling forward over its gleaming eyes, its sides heaving, its quarters already gray with the dust of the herd. There is a twist of the rope about the horn of the saddle, and all is

over with the wild life of the curly, bawling calf. It
is flipped lightly upon its side, and away it goes, skating along over the sagebrush, regardless of cuts or
bruises, up to the fire where the irons glow and where
the tally man now has his pencil sharpened. Two
men seize it as it comes into their field of operations.
One catches it by the ears and twists its head side-
ways, sitting down upon it so that the little creature
can not move. Another man casts free the rope and
lays hold of its hind legs, pushing one far forward with
his own foot, and pulling the other back at full length
with both his brawny hands. Helpless, the calf lies
still, panting. A man approaches with a glowing iron
fresh from the fire, and claps this, hissing and seething, upon the shrinking hide. A malodorous cloud of
smoke arises from the burning hair. The iron cuts
quite through the hair and full into the hide, so that
the mark shall never grow over again with hair. A
piteous bawl arises from the little animal—a protest
half drowned by the rush of mingled sounds about.
Meantime a third man trims out with a sharp knife the
required slice, if any, which is to be taken from the
ear or dewlap to complete the registered mark of the
owner. In a moment the calf is released and shoved
to one side to rejoin its mother, who mutters at its
injuries, and licks it soothingly. The calf stands with
legs spread wide apart, sick and dizzy, indisposed to
move, and shorn for many days of much of its friskiness. Mother and calf alike are hustled out of the way.
The tally man calls out, " Bar Y, one calf." Another
calf is by this time coming skating up to the fire, and
again the iron is hissing. Meantime the hubbub and
the turmoil increase, until all seems again lost to chaos.
Taut ropes cross the ground in many directions. The
cutting ponies pant and sweat, rear and plunge. The

garb of the cowpuncher now is one of white alkali, which hangs gray in his eyebrows and mustache. Steers bellow and run to and fro. Cows charge on their persecutors, amid confusion and great laughings. Fleet yearlings and young cows break away and run for the open, pursued by cowboys who care not how or where they ride. The dust and the lowings and bellowings and runnings wax until all seems hopeless. Yet all the time the irons are busy, all the time the calves are sliding up to the fire, all the time the voice of the tally man is chanting, and all the time the lines of figures are growing longer on his grimy pages. The herd lessens. The number of calves visible among the cattle becomes small. Finally the last calf is cut out and branded. The cowpunchers pull up their heaving ponies. The branding men wipe their faces. The tally man again sharpens his pencil. The herd is " worked." It may scatter now as it wills. This field has been reaped. It remains now to go on to other fields.

At the close of the day's work the men have less disposition to romp and play pranks than they had at the start in the morning. They are weary, but weary with that fatigue readily shaken off by a man in fine health and good condition. The cooks and teamsters have prepared the camp, and the professional duties of the cowpuncher close when he takes off his saddle. Until bedtime, which comes soon after the evening meal, he may lounge and smoke. The cook has prepared abundance of food for these hard-working men, whose constant exercise in the fresh air gives them good appetites. In the *menu* of the round-up fresh beef is sure to figure, and beef of the best sort running in the herd. It makes no difference whose brand is on the animal desired for the mess; if wanted, it is forthwith roped, thrown, and butchered. In the old days no account was kept of the round-up beef, but of later days the owner of an animal killed for beef is usually credited with it on the round-up books. Sometimes, when time and opportunity offer, the cowpuncher has for his dinner a dish probably unknown elsewhere than on the range, and not common there. A choice bit of " porterhouse " steak, cut thick, is placed between two steaks of similar size and excellence, and the whole buried under a bed of hot coals. In this way the middle steak retains all the juices of its double envelope, and offers a morsel which might well be appreciated by a man less hungry or more particular than the tired cowpuncher. A pound or so of beef, with some tinned vegetables, taken with a quart or so of coffee, and the cowpuncher is ready to hunt his blankets and make ready for another day. He does not work on the eight hours a day schedule, but works during the hours when it is light enough to see. The end of the day may find him some miles from where the cooks' fires are gleaming, and the swift chill of the night of the plains may have fallen before his jogging pony, which trots now with head and ears down, brings him up to the camp which for him, as much as any place on earth, is home.

Such is something of the routine of the round-up, and one day, barring the weather conditions, is like another throughout the long and burning summer, one round-up following another closely all through the season. The work is a trifle monotonous to the cowboy, perhaps, in spite of its exciting features, and is to-day more monotonous than it was in the past, before the good old days had left the plains forever. In those times the country was wilder, and there was more of novelty and interest in the operations of the

range. To-day the great plains are but a vast pasture
ground for the cattle belonging to the community of
cowmen, and the highly differentiated system of the
round-up progresses as a purely business operation,
whose essential object is the establishment of the individual rights of each member of that community.
The methods of the round-up seem of necessity rude
and inaccurate, but really they are singularly efficient
and precise. The skilled labour of the cowpuncher
gives to each man that which belongs to him, and
nothing more.

It is a curious review, that which passes under the
eyes of the tally men and branders during the calf
harvesting. Sometimes a calf comes up with a cow
whose hide is a network of confused and conflicting
brands, so that it is impossible to tell justly whose
property she is. In such a case the calf is not branded
at all to any owner, but is thrown into the association
credit, where it belongs equally to all, and where its
value will be equally divided. Sometimes in the hurry
of the work a calf is branded with the wrong iron,
and is thus given the sign of a man to whom it does
not belong. This would seem to be a puzzling proposition to the cowpuncher, for the brand is something
which, to use the cowpuncher's phrase, does not " come
out in the washin'." Yet the remedy is very simple.
Another calf is " traded back " for the calf wrongly
branded, the proper brand of the former calf being
placed upon the " traded " calf. Of course, this leaves
two mismatched calves on the range, whose brands
do not tally with those of their mothers, but within
the year time will have equalized the error, for the
calves will have left their mothers, and the one will
probably be worth about as much as the other.

Mingled with such questions as these during the

branding operations are always the complex ones of
strays and Mavericks. Sometimes a stray cow is found
during the round-up bearing the brand of a man foreign to that round-up district, or one not represented
in the round-up. The increase of this animal is
branded with the brand of its owner, who has been
no party to the transaction at all, but who has been
safe under the system of the round-up. In the case
of Mavericks found during the round-up, a like intelligent and just method obtains. Roughly speaking, an
animal must be a yearling to be a Maverick, and on
some ranges this rule is laid down, though really a
Maverick becomes such at the time when it ceases to
follow the cow and begins to shift for itself. If it is
missed in the first round-up of its life, it falls under
the rules or laws governing the handling of Mavericks, such rules offering considerable local variations.
On some ranges of Wyoming, for instance, the cowmen
have agreed lines establishing the borders of their
respective ranges, and a cowman may brand for his
own a calf running on his range and not following
any cow. This right is merely one of comity among
the local ranchers, and one which it is not expected
will be abused. Indeed, the comity goes still further,
showing yet more clearly the interdependence and
mutual confidence of the cowmen. If after the round-
up a rancher finds a neighbour's calf unbranded, but
following the cow upon his own range, he brands the
calf with the owner's proper brand, and not with his
own. This is simply a matter of individual honesty.
The cowman knows that his neighbour will do as
much for him. Each ranch keeps its own separate
tally-book in this way, and these are exchanged at
the end of the season, so that each man gets what
belongs to him, no matter where it may have wan-

dered, and no matter whether he ever sees it again or not. It has been elsewhere mentioned that on some parts of the range all the Mavericks are sold at auction before the beginning of the round-up (always to some resident cowman who is known to be responsible). In this case, when a Maverick is found in the round-up it is dragged to the fire—perhaps by two ropes, for it is big and lusty—and has put upon it the "vent brand" of the association, thus securing an abstract of title which it is to carry with it through life, and which will hold good in any cattle market of the land.

It may readily be seen how honest and how expert must be the men who carry out so intricate a system. It should be borne in mind that brands do not show so distinctly upon hide as they do upon paper, and, of course, it must be remembered that a range cow may carry more than one brand, and perhaps a "vent brand" or so, if she has changed ownership before. Here again there may be exceptions arising out of local conditions. For instance, if a herd of cattle is brought from a far Southern range to one in the North, where that brand is not met and is not recorded, it is not always the case that the owner will have these animals counterbranded; for it is known that no confusion will arise if they are left as they are, and, of course, the fewer brands an animal carries the easier it is to tell whose it is. It is justice, and justice by the shortest and most practical route, which is the desire of the cowman, whether that imply the branding of a Maverick or the hanging of a cattle thief.

After the calf round-up comes the beef round-up, and this, too, may be called the cowman's harvest, or his final harvest. The beef round-up may begin in

July or August, and perhaps it may be conducted by the joint efforts of two districts instead of one. The joint outfit acts under much the same system of gathering up the cattle as has been described for the calf round-up. All the cattle of the range are gathered in great herds, and the latter are handled as during the calf round-up, though the operation is somewhat simpler. Only the mature or fatted animals are cut out from the herd, the rest being left to scatter as they like. The separated number goes under the name of the " beef cut," and this " cut " is held apart and driven on ahead from place to place as the round-up progresses, the beef herd thus growing from day to day until all the range has been worked. The herd is then driven in by easy stages to the shipping point on the railroad, where it is perhaps held until the arrival of the herd from the adjoining district, so that the shippers may be reasonably sure they have in all the beef fit for shipment from their ranges. Then the long train loads of cattle go on to the great markets, and the work of the ranchman proper is done for the season. Perhaps in the shipment of beef there may be a few animals picked up on the range during the beef drive which belong to some owner or owners not represented in the outfits. Such animals, if fit for shipment as beef, are driven along with the main herd and shipped and sold without the owners' knowledge, the money being returned to the owners in due time through the inspectors at the markets. Obviously this is better than allowing these animals to run wild and unutilized as strays upon the range, of no profit to the owners or any one else. The common sense and the fairness of the cowman's system prevail on the beef round-up as in the harvesting of the calves.

So perfect is this great interdependent system of the

round-up on the main cattle ranges of to-day that the ranchmen trust to it almost entirely for the determining and the handling of their yearly product. Range riding is now nearly done away with in some of the more populous districts, the cattle ranging in common over the country as they like, with no efforts made to confine them to any given range. All these things are modified by local conditions, and the whole system of ranching cattle is becoming modified by the advance of time. To-day the rancher uses more and more feed about his ranch. He raises hay for his stock, a bit of grain for his horses in winter time, or perhaps he buys hay or grain of the " grangers " who are moving in about him. Speaking in the original and primitive sense, this is not range work at all. The cowman proper depended solely upon the standing grass for his cattle food, upon the saddle for the assembling of his wealth, upon his own iron for the marking of it.

If it be now obvious what is the intention of the cowman in the round-up and what the method by which he obtains his purposes, we shall none the less fail of a fair review of this business system if we lose sight of the chief actor in all these operations, the cowpuncher himself. His is the tireless form that rides day after day in rain or shine throughout the long season, collecting the cattle upon their wild pasture ground, and his the undaunted heart to meet all the hardships of one of the hardest callings known to men. From May until November he may be in the saddle, each week growing gaunter and grimmer and more bronzed, his hair and mustache becoming more and more bleached and burned, his eye perhaps more hollow though not less bright and keen. If he be tired, none may know it; if he be sick, it shall not appear;

if he be injured, it must not be confessed until confession is unnecessary. His creed is one of hardihood, his shibboleth is to dare, his etiquette is not to
complain. Such doctrine is not for the weak. It is
no place for a timid man, this grinding crush in the
middle of the herd, and the cowardly or considerate
horseman would better ride elsewhere than in the mad
and headlong cross-country chases of the round-up.
The goring of a steer, the fall from a pitching horse,
the plunge over a cut bank, the crushing of a limb
in the press, or the trampling under a thousand hoofs
—such possibilities face the cowpuncher on the round-
up not part of the time, but all the time. He accepts
them as matter of course and matter of necessity, and
with the ease of custom. Yet he is mortal and may
suffer injury. If the injury be not fatal, he accepts
it calmly, and waits till he is well again. If a round-
up knows a burial, it is not the first one which has been
known. Men of action must meet fatality at times,
and other men of action will have small time to mourn
them. The conditions of life upon the range are severe, so severe that had they been known in advance
they would have been shunned by hundreds of men
who in their ignorance thought themselves fit for cowboys and learned later that they were not.

It goes without saying that so hardy and healthy
a creature as this cowpuncher must have his amusements, even at his times of hardest work. The round-
up is by no means a succession of dreary experiences,
for it is there that one will find the most grotesque
exhibitions of cowpuncher vitality and cowpuncher
merriment. There probably never was a round-up
where the boys did not rope a steer for some ambitious
cowpuncher to ride bareback for a wager. This feat
is not so easy as it looks, for the hide of a steer, or,

worse yet, the hide of a big fat bull, is loose and rolling, so that, as the cowpuncher would say, it "turns plum over between a feller's legs." Sometimes a yearling or a runty little "dogy" is roped for this form of sport, the cowpuncher wreathing his long legs under its belly to its intense disgust and fright, though he probably sits it safely when the ropes are "turned loose" in spite of its antics, for it is the boast of a first-class cowpuncher that he can "ride ary thing that wears ha'r." Sometimes the cowboys enter into competitive tests of skill, trying to see which man can, alone and unassisted, in the shortest space of time, "rope, throw, and tie" a full-grown steer. It would seem almost impossible for one man to perform this feat, yet a good cowpuncher will do it so smoothly and swiftly that neither the steer nor the spectator can tell just how it happened. Yet another little sport on the round-up is sometimes to hitch up a cow and a broncho or "mean" horse together to a wagon, the horse jumping and plunging over the cow to the intense delight of these rough souls, to whom the wildest form of action is the most congenial.

It is taken for granted that all the men engaging in a round-up are good riders, and if it should chance that any one becomes entangled in an argument with a pitching pony, the event is one of great pleasure to his friends, who gather about him and give him encouragement of the cowpuncher sort, with abundant suggestions as to how he shall ride and much insistence that he must "ride him fair." If the cowpuncher is thrown, he is sure to get more jeers than sympathy, but it is his business not to be thrown. Nowadays the horse herd, always one of the picturesque features about the round-up, is losing some of its old interest with the gradual passing away of the habit of bucking or pitching among the range horses. The horse herd is to-day much graded up, as are the herds of cattle, and the modern cow pony may be quite a respectable bit of horseflesh. It is apt to be a more solid and "chunky" animal than the old Spanish pony, just as the cowboy himself is apt to be a more bulky man than the first cowpunchers who came up the Trail. One may note yet other changes. At the strictly modern round-up of to-day one will see few leather "chaps," few heavy hats with wide leather bands, few bucking horses, and no "guns." If we would study the cowpuncher we must do so soon, if we wish ever to see him as he once was at his best; and if we would see a round-up on the range we should not tarry too long, for yearly it becomes more and more restricted, modified, and confined, less and less a wild gathering of the plains, more and more a mere barnyard fixture. The days of the commonplace have come, and well may we mourn the past that has gone by.

The stirring scenes of the round-up, the rush and whirl of the cutting out, the hurry and noise of the branding, the milling of the main herds, and all the gusty life of the wild *mêlée* are things to remember as long as one lives, and they readily invite the multifold descriptive efforts that have been given them. Yet aside from the common or conventional pictures there may arise detached ones, some perhaps from out of the past, perhaps wilder and more picturesque than those we may easily find to-day at the focus of affairs upon the range. Memory brings up a little scene far down in the dry and desert region of the Neutral Strip, where once our party of antelope hunters crossed the range where a round-up was in progress. We had noticed the many hoof prints of cattle and horses, all trending in a certain direction, and guessed the cause when we saw the long lines of dust rising and stringing out on the hazy and trembling horizon. In that barren and flinty-soiled region water is a rare thing, and he who does not know the water holes for the country a hundred miles about would far better do his antelope hunting elsewhere. Yet we knew we were near the line of the old cattle trails, and indeed just before noon one day fell upon the wide parallel lines ground out of the hard, gray soil by the thousands of hoofs that had crossed the country in earlier years. Thinking that we should thus come upon water at some time either that day or the next, we followed along the trail, and, as luck had it, within a couple of hours we fell upon a little pool of water by the wayside. It was a very baddish bit of water, muddy, discoloured, trampled, shallow at best, and now hardly sufficient to fill the hoof marks with its greenish-yellow fluid that fairly boiled under the downright rays of the sun. Yet it was water, and such as it was we were glad to find it, since it was the first for more than twenty-four hours. We camped beside it joyfully, feeling that now all the trials of life were past. As we lay there, under such shade as the wagon offered on the blindingly hot day, we saw a trail of dust coming from the line of hills about us, and with the glasses soon made out a squad of mounted men. These came on down to the water hole, and in time were joined there by other men who came from various directions. The party was the mess of a Strip outfit that had been out all day rounding up cattle back of the watering place. The men were hot and tired and covered with dust, but if any one was disposed to grumble he kept it to himself. The cook unfastened the tail-gate of his wagon, and in a twinkling had a kitchen table and pantry right at hand,

with flour and meat within reach. Some of the boys
kicked together enough of the abundant prairie chips
—the only fuel within sixty miles of that point—and
soon the preparations for the hurried meal were in
progress. When the cook wanted water for his coffee
he walked to the pool—in which, by the way, several
dead carcasses were lying—and, picking out the point
where the water seemed clearest, he calmly dipped up
his coffeepot full and returned without comment to
the fire. No one said a word about the quality of the
water, which really was of a sort to make one shudder
at the memory years later, and if the coffee was not
good no one complained of it. From the mess box the
cook produced his tin dishes, his knives and forks, and
table was spread without cloth flat on the dusty and
hoof-beaten soil. The heat was glaring, and in it,
without suspicion of shade, the men sat, their flannel
shirts covered over the shoulders with the white dust
of the plains, their broad hats pushed back upon their
foreheads as they ate. It was a scene for some better
painter or writer than has yet appeared, this dusty,
weather-beaten, self-reliant little body of men. Each
face of the circle comes to mind clearly even after
years of time. They were silent, dignified fellows,
these men, not talking much among themselves or with
us, though they offered us of what they had, we having apparently convinced them that we were not " on
the rustle," we in turn sharing with them what our
mess box offered, as it happened some fresh game,
which was much appreciated.

Before the meal began each man unsaddled his horse
and turned it loose upon the prairie, where it first went
to water and then set to feeding on the short sun-burned
grass. When it came time to leave camp, the horses
were rounded up by the herder, a young boy not over fif-

teen years of age, whom all the men called "Kid." In their rough way they seemed fond of the boy, who had evidently shown the quality demanded on the plains, and as the boy gathered up his horses into the rope corral made by two or three cow ponies and a couple of men as supports, the round-up boss looked on at his businesslike movements with approval, and remarked aside to one of the men, "That's a d—n good kid all right." To which the other replied with an approving grunt. The Kid rounded up his charges swiftly, and got them into a many-coloured mass of mingling heads and tossing manes within the confines of the rope corral, after which the work of roping the mounts followed. The Kid begged of the foreman the privilege of doing the roping, and the latter, smiling in rough fashion, gave him what he asked, not laughing at his failures, but giving him a bit of advice about his work now and then when he had a specially wily pony to capture from out the moving and plunging bunch of wild range horses. It was a good instance of the chivalry sometimes shown by stronger natures to ones weaker or less skilled, and it afforded also a good example of the development of the cowboy from youth to manhood, from inexperience to skill.

Presently each man had out his mount, and had saddled the grunting and complaining beast in the effective fashion of the plains. There was a little mild pitching, but not enough to interest the tired cowpunchers. In a trice the rope corral was down and the ropes coiled at the saddle horns of their owners. The cook had his mess wagon slapped shut, and the teamster his team "hooked up." The men rode away as silent as they came, the foreman and some of those passing most closely to us saying as they rode by, "So long, fellers." No one looked back as he rode away, for this would have been a bit of curiosity not in good form on the range. They passed away into the edge of the rim of hills, and we saw them no more.

Such is one picture of the range, and it shows the cowboy not as a devil-may-care, roistering fellow, full of strange oaths and uncouth conduct, but, as he should perhaps better be seen, as a steady, hard-working, methodical man, able in his calling, faithful in his duties, and prompt in their fulfilment. These men were grimy with toil of a most exacting sort. Their fare was coarse and common, and even the first necessary of comfort was denied them. They were rudely clad, and all armed to the last item, for that was a country where arms were at times needful. Yet hard as was their apparent lot, and rude as they who shared it, their simple and uncomplaining hardihood and self-control, their dignity, and their generous conduct to the younger member of the party left a lasting impression—perhaps a good one of its kind—of the cowboy as he is in actual life upon the range.

13

CHAPTER X.

THE life of the cowboy in the early days of the West was a series of pictures of unusual and striking themes. The panorama of the plains dealt with no small things for subjects, not the turn of a gown nor the poise of a fan nor the cast of a gesture, but with things of gravity and import. The wars of man with brute, of brute with Nature, of man with brute and Nature both, such were the topics of that vivid canvas. It was a time of large actions, large pictures.

One can see it now, the great cold landscape of the cattle range in winter. It is a picture of scant lighting and low values. The monochrome of winter, the blue-gray of cold desolation, oppresses it all. The white hills set on the farther edge are cold and bluish. The sky above is forbidding with its sunless gray. The dust-grimed snow in the *coulees* is gray, and the un-covered soil of the wind-swept hill is gray and cheer-less. Not a rift of light falls anywhere, not a touch of sun to soften the hard, metallic composition. All the greens were gone long ago. The ragged and clutching hand of a sagebush reaches up in despair from the uncompromising desert, but it, too, is gray—gray with the withered spirit of the iron earth and icy air. The sky is even in its colours, except that now and then there scuds across it a strange and

182

ominous thing, a wisp of flying white, misplaced and
unregulated. For the air is altogether still. No
breath waves the mane of this pony which stands on
the little ridge, its head up and its gaze bent fixedly
upon the far horizon. There is something strange in
the air. It is not so extremely cold, but the silence
is so deep, so startling. Back of the very silence there
is something, something of portent, of warning. Now
and again a long shivering moan goes across the plain,
borne from no one knows what origin. The image
of dread is stalking forth this day. All animate nature
feels it. Whither are going these great gray wolves,
slouching along, their tails low, their heads over their
shoulders, looking backward at this unseen pursuing
thing? They do not trouble the cattle now, nor do
the cattle fear them as they pass through. What, then,
is it that the cattle dread, so that they sniff and snort
and toss their heads, looking wildly toward the north
as did this pony now? Written on this inscrutable dull
sky there must be some awful sight invisible to human
eyes. These wild creatures of the plains see it. They
feel the dread. They know their weakness to meet
this coming thing. They moan, the note of despair
in their voices. They start now and then and run
swiftly for a short distance, then turn and come back,
pitching their heads high and bellowing. They lower
their heads and shake them, and mutter hoarsely,
with their muzzles near the ground, emitting their
breath in sharp puffs.

Look! The breath of the cattle has grown white.
It shines like fresh steam in the air. A moment ago
the air was warm. And now that weird white scud
flitted again across the sky, across the earth rather,
low down, flying like some wraith of the mountains.
Back there, upon the horizon where the cattle have

looked so long, there arises a tiny cloud of white, soft, fleecy, innocent as the garb of a babe. Alas! it is the shroud of the range. It is the vestment of death for thousands of these creatures here!

It comes, this little cloud, rising and growing and spreading as though it were some vast curtain drawn quickly up and forward. Before it run long, ragged hissings in the air, and on the edge of these hissings fly always these scuds of the sky, little venomous spirits of fury, as they may now plainly be seen to be. With the mutterings of the gathering cattle, which now crowd together in the blind wish for aid and comfort, there blends the first low voice of the storm, a far-off sighing wail, of cadence at first indicative of anything but malice. This voice rises and then falls and is silent for a moment. It rises again, nearer and changed in import. It dominates the mingled voices of the herd, now crowded together, their feet scuffling, their heads thrown high and confusedly. Again the storm speaks, this time very near, and as it falls a great sigh goes over the breast of Nature, the sigh for that which is to happen. It is the last warning, as useless as the others. The storm has crept on until it is sure of its prey. There is a whirring, rasping crash as the blades of the wind meet and sweep on, and then a wall of icy white smites the shivering beasts as they stand huddled and waiting for that which they know is doom!

On the narrowed horizon, leaning forward as they ride and coming to the herd as fast as their horses can bear them, are two figures, the men of the line camp nearest to this spot. If they can head the cattle into the broken country beyond perhaps they can find shelter enough to stop the drift. If they start straight down before the wind, nothing can stop them till they reach the first fences many miles below. It will be

the emptying of the range! Once under the hills before the drift begins, and perhaps there will be shelter
enough to enable the cattle to live through the storm.
Perhaps they, too, can live through it in some way;
they have not paused to ponder how. Well enough
they know that anything they do must be done at once.
Well enough they know, perhaps, that every human regard for their own safety would take them just the
other way, back to the little dugout in the bank which
they have left. But at least they will try to save a part
of the herd which has formed here. They must be
young men. Old hands would know that when the blizzard has set in there is no power on earth that can stop
the drifting of the cattle.

And now the storm bursts with a blinding, smoth-
ering wave of white, fine snow, driven to atoms by
the flat wind that hurls it on. This *poudre* of the
north cuts like a set of knives revolving on the skin.
No man, no creature can face it. The stings of the
thousands of whips smite unceasingly, all this under
the exhaust of the storm, which steals away the breath
so that one must turn down wind to live. The air has
grown icy cold at once. All around the world is now
blotted out. The eye strikes a continuous dancing,
glittering whirl of particles of ice, which confuse and
bewilder with their incessant glinting flight. All
sense of direction is lost at once. There is but one
direction, and that is with the wind. The ground
itself is almost gone. The mountains, the hills, the
ridges, the *coulees* have all disappeared. Only close at
the feet of the horses and cattle can one see a bit of
earth, this veiled by the suffusing white breath of the
animals, turned into vapour on the instant that it
strikes the arctic air.

At first the cattle turn their backs to the wind,

and so stand huddled and motionless, the little calves pressing deep into the mass of the shivering creatures and bleating piteously. In a few moments the whole herd is covered with a blanket of white. The two men who are now up with the herd strive to break apart this blanket of white, riding along the edges with bent heads, seeking to open out the cattle so that they can get them moving. It is useless! The white veil shuts down too sternly. The men can no longer breathe. Their eyes are blinded by the stinging riffs of fine ice. They are separated in the storm. A shout is answered by a shout, but though the one ride toward the other as best he may he can not find him now, for ever the voice calling seems to shift and evade as though the spirits used it mockingly. Crack! crack! comes the note of the six-shooter, but how small, how far away it is! Again and again, and again also the answer! These two men have not lost their heart. They will yet find each other. They will turn the herd, they two alone, here on the wide, white plain, in this mystery of moving white! But where was the last shot? It sounded half a mile away. It might have been a hundred yards.

There comes a mightier wail of the wind, a more vindictive rush of the powdery snow. All trace of the landscape is now absolutely gone. The cowboy has wheeled his horse, but he knows not now which way he heads. The hills may be this way or that. A strange, numb, confused mental condition comes to him. He crouches down in the saddle, his head drooping, as he raises his arm yet again and fires another shot, almost his last. He dreams he hears an answer, and he calls again hoarsely. The scream of the wind and the rumbling of the voices of the cattle drown out all other sounds. He is in with the herd. His partner is in with it too. But neither he nor they both will ever turn or direct this herd. This he knows with sinking heart. They are lost, all lost together, out here upon the pitiless plains. And there are firesides of which these men may think!

The herd moves! It recks not human guidance now, for the storm alone is its final guide and master. The storm orders it to move, and it obeys. With low moans and groanings of suffering and of fear there ensues a waving movement of the long blanket of white which has enshrouded the close-packed mass of cattle. They stagger and stop, doubting and dreading. They go on again and stop, and again they sway and swing forward, the horns rattling close upon each other, the heads drooping, the gait one of misery and despair. The drift has begun!

Lost in the drift are the two boys, and they know they may as well follow as stop. Indeed, they dare not stop, for to stop is to die. Down from their horses they go and battle on foot among the dull-eyed cattle. Over their hearts creeps always that heavy, wondering, helpless feeling. They freeze, but soon cease to know they freeze. Their stiff legs stumble, and they wonder why. Their mouths are shut fast by the ice. The eyes of the cattle are frozen over entirely by the ice that gathers on their eyelids, and their hair, long and staring, shows in frosty filaments about their heads and necks. Icicles hang upon their jaws. They moan and sigh, now and then a deep rumbling bellow coming from the herd. The cows low sadly. The little calves bawl piteously. But on and on goes the drift, all keeping together for a time. And with it somewhere are the two cowboys, who should have known the import of the blizzard on the plains.

This horrible icy air can not long be endured by

any living being, and soon the herd begins to string
out into a long line, the weaker ones falling to the
rear. If the cattle be strong and well-fed, they can
endure any cold, but starvation has here been long
at work. The horrible and inexorable law of Nature
is going on. The strongest alone may survive. Those
which fall back do not at first stop. They stagger on
as far as they can. A little calf falls down, sinking
first to its knees, and then dropping stiffly, its head still
down the wind. Its mother stays with it, pushing at
it with her own frozen muzzle. It can not get to its
feet. The mother looks after the indistinct forms
slowly disappearing in the driving mist of white, but
goes no farther on. In the spring they will find the
mother and calf together. Farther to the south are
the bunches of yearlings which were weak and thin
of flesh. Then come the heifers and cows and steers
as they fell out and back in order in this white cold
mist of the great drift that cleared the range from the
foothills to the railroad fences. In places the followers of the drift may find gullies or deep ravines packed
with carcasses of animals which here met their death.
When the wind had swept the *coulees* full of snow the
treacherous white surface looked all alike to the dull
eyes of the drifting cattle. They walked into the
yielding snow and fell one above the other in a horrible confusion, those above trampling to death those
beneath until all was mingled in a smother and crush
of passing life. Again there may be noted a spot
where, under the lee of some cut bank or bluff, the
cattle paused for shelter from the storm. Here the
snow piled up about them, drifting high around into
an icy barricade, until they had left but a tiny feeding
ground, swept bare by the eddying winds. Here,
hemmed in and soon without food, they stood and

starved by inches, perhaps living for days or weeks before the end came. Here, had rescue been attempted, they would have charged furiously, with such strength as they had left, any human being daring to come near, for the greater the strait of the range animal the greater the unreasoning rage with which it resists all effort at its succour.

All day and all night and into the next day, perhaps, the cattle drift, their numbers less and less with each passing hour, leaving behind a trail of shapeless heaps, thick and thicker as the long hours drag by, the numbers of the survivors growing still fewer and fewer, weaker and more weak. Out of the whole herd which started there are but a few hundreds or thousands which come to the fences of the railroad, seventy miles from where the drift began. Here it ends— ends in a row of heaped-up carcasses along the wires that held the remnants of the herd from further travel; ends as you may see as you gaze from the car window in the spring as you are whirled across the great plains—ends in a blanket of hide a hundred miles in length. The skinning parties which follow the drift when the weather has grown warmer use the wire fences as their drying racks.

And of the men who were caught in the storm? One they found in a *coulee* back toward the beginning of the drift, where he crawled under a little ledge and thought he could weather out the storm. He had no fire nor fuel nor light of any kind, and neither had he any food. He cared nothing for these things. He felt cheerful, and he fell asleep, dreaming. The other man went much farther before he lay down. Then, resourceful to the last, he shot and killed a steer in a little hollow where the wind was least. They found him crouched up close to the body of the ani-

mal, his arm between its fore legs and partly about
its neck, his face hid in the hair of the creature's chest.
But the blood of both had turned to ice before they fell.

In the spring the sky is blue and repentant, and
the wind sings softly in the prairie grasses. But one
can not forget that awful picture of the blue-gray time,
and ever he hears the death songs of the legions of
the air which urged on the herds in their solemn march
into annihilation. Such is one picture of the range.

There is another picture of a strenuous sort. This
time it is summer, and it is at night. At evening, when
the great herd of trail cattle bedded down on the hillside, the sky was clear and the stars were shining
luminously large in the pure air of the plains. It
needed an old plainsman to know what this foreboding
quiet meant, this ominous hush, and he alone would
have noted anxiously the dark line of cloud along the
horizon. Any of these hardy riders could tell you a
storm was breeding, but they have seen many storms
and do not fear them. The cook whistles as steadily
and discordantly as ever as he washes his dishes in
the dusk, swearing fluently when a stray whisk of air
blows the ashes out of his fire pit into his eyes. The
cook pulls the wagon sheet tight to-night, however,
and he makes his own bed inside the wagon. The
night herder turns up his collar as he goes on watch
with the horse herd. The drive boss sits with his
knees between his hands smoking a pipe, which glows
dully in the darkening night. The camp is quiet.
All about come up the faint night sounds of the plains.
The men are tired, and one by one they unroll their
blankets and lie out in huge cocoons, each with his
head in the hollow of his saddle and his hat pulled
down over his face. Jim, the foreman of the drive,

does not go to sleep just yet. He sits smoking and watching. Now and then a wandering whiff of wind blows the ashes in a fiery little stream out of his pipe bowl. Jim puts an extra man on the night watch, who departs into the dark, singing softly to himself.

Jim sits thus for some time with his knees up between his hands, perhaps nodding now and then, but afraid to go to sleep. He notes the steady play of the lightning on the rising bank of clouds, and before an hour has passed he begins to hear the low, incessant muttering of the thunder. In half an hour more he is going down the line, kicking the long cocoons with the toe of his boot and calling out:

"Tumble out, fellers! Git up! There's goin' to be a hell of a storm."

With grunts of protest the cowpunchers roll out of their blankets and sit up in the night, rubbing their eyes. They see the bank of cloud now reaching over them, and hear the steady roar of the thunder approaching. The wind begins to sob in the grass, and little particles of dust go whirling by. The head of the cook pokes itself out from the wagon.

"What in hell!" says the cook.

"She's goin' to be hell all right, cookie," says a voice cheerfully. "You better picket your dough-pan."

"I would not live al-l-lwa-y," comes the faint voice of the night herder as he makes his rounds.

"Saddle up, fellers!" says Jim. "There's shore goin' to be hell a-poppin' here before long. If they ever break out of here they'll run to hell an' gone with us to-night."

"That's right, pitch, you wall-eyed son of misery!" says an injured voice in the dark, from where some cowpuncher is having an argument with his pony, which resents the saddle thrown across its back in the dark.

"Oh, then, Susannah, don't yer cry fer me!" sings another voice, as the owner of it, wrapped in his yellow slicker, gets into his saddle and turns toward the herd.

"Good-bye, cookie!" calls another. "You can git breakfast fer us on the Cimarron, I reckon."

They all take up their round about the herd, falling into their work with the philosophy of their calling, which accepts things as they come. As they ride in line along the edge of the herd the thunder is booming loudly, and the rain begins to fall in heavy, irregular drops. Then suddenly with a gusty rush the torrents of the air break loose, and a solid wall of rain sweeps over the place, hiding in a whirling mist the outlines of men and animals. The thunder now bursts with deafening volume. The cattle have sprung to their feet and now push about among themselves uneasily, their long horns clanking together in the darkness. They are wet, but the rain is not chilling, and in a moment the cloud-burst is over and gone, and nothing remains of the storm but the lightning and the wind. The sky lightens queerly, so that objects may be faintly seen, men riding along the edge of the herd, keeping the cattle back and closing them up. Sounds of confused sort come from among the cattle, grumblings and mutterings, mingling with the chanting of the cowboys riding. The storm is nearly past, but the whole air is alive with electricity. The discharge of the thunder is as the noise of cannon. The lightning falls not in jagged lines, but in bursting balls of flame, which detonate with terrible reports. Along the tips of the horns of the cattle the faint flames play in weird way, as the fires of St. Elmo upon the spars of a ship caught in a storm at sea. The men still hold the line, calling to the cattle, which are now clattering and shuffling about in a way not pleasant to hear, though still they do not break into any concerted rush. Now and again a start is made by some frightened animal, but the nearest cowboy turns it back, riding against the head of each break showing toward the edge. The herd is shifting ground a little, edging a trifle down wind. This brings it nearer to the camping place, nearer also to the wagon of the cook, which stands with its white cover broken loose and flapping upon the gale. There is a call of a voice, which begins to shout out something.

But this voice, and all the voices, and all the other sounds are swallowed in a mighty, dreadful roar. The white cover of the wagon has broken loose at the other end, the rope parting with a crack like the report of a gun. The wagon sheet whips madly up and down as though with deliberate intent of malice, and then goes sailing off across the prairie. No studied effort of evil could have been direr at this very moment! The herd, keyed up to the last pitch of nervousness and only held by the utmost efforts of the cowboys, needs only this devil's device to set it off. " Good God A'mighty! " bursts out the foreman. But even as he shouts he, in common with every other man of the outfit, digs in his spurs and rides for the head of the herd, the front of this plunging, rushing, stumbling, falling mass of panic-stricken creatures which are off in the curse of the drive—the dreaded stampede in the dark!

The sound of the rushing hoofs of near ten thousand cattle is imposing enough at any time, but heard mingled and confused in the running in the dark it is something terrible. A loud cracking of hoofs comes through the fog of sound, and the mad rattling of the great horns swung together in the crush as the cattle struggle to head out of the suffocating press behind them and on all sides. Mad indeed is this chase to-night, and far will be its ending, this ride with the accompaniment of the booming thunder and with the ripping flight of the lightning for its only beacon. Ride, Jim! Ride, Springtime, and Tex., and Curley, and Kid, and Cherokee, and all the rest of you! Now if ever you must be men of proof! Into the rattle of it, up to the head of it, press, spur, crowd! Shoot into their faces, frighten them back, turn them aside, ride into them, over them, but ride fast and thoughtless of yourself! There is no possibility of taking care. The pony must do it all. The pony knows what a stumble means. The herd will roll over horse and man and crush them as if they were but prairie flowers. The ground is rough, but there must be no blunder. Ah, but there was! Something happened there! There was a stumble! There was a cry, smothered; but all that was half a mile back. The herd sweeps on.

Into the thick of the leaders of the herd the cowpunchers crowd in from the flanks, meeting there the men who were swept away in the first mad rush of the cattle. They can not now escape from this position, nor do they seek to do so, but ride with the stampede, their horses with ears flat, struggling on at top speed, bounding from side to side to escape the jostling of a steer, leaping ahead when the press clears in front for a moment. Through the noise of the pounding hoofs comes the panting of the cattle and the sobbing but valiant breath of the brave little horses which carry these wild and reckless men. A faint shout is heard at times or the " Whoa-o-o-ope! " of a voice call-

ing to the cattle in attempt at soothing them. Now
and then may be seen an arm thrown up and waved
in gesture to a near-by rider, or at times may shoot
forth the flash of the revolver as some daring man
heads across the front and tries to frighten the herd
into swinging from its course.

The thundering hoofs now seem to pound upon
harder ground. The broken country near the bluffs
of the river is at hand. Down into gully and ravine
go men and horses and cattle in the dark, and welter
out of it upon the other side as best they may. Many
an animal goes headlong in the dark, but it is not
noticed or deplored. Each object makes a tiny rock
to stem the flood of pouring cattle. But suddenly,
without warning, the whole front of the herd plunges
down utterly out of view! It has dropped down into
the earth, has been swallowed up bodily! Some of the
cowpunchers went down too. At the brink of the
bluff the following numbers of the cattle pile up and
back in a horrid mass, seeking to crowd back, but yet
pushed on by the herd behind. The remnant of the
herd splits, and turns along the side of the bluff.
The remaining cowboys follow, pressing and crowding
in, still spurring up to the heads of the panting cattle
and seeking to turn them. The head of the herd
finally swerves, it turns gradually more and more.
The cowboys are still in front, shouting, crowding,
firing their revolvers across the faces of the cattle, and
urging them back and away from the bluffs. The
cattle turn now and traverse a circle. A moment later
and they round the same circle, their ranks now closer
together. The circle grows smaller and smaller. The
mill is begun. Round and round they go until they
no longer seek to break away, but stand and clatter
and shuffle and pant. Round and round the mill the

cowboys ride, talking to the cattle now in proficient profanity, but doing nothing to startle the terrorized animals into a further flight. Gradually the panic passes. At length the cowpuncher takes a chew of tobacco and pulls up his pony even from the walk in which he has been going about the herd.

The men who were at the head of the herd at the place where it went over the cut bank had no warning and no alternative. The ponies leaped with the cattle, and all took their chances together at the foot of the bank, a dozen feet in height. But here the ground was soft, and it was but a few steps to the water. In a moment the river was full of struggling, frantic creatures, all swimming for their lives, and all acting blindly except the cowpunchers, who retained their grim energy and had no thought of giving up their lives. These swam clear of the crush of cattle and dropped down to a bar below. Scattered animals came drifting down stream and took the shore as they had done. Many dead cattle floated past the bar, and at the foot of the bank a heap of dead and crippled ones lay tangled. Not till morning, of course, could the task of roping and pulling out the cattle from the water and from under the banks begin. These cowpunchers as well as they were able rode back to the path of the "split," and so found the main mill and joined their companions.

"I shore thought I was a angel when we took the bank," says Curley, wiping his face with his wet neckerchief.

"Where's the Kid?" asks Jim gruffly.

"Dunno," is the answer. "I ain't seen him nowheres near me."

It is hard to tell where any one may be at this time, past midnight, with the storm just muttering itself away. Some of the cattle may be running yet, and some of the cowboys may be with them. It may be twenty miles away that the last cowpuncher will pull up. The cattle will be scattered over miles and miles of country, and it will take days to get them together, less the losses which are sure to ensue upon the stampede. Nothing remains to be done now by those who are assembled but to hold their remnant of the herd till morning. And morning finds the men still holding the herd, their eyes now heavy and red, their faces haggard, their clothing covered with the mud of the mad ride in the night. A detail is made to keep watch here, while the rest of the men go back to camp to bring on the cook wagon and pick up the frayed ends of the rout. As these men ride in they see occasional scattered groups of cattle, which are turned back toward the main body. No one says much, for all are tired. As they pass on toward camp, or rather toward where camp was, a draggled figure rides up from out a little gully—one of the boys who has followed off a bunch of cattle by himself, and so been widely separated from the others.

"Hello, Cherokee!" says Jim. "Where's the Kid? We can't none of us find him nowhere."

"I ain't seen him neither," says Cherokee. "There ain't nobody at all been with me."

But as they ride on along the torn and trampled trail left by the cattle in their flight of the night before, they all see the Kid—see him, every one of them, before any one of them dares to say a word. They know what is this dark mass lying on the ground on ahead. Something strange chokes every throat, and each man adds an oath to the heap of pity as they draw up by the body. The boy's face, washed white and clean by the drenching rain which has taken away

14

the grime of the ride, lies upturned in the morning
sunlight, which kisses it gently. His hair, sodden with
the flood, trails off into the miry earth, of which he
was a part, and into which he is now to return. His
pony, with its fore legs broken, lifts its head as high
as it can and whinnies.

"Kill the horse, Bud!" says Jim at last, as they
stand about the straightened figure of the boy. A
shot is given the pony, and the saddle stripped from
its back. Jim mounts his horse, and reaches down to
the burden which Springtime hands up to him from
the ground. He takes the dead boy in his arms, riding
with his reins loose over the horn of his saddle and
holding up his burden carefully across his lap. He
says nothing till he gets near camp, muttering then
only, "It's too d—d bad!"

When they get to camp the cook has breakfast
ready, such as it is. The flour and sugar and everything else is wetted to the point of dissolution by the
rain. More talkative than his fellows of the saddle,
the cook breaks into loud exclamations of lamentation
when he sees what is this strange burden the foreman
is carrying.

"Shut up, d—n you!" says Jim to the cook. He
knows that it was not the fault of the cook that all
this trouble occurred, but he feels that he has to blame
somebody for something, in order to relieve his own
overburdened heart. "It's yore own fault," he says to
the cook, "lettin' that wagon cover blow off. You
do it again, an', d—n you, I'll kill you!"

It is primitive, crude, and hard enough, this little
group here on the muddy plains this morning. For
them there is not a voice of comfort, not a sign of help,
not a token of hope. The tired, worn faces show hard
and grim in the unflattering light of morning as they

stand about, some holding the bridles of their horses, some leaning against the wagon or sitting on the wagon tongue. There is no house nor home here nor anywhere near here. It is a hundred miles to a ranch, two hundred to a town. There is no church nor minister. Not one hypocrite is to be found in this knot of rude men, and as none has professed any religion before, so none does so now. Jim, who is the leader, straightens out the boy's limbs as he lays him upon the ground and spreads a blanket over him.

"Git breakfast over!" he says grimly. And after breakfast the shovel of the cook which dug the trench for the fire digs the grave for the boy. There is no funeral service. He is buried in his blankets, with his hat over his face and his boots and spurs in place, as he slept when he was alive. A soldier of the plains, he dared the risks of his calling, and met them like a man. Such is another picture of the plains.

CHAPTER XI.

DURING days, or perhaps weeks, of the busy season, when most of the men are absent on the round-ups, the door of the home ranch may be closed. It may be closed, but it is not locked, for on the frontier locks and bars are unknown. The necessities of a country make its customs, and in the remote parts of the plains and mountains hospitality is practically a necessity. The traveller is perhaps far from home, and is hungry or athirst when he falls upon the cabin of some man to whom he is a stranger. When that occurs the stranger goes into the unlocked house, helps himself to the bacon and flour, cooks his meal, and departs as he came. In time he may repay the courtesy himself at his own cabin and perhaps in the same way. There was a touch of feudal largeness and liberality in some of the customs of the earlier cattle days, and the fact that they were necessary rendered them none the less beautiful. Perhaps the state of the social relations among the cattle men of the early range was approached most closely by the life of the great Southern plantations in *ante bellum* days, from which, indeed, it may in part have had its origin. The ways of the South always flavoured the life of the cattle country, whether in Texas or Wyoming, far more than the ways of the North and East. Perhaps

the zest which many Eastern men found in ranch life
was the zest of novelty, and this a novelty to be meas-
ured by degrees of latitude and not of longitude. We
must credit the South with the origin and establishment of the cattle trade, and with many of its most
interesting, its broadest, and most beautiful features.
The more exact methods, the better system, the perfection of detail, and utilization of things once neg-
lected came from the North, and came, alas! with a
shock fatal to some of the customs of the good old
days. In the past the lock of the ranch door was
nothing but a rude wooden latch, as easily opened
from without as from within. To-day there may be
iron padlocks upon some of the doors of the houses on
the range.

There is no lock upon the door of our ranch house,
whether it be empty or occupied. Such as it is, it constitutes the only home the cowboy has. Hither he
returns from the more active duties of the round-up
or the drive, and takes up the less exacting routine
of everyday ranch life. Of work proper, as a farm
labourer would consider it, the cowboy has little real
conception. He is a horseman and nothing more,
and has little inclination for any work that can not
be done in the saddle. Thus, if he feels obliged to
go out for wood, he goes out on horseback, and his idea
of the correct way to get a log of wood to camp is to
drag it at the end of his lariat. If a wagon is mired
down in the quicksands of a soft crossing, the cowboy
who comes to the aid of the driver does not dismount
and get himself muddy in the labour of getting the
wagon out, but makes fast his rope to some holding
place on the wagon and trusts to his saddle girths for
the rest, knowing that his plucky little pony will in
this way pull a considerable load, though it would

break its neck in rebellion if hitched up to the wagon. The cowboy has a mild contempt for all walking and driving men. In his own line of work he can be a miracle of tireless energy. Out of that line he is a prodigy of more or less good-natured laziness.

We may suppose, then, that a day of ordinary ranch life is not one of great activity or haste. The chores which the cowpuncher considers within his province are very few and simple. If in the winter some horses are kept up under feed in the ranch stables, he may feed his own horse, but no other man's. In the later days of ranch life the cowboy has come to be more of a hewer of wood and a drawer of water, more interested in the haying operations and other portions of the ranch economy, but primarily and properly the genuine cowpuncher had to do, as he understood it, only with cows, which were to be handled by himself only while he was in the saddle. It was the chief concern of the rancher in the early days to see that his cattle had a fair show in the struggle with Nature. Efforts toward ameliorating the conditions of the animals were very crude and little considered. Food and shelter were things which the cattle were supposed to find for themselves. The ranch proper has none of the grinding detail of the farm, and the cowboy proper is as different from the farm labourer as a wild hawk from a domestic fowl.

The day at the ranch begins early, for by daybreak the men have slept enough. There is little to induce them to sit up late at night. Sometimes a trapper or wolfer stops at the ranch, and there may be spirited games inaugurated over the well-worn and greasy pack of cards, the currency being what money the cowpunchers may have, together with due bills against their coming pay day, these perhaps staked against

strings of coyote feet and wolf scalps which are good
for so much bounty at the county seat. Of reading
the cowpuncher does but little, and his facilities for
obtaining literature are very limited. The periodicals
reaching the cow camp are apt to be of the sensational,
pink-tinted sort, with crude pictures and lurid letter-
text. His books are too often of much the same type,
though at some of the ranches there may be some few
works of fiction of a better sort. Whatever the books
at the ranch may be, from society novel to farrier's
guide, the cowpuncher reads them all over and over
again until he is tired of seeing them. Not having
much more to do of an evening, he goes to bed. It is
supposed by some misguided souls that when the so-
called wild cowboys of a ranch have met at night
after the close of their exciting duties the scene at the
ranch house is one of rude hilarity and confusion.
Really quite the opposite of this is true. The interior
of a ranch house of an evening offers rather a quiet and
orderly appearance. Liquor is something rarely seen
there, because it comes very rarely, and does not last
long when it comes. As a rule, the cowpuncher is
rather a silent man, though not so silent as the melancholy sheep herder, who rarely endures the terrible
monotony of his calling for more than seven years
without becoming insane. A cowboy who is very
"mouthy" is not usually in high repute at a cow
camp, and one disposed to personal brilliance or sar-
castic comment on the peculiarities of his fellow-men
is apt to meet with swift and effectual discouragement.
Rude and unlettered though he be, and treating his
companions with a rough and ready familiarity, the
cowpuncher yet accords to his neighbour the right to
live the life and go the gait which seems most pleasing
to himself. One does not intrude upon the rights of

others in the cow country, and he looks to it very promptly that no one shall intrude upon his. In the cow towns or at the cow camps one never hears the abusiveness or rude speech common in the older settlements. On the range, especially in the earlier days, if a man applied to another an epithet which in the States would be taken as something to be endured or returned in kind, the result would have been the essential and immediate preparations for a funeral.

In all countries where the home is unknown and the society is made up of males altogether, the men grow very morose and surly, and all the natural ugliness of their dispositions comes out. They are more apt to magnify small slights and slips, and more apt to get into trouble over small matters of personal honour. Upon the other hand, the best possible correction for this tendency is the acknowledged fact that it is not personally safe to go into a quarrel. It was never safe to quarrel on the cow range.

The cook, of course, is the first one up about the camp, and he " makes the breakfast " in his own room. The toilet of the cowpuncher is simple, and, after he has kicked off his blankets, it is but a few moments before he is at the table eating his plateful of beef or bacon and beans. The meal does not last long, and those which follow it later in the day are much the same. The city club man is fond of wild game as an adjunct to a good dinner. The " granger " sets oysters and ice cream as the highest possible luxuries of life. The cowboy thinks of fresh green vegetables in his epicurean dreams, and he longs for the indigestible pie of civilization. Any pure cowpuncher would sell his birthright for half a dozen pies. The cow cook can not make actual pies, only leathery imitations encasing stewed dried apples. One remembers very well a cer-

tain Christmas dinner in a little far-away Western
plains town which cost two men twenty-five dollars,
and which consisted of some badly cooked beef, one
can of oysters, a frosted cake, and five green onions,
the latter obtained from somewhere by a hothouse
miracle. This dinner was voted a very extraordinary
and successful affair. The men at the ranch house are
not averse to an occasional change in their diet, and
fresh game is appreciated. Deer, antelope, wild turkey, and sometimes smaller game often appeared on
the *menu* of the ranch in the old days, but big game
is scarce now over most of the range, and small game
has rarely had much attention from the cowboys, who,
as a rule, do not at best do a great deal of hunting.

After breakfast, if this be in the winter season
and in a cold Northern country, the first work is attending to the riding horses kept in the stables, which
are in such a country a necessity. Behind each horse
in the stable is a long wooden peg, upon which hang
the bridle and saddle. Each man has his own place
reserved, and resents any intrusion upon his rights
as to saddle, bridle, and rope. One man may use freely
the tobacco or whisky of a fellow-cowpuncher, but he
may not touch his rope, quirt, or other parts of his
riding outfit. Of course, one man will not want to
use another's saddle. " I wouldn't ride a mile in that
thing o' yourn fer the best heifer that runs the range,"
says the cowpuncher, referring contemptuously to the
prized saddle of another. " I'd plum have a misery
if I had to ride yourn," is the reply.

Part or all of the horse herd will not be kept up
at the ranch house, but will be watched, so that their
whereabouts will be known. A man may be sent out
in the morning to bring in the horse herd, and then
ensues one of the most picturesque events of the day.

The bunch of horses comes up on a gallop, urged by the cowpuncher behind them. All sorts of horses are in the collection, all of them rough of coat and hard of form, and not one of them has a pleasant expression of countenance as he turns into the ranch corral, with his ears drooping and his eye rolling about in search of trouble. Inside the corral each horse runs about and dodges behind his fellows when he fancies himself wanted, doing his best to escape till he actually feels the circle of the rope, when he falls into meek but mutinous quiet. The cowpuncher leads him out, and throws on his back the heavy saddle, the pony meanwhile standing the picture of forlornness and despair, apparently upon his very last legs and quite unfit for travel. To his airs and attitudes the cowpuncher gives no attention, but proceeds to cinch up the saddle. As he begins this the pony heaves a deep, long breath, which converts him temporarily into something of the figure of a balloon. The cowpuncher knows what this means, and, putting his foot against the side of the pony, he gives a quick, strong pull on the girth, which causes the pony to grunt in a grieved way and to lessen his size abruptly. The hind cinch is not drawn tight, for in regard to that a cow horse feels that it has certain rights to breathing room which even a cowpuncher is bound to respect. In any case, the pony may pitch a little when the cowboy swings into the saddle, especially if it has not been ridden for some time. It may do this because it is happy or because it is not happy, but the cowpuncher does not pay much attention to it unless it be very violent, in which case he may join the yells of his companions as the pony goes thumping stiff-legged over a dozen yards or so before it settles down.

The conventional picture of a cowboy shows him

going at a sweeping gallop over the plains, his hair
flying wildly and his horse *ventre a terre*, its eyes bulging out in the exultation of speed. Sometimes the
cowboy rides hard on the round-up or when he comes
to town, but when he sets out across the range on his
day's work at the ranch he does not spur and gallop
his horse. He goes at a steady, ceaseless, choppy little
trot, which it tires the life out of a tenderfoot to follow
all day. This short trot is a natural gait for the cow
pony, and it will maintain it for a long time if not
crowded too hard. These little horses make very enduring driving horses when broken to that work, and
a team of them has been known to pull a light wagon
eighty miles in a day's drive—a feat which would
be impossible upon Eastern roads and in the Eastern
atmosphere.

As Jim, our cowpuncher, rides along on his day's
work, quite alone, of course, he sees many things which
the tenderfoot would not notice. He notes where a
deer has crossed the ranch road, where the wolves have
been playing in the sand, where the "bob cat" has
walked along the muddy bank. He sees the track of
the horse which crossed, and can tell whether or not it
is a fresh track. Perhaps it is part of his day's work to
look up some of the ranch horses which have strayed
away. Perhaps his ranch is under fence, and if so he
must ride the line to see that the fence is not down
at any point. In the early days no man needed to
worry about fences, but of later times the faithful
cowboy who works on a fenced ranch is sometimes
called contemptuously a "pliers man" by the rustlers" who have no fences of their own, this name
coming from the tools which the cowboy carries in
order to mend a break if he finds one in the wire fence.
The cowpuncher's eye, from force of habit, is keen to

note any unbranded animal that may be running on his range. If the law or his conscience in regard to Mavericks permit it—and as to Mavericks the conscience of all good cowpunchers is wide—our solitary rider may forthwith set about correcting the deficiency in the unbranded calf running with or without the company of the cow. It is not unknown that a cowpuncher has built a fire, heated his iron, taken his place again in the saddle, roped and thrown his calf, and then dragged it up to him as he sat in the saddle, finishing the branding without dismounting. This, however, is the act of a stylist in cowpunching.

The range in summer time is a breezy and not unpleasant place to be, in spite of the brilliant sun. The cowpuncher has the equanimity of good digestion and well-oxygenated blood as he goes on his morning ride across the country. Always his eye roams over the expanse ahead. He can tell farther than the tenderfoot can see what is going on out on the horizon. He knows what is this distant horseman crossing the flat ahead. If it is a cowboy, he knows him because he rides straight up in his stirrups, with no crooking-back of the leg. If it is an Indian, he will be sitting hunched up, with his stirrups very short and his leg bent back under the horse's belly, riding with the calf of his leg rather than with the thigh or knee, and, moreover, kicking his horse all the time. If Jim, the cowboy, does not think this horseman should be there at this part of the range, he may stop and unsling the big field glasses which he sometimes carries with him as an aid in his work. With these glasses he swings his gaze across the whole sweep of country steadily, seeing a strange panorama, not all of which would be visible if he waited to ride up close enough to see with the unaided eye. He sees a little bunch of young cows running up out of a draw, and suspects that the gray wolves may have pulled down a calf there. He sees the coyotes, reddish in the warm sun, sneaking off across the plain. He notes the low swoop of a big eagle, and he watches a long time the actions of a bunch of antelope. A little cloud of dust arising steadily from one spot attracts his attention, and, looking for a long time at this, he sees it is caused by two big bulls which are waging one of the stubborn and exciting combats of the cattle plains. Interested in this, he closes the glasses and rides over to " see the fun " ; for a fight of any kind is not foreign to his preferences. He draws up by the side of the intent fighters, not close enough to disturb them, and, taking a chew of tobacco, throws his leg over the horn of his saddle as he sits, offering mental wagers on the winner. The two great animals charge and charge again, their solid foreheads meeting with dull thumps, their backs bowing up strongly, their muscles cording out in relief as they thrust and shove, each trying to get at the side of the other, their hind legs going fairly up on their toes as they clash in the encounter. The herd stands near by, watching the contest with eager interest, the heads of the cows thrown high, occasionally an animal running away a bit in fright, only to return to the fascination of the spectacle. The eyes of the fighting bulls glare, and foam hangs from their mouths. They pant and grumble, their sides momentarily growing more densely covered with the white dust. Thus they fight till at length one tires and can no longer withstand the steady shove of his antagonist. He weakens, turns swiftly to one side, swerving cunningly clear of the rapid thrust at his side which follows, and runs off discomfited, the other retiring pawing, shaking his head, and bellowing. This will give the cowpuncher something to talk about to-night.

As he rides on over the range, the cowpuncher keeps out an eye along the watering places to note any animal that may have become mired down. When he sees a big steer thus entrapped, and with life enough left in it to warrant an attempt at its rescue, Jim rides up to the edge of the boggy place and sets about pulling out the animal. He does not like to get his rope muddy for the sake of a Texas steer, but still he may do so upon occasion. With a sweep of the wrist he lands the rope about the horns of the creature, the latter meantime snorting and shaking its head in resentment, and having no understanding of the intention of it all. Heading the pony up the bank, Jim sets in the spurs, and the sturdy little horse, which takes as much delight as its master in showing its superiority over all horned things, stiffens its muscles and strains at the rope. If the steer's neck holds together, it comes out of the mud. Then, if it has not been bogged down for very long, and still has most of its quota of original sin, the steer is extremely apt to reward its rescuers with a sudden and determined charge as quickly as it gets on its feet, for it knows nothing about the service that has been rendered, and feels only that its dignity has been injured by these creatures which it hates. But the charge is not rapid enough to catch the swift-footed little pony.

Perhaps Jim notes in his rounds a steer that is standing apart by itself, with its head down, dull and stupid. Or perhaps it will so stand for a time, and then run about frantic and crazy, as though intoxicated. Jim knows what is the cause of this. The animal has been eating the " loco weed," against which instinct gives it apparently no protection. The effect of this herb is to stupefy or render crazed the animal eating of it. From the Spanish word *loco*—"mad, crazy" —comes the expression common on the range, "locoed." To say that a man is "locoed" means that he is foolish, absurd, crazy. If Jim sees too much loco weed about, he may drive the cattle away from that part of the range.

Jim does not love a rattlesnake, nor does his pony, and the latter can smell one a long way, turning its head to where it lies curled up under the shade of the Spanish bayonet. Jim takes a shot or so at the snake with his six-shooter, not heeding the objections of the pony to the gun. A cow horse has to get used to a great many strange things that go on upon its back. Or Jim may dismount and kill the snake with his quirt, rather a short-range weapon for such a case, though this does not seem to trouble him. He may skin the snake if it be a very large one, turning the skin back from the neck, and pulling it free as he holds the head down with his foot. Snake fat is good for softening leather, and so is the fat of the prairie dog, at which Jim occasionally tries a shot, just to "keep his hand in."

Thus on the cowpuncher rides in the course of his day's work, across wide flats and around high, red buttes, over rough gullies and *coulees* (" *arroyos* " these would be called in the Southwest), and all the time he is observant of all that transpires about him, near at hand or at a distance. Perhaps he takes a straight course across country, on his way out to one of the "line camps" of the ranch, to see how matters are progressing there. He may take out a letter to one of the boys at that camp, a letter which has perhaps lain at the nearest post office for a month before the ranch wagon went to town, and which has been at the ranch a couple of weeks or more in addition, but which none the less seems fresh to the cowboy receiving it. It may be from his "girl," as he calls it (his "*dulce*," it would be in the South), and if so Jim will not take the answer back with him, even though he stay overnight at the line camp, for the composition of the cowpuncher's reply is perhaps a portentous thing, to be accomplished only after long and studious effort.

As Jim turns back in his course, and rides toward the home ranch again, if it be among his plans to return to the ranch the same day, he may be a trifle hungry, but he does not mind that. It may perhaps rain, and make the going bad over the soft flats, but he does not mind that either. It is a part of his daily training to be calm and philosophical. If he be thirsty, he dismounts at the first water hole and drinks, fearless of the alkali which would nearly kill a tenderfoot, but which does not trouble him any more than it does the hardiest steer. He is fitted to survive in these hard surroundings. He belongs in this landscape of butte and plain and scarp and valley, this rugged, hard-faced man who so confidently holds on his way, from his narrowed eyes seeing all the wide sweep of the earth and air about him.

Perhaps it is night by the time he gets back to the ranch house, coming in after a wide circle in a direction opposite to that in which he went out. Perhaps he does not get back to camp at all that night, even though he wishes to do so, for even the cowpuncher can go astray in the labyrinth of the wilderness. One occasion comes to mind in which an able cowboy lost his way in a big Texas "pasture," all of which was under fence. He had, almost unbelievable thing, gone out on foot into the *chaparral* to get his horse, which led him a chase into the heart of the dense thicket, where the blended cover stood higher than his head, matted and almost impenetrable. In spite of the fact that he knew the country perfectly, he got lost and wandered directly away from the ranch house, and spent three days in the *chaparral*, all the time, it seems, getting farther and farther away from home. He had water but once in that time, and was in a desperate plight. At last he met a bunch of horses, and noticed that one had a bit of rope about its neck, and which he therefore thought might prove gentle. His belief was correct, and he was able to go up to this horse and catch it. Mounting it bareback, he urged it on and gave it its head, and soon the horse took him to a road, which later led him to a town at the edge of the " pasture," thirty miles from the ranch house.

Perhaps on some of his daily rides about the range Jim spies one or more cows with calves which have escaped the round-up, and to which the attention of the branding iron should be given. If he does not have any branding iron with him, which is very likely the case, and if the calves are anywhere near the home ranch, he rounds them up and drives them in ahead of him, perhaps having four or five in his herd by the time he gets to the house. These he turns into the big ranch corral, and soon a miniature branding bee is going on. The fire is built near the mouth of the corral, and Jim rides into the corral to get the calves. He knows far too much to go in on foot, for a range cow will often charge a footman, not recognising man in that segregated form, and taking him to be some enemy less redoubtable. The cows and calves run around the limit of the corral, Jim leisurely follow-

15

ing, his rope trailing out in the dust behind him. Jim has just eaten his dinner, and is in no hurry. Between his teeth still rests the toothpick which he has whittled for himself from the tough yellow wood of the *Palo à Maria,* and on this Jim chews meditatively as he lazily follows after the little calf which is with the big dun cow. Jim slowly takes up the slack of the trailing rope, coiling it in his left hand, and then he lets drop the great noose, bending back a few inches of the noose upon the rope, and grasping both together a little way from the eye of the rope. He then rides on a trifle faster, and with a swift whirl the rope now begins to move about his head, the wrist turning smoothly with it, and the noose of the rope waving in its line like the back of a snake, undulating up and down as well as circling about. The cow pony knows all about this, and Jim pays little attention to the horse. The pony takes him to just the right distance from the right calf, and Jim launches the rope with a swirling swoop which rarely fails in its aim. Enjoying this very much, the little cow horse sets back on its hind legs, and the poor calf comes over, to be dragged to the iron and treated as it would have been on the spring round-up if it had not in some way slipped through the lines. And as it staggers away free of the corral, the heartless cowpunchers say blithely, " Did you hear the ten dollars drop in the box? "

Some day, as the cowpuncher is riding his rounds about the range, his quick eye may note out on the horizon a faint cloud which has not the appearance of a dust trail. This he regards intently, stopping his pony and looking steadfastly toward the spot. The little cloud does not pass away or grow less, but widens and rises, and all at once fans out on the wind, taking

on the unmistakable blue of smoke. There is fire! One
might think there would be no harm in a simple little
fire, but not so impressed seems the usually unper-
turbed cowpuncher. There is something in the sight
of this little crawling fire which causes him to turn
his horse and ride as hard as he can for the ranch
house. He knows that the whole range may burn, that
the stock may be utterly robbed of their only food,
that the ranch is to be ruined and the cattle are to
starve unless that little creeping line of blue can be
quickly met and conquered. He does not pause to ask
how it was started—perhaps by accident of some camp
fire left uncovered, perhaps by the deliberate act of
some malicious rustler, who would be shot like a dog
if found in the act of firing the grass. There is no
time to think of anything but the remedy, if any still
be possible. On parts of the range, especially that
where the ground is high and dry and the grass chiefly
the short and scattered buffalo grass or gramma grass,
the fire will not spread so rapidly, and can be more
easily handled, though even there the food of the
range can be entirely destroyed by the flames which eat
slowly on. If the grass be full and high, as it is on
some parts of the cattle country, more especially along
the streams and valleys, and if the wind be strong and
in the right direction, the prairie fire will soon be a
terrible thing. A swift sea of flame will roll across
the range, driving forward or destroying everything
in its path. Fences and buildings, if there are any,
corrals and stables, everything is in danger. If there
has been a little hay put up for winter feed, even the
ploughed fire guard may prove insufficient to protect
the stacks. There is danger that the entire profit of
the season will be destroyed, and all the possibilities
for the ensuing season jeopardized. The cowpuncher

swears sternly as he rides, and every man who rolls out of the house and into saddle swears also as he rides for the flames. There is excitement, but there is no confusion, for each exigency of the calling is known by these men, and they are ready with the proper expedient to meet it. Some of the men look to the buildings carefully, back-burning a broad strip about them, so that the full sweep of the fire will not need to be met there. This is done by lighting fires, a little at a time, farther and farther back against the wind, not enough grass being allowed to burn at once to make a serious blaze, and the fire being under the control of the men, who stand ready to whip it out with wet blankets, green rawhides, or anything which comes handiest.

If the haystacks and the houses be considered safe, all the men unite in fighting the main fire, which is a more serious and difficult matter, a dangerous one if the grass be heavy and the wind high. Riding along the edge of the line of the flame, two cowpunchers drag at the ends of their ropes a wet, green hide, a pile of wet blankets, anything which will serve to drag down and beat out the flame which is eating on. The men "straddle the fire," one riding on each side the line of fire, so that the hide drags along the burning grass, the two riding along the edge of the burning in this way, back and forth, until they have dragged out and smothered down the flames, or found their attempt a hopeless one. Sometimes this work may go on for hours, and it may be either in the day or the night, as the case may happen. Though they be hot and tired and thirsty from the long hours of work in the withering heat, they do not pause, but keep on until the fire is checked or until it has burst away from them, beyond all human control, and so rolled on across the range in its course

of desolation. It must be a bad fire if the cowboys
do not check it, for they rush into the work with all
that personal carelessness of fatigue or danger which
marks them in all their work, and so labour as long
as they can sit their saddles, sometimes coming out
of the smoke with eyebrows singed off, hands blistered,
and faces black and grimed, their eyes small and red
from the glare and heat of the battle with this enemy
of the range. When they are through the fight they
sleep, eat, and vow revenge. Ill fares it with the man
who fires the range if his offence be ever traced to him.
This disastrous disturbance, which imperils the welfare of so many and so much, which sends the cattle
in a frightened mass hurrying across the range, mingled with the antelope and deer and wolves, which
must also move before the flames—this is something
too serious for even the cowman to face with uncon-
cern. He dreads nothing more than a fire. But his
diligence and skill in fighting the fire usually confine it in such way that it will burn itself out without
a general destruction of the range. If there is little
wind, the fire may be caught and stopped at a roadway, or at a dry creek bed, or on high, hard ground,
where the rocks and bare earth give the fighters a
better chance to wipe out the flames. Behind the ultimate edge of the fire's progress, back to the point
where the cowpuncher first saw the tiny line of smoke,
there may lie a dozen miles of blackened, smoking
prairie, where in the spring the wild plovers will
whistle and the big curlews with bent bills will
stalk about and utter their wild and shrilly mellow
calls.

Such may be some of the incidents of a day on
the ranch in one part or another of the cattle country, local conditions, of course, affecting the daily

routine and the general features of the work. It may be seen that the cowboy is rather a watchman than a labourer, a guard rather than a workman. His life at the ranch is rather one of alertness than of exertion. Yet his is no easy or idle task, as any one may find who, not bred to the work, undertakes to do it for the first time. What seems so easy is really difficult. It would take years of practice to rival the cowboy in some of the simplest features of his daily occupation. He is in a way a skilled labourer, competent only after long and hard years of apprenticeship. To measure the force of this assertion, let us suppose that the affairs of a single ranch district were left for a season in the hands of other than skilled cowboys, the place of the latter being taken by men who could not sit a "mean" horse, who could not rope and throw a steer, and who had had no experience in reading range brands. Would not a round-up conducted by such gentleman be a pleasing affair? Would not a drive left to such hands be a reminiscence to dwell upon in after years? How would the season's profits come out if many ranch owners had cowboys about as skilful, let us say, as they themselves in the practical profession of the cowpuncher? No one ever heard of a cowboy's union or of a strike of cowpunchers; yet, if ever a department of labour had capital at its mercy, these riders of the range could have if they chose. Suppose that there was a general walk-out of the cowboys on a round-up just as the herd was formed for the cutting out, it being further added that each cowpuncher had a gun and a playful way of using it! There is a theme for some writer of short stories on Western life, and sufficiently inaccurate to be inviting. Such a scene could never occur in actual life, because the cowpuncher does not hold himself as a servant, but as his own master. He has no delegates, and belongs to no society save that of the plains, which has time out of mind been a society of the individual, embraced under no classification and subject to no control beyond that of personal honour.

Our friend Jim—and proud may you be if he calls you friend!—is a man able to read brands and ride horses, to follow sign and mark calves, to ride all day and all night, to go hungry and thirsty, to go without shelter or home or guidance, always having in mind the thing he started out to do, the duty that is to be performed. This duty he will do without overseeing. He is his own overseer. He needs no instruction nor advice. No higher type of employee ever existed, nor one more dependable. The rudest of the rude in some ways, he is the very soul of honour in all the ways of his calling. The very blue of the sky, bending evenly above all men alike, has reflected into his heart the instinct of justice—that justice which is at the core of all this wild trade of the range. It is not the ranchman, the man who puts the money into the business, who is the centre of the occupation. It is not he who has made the cattle business. It is the cowpuncher, whom you may be glad to have call you friend.

The actual life in the saddle of an active cowboy is not a long one upon the average, for the hardships of it are too steady, the accidents too common. Any injury received in the pursuit of his calling he bears stoically, after the fashion of the plains, whose precedents were established where there was " lack of woman's nursing, there was dearth of woman's tears." Under all the ills of life the cowboy " 'quits himself like a man." That is his standard. There are some who ask for the gallop of the cowboy, and not the quiet trot, some who think his crudeness and his wildness should be made his distinguishing features. Rather let us say that his chief traits are his faithfulness and manliness. There is his standard—to be a "square man." If you called him a hero, he would not know what you meant.

CHAPTER XII.

THE COWBOY'S AMUSEMENTS.

THE man who is strong rejoices in his strength. The man who is skilled takes pleasure in the renewed exercise of his skill. The old and staid cowboy might not care to run his horse and rope his friends as the younger members of the ranch staff took delight in doing, and the foreman of the ranch might not take the interest in rifle and pistol practice that the younger men did, because he knew that he could shoot well enough already; but each, young or old, followed the life because he loved it for its freedom and its outdoor quality, the sheer attraction it offered to a vigorous and energetic man who needed outlet for his vitality and exercise for his muscles. It was natural, therefore, that the chief amusements of the cowboy should be those of the outdoor air and those more or less in line with his employment.

The cowboy was accustomed to the sight of big game, and so had the edge of his appetite for its pursuit worn off; moreover, he had his regular duties to perform, so that he had not always time to go hunting. Yet he was a hunter, just as every Western man was a hunter in the times of the Western game. The weapons of the cowboy were the rifle, revolver, and rope; of these, more properly the latter two, as these he had always about him. Of the " scatter gun " he knew nothing at all, and entertained for it a pronounced contempt as a weapon unfit for the use of a man. With the rope the cowboy at times captured the coyote, usually after it had been run hard by the dogs, and under special circumstances he has taken deer and even antelope in this way, though this was, of course, most unusual and only possible under chance conditions of ground and cover. Elk have been roped by cowboys very many times, and it is known that even the mountain sheep has been so taken, almost incredible as that may seem. The buffalo was frequently the object of the cowpuncher's ambitions, though sometimes such a vaulting ambition overleaped itself. An old cowboy who once roped a full-grown buffalo bull described his emotions as decidedly far from pleasant when he found himself attached to such a monster. " I thought I could shore throw ary bull there was," said he, " but that there thing plum run off with me an' the bronch' both, an' the only thing I was thinkin' of was how to turn it loose."

The young buffalo, especially the calves, were easy prey for the cowboy, and he often roped and made them captive. Many instances are known where these animals were found in the round-ups of the early days, and in such case some of them were sure to fall victims to the cowboys, who often took them home and kept them. Buffalo nearly full-grown have in many instances been roped, thrown, and branded by these enthusiasts, and then turned free again upon the range. The beginnings of all the herds of buffalo now in captivity in this country were in the calves roped and secured by cowboys, and these few scattered individuals of a grand race of animals remain as melancholy reminders alike of a national shiftlessness and an individual skill and daring.

It required an expert man to rope and capture a buffalo, even a calf but a few weeks old, for the little fellows were incredibly swift, and asked the limit of a horse's speed and staying qualities. On a hunt for buffalo calves in the Panhandle of Texas, in which our party was so fortunate as to take thirteen buffalo calves, much of the roping was done by a cowboy not yet twenty years of age, who was very skilful in his calling, and an especially fine roper. He enjoyed to the utmost the exciting sport of the buffalo calf chase, as well he might, for few forms of sport ever had a keener tang than this. At times the calves were run hard for over a mile before the swift horses could be urged up close enough, and, after such a chase, it behooved the roper to be sure of his cast. Nor after the successful cast had been made was all the trouble over, for very often the buffalo cow would charge the man thus taking liberties with her calf, and then an interesting situation was developed. The cowboy did not like to release his calf after the pains of the long run, and he did not like to lose his horse on the horns of the enraged cow, which pursued him steadily and viciously. There was sure to be a constricted but exciting chase about a narrow circle, with the rope as its radius and the calf as the pivotal point. In two instances it was necessary to kill the cow to save the cowboy from death or serious injury, but it was rarely he missed his calf if the horse could carry him up, and he never let one free in order to escape the charge of the mother. The offspring of some of these calves live to-day in the largest herd of buffalo now alive in the world.

The buffalo has for years now been gone from the range, and the cowboy will no more rope the little red calves of the curly cattle. It will be rarely, too, that he will ever again see out on the cow range the great grizzly bear, which once lived far east over the prairie country, but has now gone far back into the mountains. In the past the grizzly was at times seen by the cowboys on the range, and, if it chanced that several cowboys were together, it was not unusual for them to give it chase. Of course, they did not always rope him, for it was rarely that the nature of the country made this possible, and sometimes they roped him and wished they could let him go, for a grizzly bear is uncommonly active and straightforward in his habits at close quarters, and his great power and ferocity make him an almost impossible customer unless all things are favourable. The extreme difficulty of such a combat, however, gave it its chief fascination for the cowboy, and in several recorded cases a party of cowboys have succeeded in capturing alive a full-grown grizzly bear with no means thereto except their horses and ropes. Of course, no one horse could hold the bear after it was roped, but, as one after another came up, the bear was caught by neck and foot and body, until at last he was tangled and tripped and haled about till he was helpless, strangled, and nearly dead. It is said that cowboys have so brought into camp a grizzly bear, forcing him to half walk and half slide at the end of the ropes. Such a bit of wild life would offer excitement sufficient for any man, it would seem, and if any man would be fit for it, then surely would be the hardy and daring cowboy. No feat better than this could show the courage of the man and of the horse which he so perfectly controlled.

One of the great pests of the cattle range was the wolves, which annually inflicted a great loss upon the young stock, and against which an incessant war was waged by the whole ranch force, this more especially

applying to the great gray wolf known as the timber
wolf, buffalo wolf, " loper," " loafer," or " lobo " wolf,
an animal quite large enough to pull down a yearling
or a heifer with the help of not more than one or two
of its kind. So great were the ravages of these animals
after the buffalo had disappeared and left them no
prey but the domestic cattle, that regular campaigns
were made against them by a class of men called
wolfers, who made an occupation of hunting, trapping,
and poisoning them, more especially for the bounty
money offered by nearly all the States of the cattle
range. It was not possible, however, for the most
energetic wolfing operations to clear the range of these
pests, for they would drift in again from great distances; so the cowboy throughout the year had more
or less opportunity of seeing wolves. Perhaps no wild
animal might better be called his staple source of sport.
A great many ranches kept good packs of hounds, usually very large and powerful greyhounds, with a few
rough-coated staghounds or deerhounds, for the purpose of hunting wolves, and no better sport was offered in the cattle country than this coursing wolves
with hounds. The cowboys kept the pack in good
hard condition, for the excitement of the horseback
running, the mad flight of the long chase, and the ensuing bitter fight at the close when a big " gray " was
" stood up," made a sort of thing exactly to the cowboy
fancy. In this way a great many wolf pelts found
their way to the walls of the ranch house.

One remembers very well a wolf chase with a ranch
pack which had killed many grays. The ranchman,
riding out over the range early in the morning, saw
a heifer pursued by a pair of big wolves, which pulled
her down in a little valley. The ranchman rode
back to the ranch at full speed and called out the

dogs, all the men, of course, piling out and getting into saddle as soon as the nature of the excitement was known. Wild enough was the scene, as the entire force of the ranch, some seventeen dogs and a dozen men, strung out at speed across the country, each man riding at top speed and the dogs bounding up at the horsemen and running eagerly about, as though beseeching that they be shown their game. The kill was at a distance of some three miles from the house, and it happened that the wolves were approached at their feeding within a quarter of a mile before they took alarm. The dogs sighted them well, and at once shot forward with their inimitable burst of speed. The wolves, already heavy with feed, could not travel at their best, and soon one of them, the larger, was reached by the head dog, a great blue hound that had killed many wolves in the numerous fights of his eventful life. This dog seized the wolf by the side of the neck and rolled it over in its stride. The wolf rose just in time to be caught upon the other side of the neck by the second hound, a powerful red fellow, also of great experience. It is very likely these two dogs would have eventually killed the wolf, large as it was, for finally one or other of them would have shifted and gotten the fatal grip on the throat for which they were both manœuvring, and which neither would have released until the wolf was dead, though possibly both would have been badly cut up before this conclusion was reached. As it was, the wolf was so very large (its skin was six feet six inches in length) that it got to its feet and was actually dragging both dogs along with it as they clung to its neck, trying all the time viciously to get its teeth upon them, which their skill in seizing prevented it from doing. Seeing that the dogs could not kill without breaking their hold, and disliking to have such valuable hounds cut up by the wolf, as would be the case if it got its jaws free for a moment, the rancher at length rode up and broke the back of the wolf with a pistol shot, so that it was soon killed by the dogs. The cowboys all loudly expressed their dissatisfaction at the shooting of the wolf, for they had all the confidence in the world in their pack, which they always allowed to do their own killing in their frequent runs. In this case the second wolf escaped from the other dogs, which had no dog among their number large and courageous enough to seize and stop a gray. The latter is a tremendous fighter and an ugly customer, so that the ranch pack usually has a war-worn aspect, nearly all the dogs being covered with scars received in fights with wolves or coyotes. The coyotes are run into and killed by good hounds without much trouble. For this wild wolf coursing the cowboys usually preferred heavy greyhounds, though at times there were good wolf dogs among the rough staghounds.

It is sometimes said that the antelope can not be taken by any greyhound, and this is practically true in regard to the single greyhound, though even then with exceptions. A pack of good greyhounds can certainly kill antelope, for the writer has known eleven antelope to be killed in one week by a pack of greyhounds. In certain parts of the country, too, the white-tailed deer offers sport to the ranch pack, or at least did at one time, though perhaps now it would be difficult to find country where the deer could be successfully coursed with hounds. In the Indian Nations the writer has been out with a pack of greyhounds, which included a good pack of ranch dogs, when three deer were killed by the hounds in one day. It was very intense sport, and none enjoyed it better or were more adept at it than the cowboys, who were sure to be in at the death if that were among the possibilities. The fleet and hardy cow horse is never seen to better advantage than in this rapid and head-long rush across country after so swift an animal as the deer, and few riders but the cowboys could man-age to keep in view of so impetuous a chase. The deer can outrun the horse on a straight course, to be sure, but if it double or swerve, as it is sure to do if pressed by the dogs, it is very likely that the cow-puncher and his horse will be near it at the turns. Then it is that the cowpuncher yells and spurs and rides his best, his kerchief flying straight on the wind, his hat front sitting back firm against his forehead under the impact of the air. In such riding one can see some of the finest horsemanship of the world, and certainly some of the most reckless.

The mountain lion is another animal in disrepute upon the cow range, because of its fondness for young calves or colts, but the range and the numbers of these animals was always so restricted that they cut less figure than the wolves in the annual estimate of losses in ranch work. Still, it was not unusual, more espe-cially upon the southern range, where this animal ranged farther out into the open country, to see one of these great red cats stealing off across the plains in its attempt to get away unnoticed. The cowboy knew perfectly well that a more arrant coward never lived than this big, hulking cat, and he had for it a contempt that not all the panther stories of the Sunday news-papers, had he ever seen such a thing as a Sunday newspaper, could have mitigated. No matter whether alone or in company, as soon as he saw the " lion," he made after him at full speed. The cat ran away with incredible great leapings, showing a good turn of

speed for a time; but the savage little cow horse, which
enjoyed such a chase as much as did its rider, was sure
to soon lay the cowboy well alongside if the country
was open enough for a little running. The cat looked
back over its shoulder, spitting viciously, but not turning to fight, and in reality scared fairly to its wits' end.
The hissing rope soon clinched it, and then, no matter
whether the noose fell on paw or neck or body, the
little cow horse quickly dragged the panther to death.
Wild enough sport, too, was such a chase as this.

The cow range did not often or not long offer any
great amount of fur-bearing animals. The wolf, the
coyote, the foxes and swifts, the antelope and deer, were
the animals most frequently seen by the cowboy in his
rounds. In the early days, or even yet, the ranch might
be on a bit of good fur country, but if the cowboy
found a beaver stream he was more apt to tell some
trapper than to trouble his own head about the beaver
harvest. At times on the cold northern range the
cowboy bethought him of a fur cap for the winter
days, and if an otter came in on some stream near
the ranch and showed sign of staying about some
creek or spring hole for a time, one of the cowboys
might undertake to get his hide. It takes a good
trapper to catch an otter, and the cowboy was not
always a good trapper. But sometimes he would take
his rifle and lie at some air hole through the ice where
the otter came up to breathe, and wait there for a
shot at his game, which he occasionally got. Once in
a while the cowboy might go out for a look after some
smaller fur-bearing animal, and he was always ready
to join any hunting party made up at the ranch for a
day or night hunt after wildcats, "leopard cats," lions,
or other sort of game which his country might happen
to produce; but left to himself, the cowboy was not

16

always an ardent hunter, especially when the hunt demanded that he go on foot, a means of locomotion not in accordance with his idea of the human proprieties. If he could ride to the game, any sort of chase suited him. Sometimes, if he lived in a country where there was timber along some stream, he might go out at night for a 'coon hunt, for he loved the noise and flurry of the fight with the dogs in the dark. Such sport was possible only over a very limited part of the cow country.

In some parts of the country the cowboy carried a rifle in the holster under his leg, but this sometimes as much for the cow thief or rustler as for any game. The favourite arm of the cowboy was really the six-shooter, and with this weapon he rarely hesitated to attack any animal that came in his way. Very often cowboys killed mountain lions with their revolvers, sometimes shooting them out of trees where they had taken refuge. In a few instances the cowboy has ridden alongside and with his six-shooter killed the grizzly, cinnamon, or " range bear." Constantly inured to the dangers of the open range, and familiar with the sight of large game, there was no animal for which he had much fear or reverence. Really there were some small ones which he feared more than any large ones. The bite of the small plains polecat he dreaded above all things, for he knew that it was practically certain to result in hydrophobia and death. Many cowboys lost their lives in this way, being bitten by this animal when it had crawled into their blankets at night. At the least move of the sleeper the venomous creature would bite, and its bite was accounted almost certainly fatal. One United States army regiment stationed at an Arizona post lost thirteen men in one season through bites of the polecat.

The rattlesnake sometimes crawled into the cowboy's blankets at night, but this was a less dangerous affair, as the snake was apt to be chilled and stupid. Yet another creature much dreaded on the range was the centipede, which was also a night traveller. It is a tradition of the range that if a centipede crawls across a man's flesh the poison left by its hooked and penetrating feet will surely produce insanity. One instance comes to mind where a cowboy was so poisoned by a centipede, and who really became crazed, although he did not die.

The tarantula was still more poisonous than the centipede, but seems to have been less dreaded. It was a favourite amusement at a cow camp, where these hairy monsters abounded, to get a pair of them and set them fighting, which they were always ready to do, tearing off each other's legs with great gusto. A winner of many of these battles was sure to become a ranch pet, and was usually kept in a tin can with a board over the top, ready for action in case anybody came along with a tarantula which he thought could fight, and which he was disposed to back for a little money. The thought comes to mind now, with something of horrified regret, of a certain pet tarantula, a scarred warrior of many battles, which was forgotten and left thirteen years ago in a tin can back of a certain ranch house far out on the cattle range. A tarantula is a hardy animal, and can live long without food, but one must admit that thirteen years is a long time for even a tarantula to go without anything to eat, and it is probable that the pet of the camp has before now departed this life in a way not deserved by so redoubtable a warrior.

The cowboy was fond of any kind of hazard, any manner of fight, any contest of speed or skill or strength. Not much of a runner himself, he would back his favourite in a foot race. Wrestling and boxing were unknown upon the range, and it is well enough they were, as they might have led to more serious matters, whose result would have been a lessening of the visible supply of material for cowpunchers. The horse race was an ever-present and unfailing source of enjoyment for the cowboy, and if a ranch had a good quarter horse the whole outfit would, if necessary, " go broke " in backing it, as a matter of pride, against a horse from some other ranch or town. Sometimes the cowboys rode their own horses in such races, or sometimes they trusted to riders of lighter weight. No more inveterate gambler or horse racer ever existed than was the North American Indian, and sometimes a ranch outfit would " go after " an Indian village with some favourite running horse, and both parties would back their convictions to the extent of their worldly goods.

Small enough, we may be sure, were the amenities of ranch life, and rude enough were the conditions out on the far, unsettled country, where these rough, strong-natured men had no society but that of their fellow-workmen, and no amusements save such as lay at their hand in the rude surroundings of their employment. Though these amusements were always about, always possible, the life of the cowboy was by no means taken up in their pursuit. He was above all things a labouring man, with much to occupy his attention beside the demands of sport. The romance of the cowboy's life is best seen at a little distance from the cattle range. The visitor to the ranch has an enjoyable time, for his is the zest of novelty. The cowboy in turn cares little for the things whose freshness delights the man from the States. The cowboy

longs to see a theatre, to have a trip to the city, to
eat an oyster stew and all the green "garden truck"
he can hold. To him it seems that all the great pleas-
ures of life must lie out beyond the range, in the "settlements." The latter term usually meant for the cowboy, over the greater part of the cattle range, some
squalid little cow town of the frontier, and ill-fitted
enough was such a community to show the quality of
civilization. It may be imagined what were the amusements of the cowboy when he left the range and visited the "settlements."

The end of the round-up or the drive, perhaps,
found the men of a cow outfit at some such ragged,
scattering little Western town. These men, reared in
the free life of the open air, under circumstances of
the utmost freedom of individual action, perhaps came
off the drive or round-up after weeks or months of unusual restraint or hardship, and felt that the time
had arrived for them to "celebrate." Each and all of
powerful constitution, of superb physical health, and
of all the daring and boldness inculcated by wild life
amid wild surroundings, these men were ignorant of
fear, ignorant of self-restraint, ignorant of life in any
but the narrowest sense of the word. Their vices
were few and strenuous. They were eager to practise
such vices as they knew, and to learn as many more
as they could in the brief time of their visit. Merely
great, rude children, as wild and untamed and un-
taught as the herds they led, their first look at the
"settlements" of the railroads seemed to them a
glimpse of a wider world. The tinsel and tawdry
glitter of it caught their eye as a bit of bright stuff
attracts that of a babe. They sought to grasp that
which they saw. They pursued to the uttermost such
avenues of new experience as lay open before them,

almost without exception avenues of vice. Virtue was almost unknown in the cow town of the "front" in the early days. Vice of the flaunting sort was the neighbour of every man. The church might be tolerated, the saloon and dance hall were regarded as necessities. Never in the wildest days of the wildest mining camps has there been a more dissolute or more desperate class of population than that which at times hung upon the edge of the cattle trail or of the cattle range and battened upon its earnings. The chapters of the tale of riotous crime which might be told would fill many books, and would make vivid reading enough, though hardly of a sort to the purpose here. It would be folly to attempt to idealize the cowpuncher in his relations with the early "settlements." He was the wildest of all the wild men of the West, and he rose rapidly into a reputation which, unjust and inaccurate as it is to-day, has clung to him ever since, so that people will have no other cowboy but him of the uncouth garb and the wild and desperate bearing, him who swears, shoots, carouses, and comports himself as a general "terror." This notion of the cowboy is grotesque in its injustice, but none the less it at one time had a certain foundation. There was a time when the name of "cowboy" was one with which to frighten children, and it carried with it everything of absolute disregard for law and order. In the early days of the drive, at the cow town it was a regular and comparatively innocent pastime to "shoot up the town." To shoot out the lights of a saloon was a simple occupation, and to compel a tenderfoot to dance to the tune of a revolver was looked upon as a legitimate and pleasing diversion such as any gentleman of the range might enjoy to his full satisfaction. If a cowboy wanted a drink, he shot a hole in a whisky

barrel and helped himself. As the revolver was thus
first in peace, so also it was first in war. All quarrels
were arbitrated with the six-shooter, and it took slight
cause to start a quarrel when the strong waters of the
settlements were doing their work. Hardly a night
passed without its " killing," though one never heard
of a murder. In the town of Newton, Kan., one of
the hardest of the hard cow towns of the early trail
days, it is said that eleven men in one day " died with
their boots on," as the euphonious expression goes.
The coveted art of the six-shooter was an essential of
a finished education in that country. The powerful
excitements of vile liquor and viler women stirred into
a malignant activity all the evil elements of untutored
and rugged natures, and the results in many cases
were lamentable enough. It is strange that the records of those days are the ones that should be chosen
by the public to be held as the measure of the American
cowboy. Those days were brief, and they are long
since gone. The American cowboy has atoned for
them by a quarter of a century of faithful labour, and
it is time the atonement were written for him in the
minds of the people by the side of the record of his
sins.

The stories of excess, the lessons of restraint were
the same upon the cattle range and in the cow towns as
they are in the cities to-day. Under it all is the same
human nature, seeking that which is forbidden, longing, daring, sinning, and repenting. The cowboy was
above all things human, and he had the failings of the
ordinary man. Yet he had his softer and his more
reflective side. The man who would carry a wounded
greyhound five miles on his saddle and nurse it for a
month as one would a child until it recovered was a
man not altogether bad. If his impulses led him

wrong at times—as whose shall not?—he could at least with those equally guilty feel regret and remorse. On the range in the old times, on the range even to-day are men drifting about like wrecks at sea. The old West was full of such characters, men who knew their own stories of self-reproach, regret, remorse, despair. The outward reflex of such feelings was a nature perhaps silent or apparently surly, at times inflammable and uncertain. The West in the good old days asked no questions of any man. It cared not whether the younger cowboys were at times wild and full of freakishness. It asked not why the older men at times seemed never more happy than when they were hard at work.

The amusements of the cowboy were like the features of his daily surroundings and daily occupation—they were intense, large, Homeric.

CHAPTER XIII.

SOCIETY IN THE COW COUNTRY.

THE West in the good old times, before the influx of the so-called better classes, was a great and lovable country. We go back to it yet in search of that vigorous individuality which all men love. In the cities men are much alike, and, for the most part, built upon rather a poor pattern of a man. The polish of generations wears out fibre and cuts down grain, so that eventually we have a finished product with little left of it except the finish. In modern life the test of survival is much a question of the money a man is able to make. The successful money-maker can buy a part of the desirable things of life, and he may found a family, the latter, perhaps, not begun in love and mutual admiration of person so much as in admiration of the tangible evidences of that which is called success. Men do not love women because they are rich, nor do women admire men because they are rich; and, after all, the only problems of life are those of bread and butter and of love. All the rest is a mere juggling of these two. Such is the society of the artificial modern life of large communities. In the West the individual reigned, and there had not been established any creed of sandpaper. Should we break up the organizations of society as it is known to-day in the focal points of civilization, should we cast abroad

237

the men of the cities and bring in the men of the old plains, what a changing about there would be then! Society and human nature and the human race might be benefited by it. But this may never be, and in this country, as in the history of all other countries, there must go on the slow story told by the ages, of more and more wealth, more and more artificiality, more and more degeneration. And yet good human nature, dragged by the hand of the spirit of complex civilization, looks back always at the past. Aside from the love of tinsel, which in time becomes a necessity for many natures, mankind has always loved the strong, because it is only the strong which is fit to be loved. So we go back continually, fascinated, and revel in the stories of strong times.

Among the little cow towns of the frontier the searcher for vivid things might have found abundance of material. Society was certainly a mixed matter enough. It was a womanless society for the most part, hence with some added virtues and lost vices, as well as with certain inversions of that phase. The inhabitants might be cowboys, half-breeds, gamblers, teamsters, hunters, freighters, small storekeepers, petty officials, dissipated professional men. The town was simply an eddy in the troubled stream of Western immigration, and it caught the odd bits of drift wood and wreck—the flotsam and jetsam of a chaotic flood.

In the life of a modern business community a man must beware of too much wisdom. The specialist is the man who succeeds, and having once set his hand to an occupation, one dare never leave it, under penalty of failure in what he has chosen as his life work. In the city he who shifts and changes his employment loses the confidence of his fellow-mortals, who agree that he should know how to do one thing and nothing else, and should continue to do it diligently all his life. In the West all this was different. Versatility was a necessity. The successful man must know how to do many things. The gleanings of any one field of activity were too small to afford a living of themselves. This fact was accepted by the citizens of the country, sometimes with the grim humour which marked the West. A young lawyer in a Western town had out a sign which read, " John Jones, Attorney-at-Law. Real Estate and Insurance. Collections promptly attended to at all hours of the day and night. Good Ohio cider for sale at 5 cents a glass." A storekeeper had on his window the legend, " Wall Paper and Marriage Licenses," thus announcing two commodities for which there was but very small demand. One of the prominent citizens of such a town was a gambler, a farmer, a fighter, and a school teacher all in one. One of the leaders of the rustlers and cattle thieves who made a little cow town their headquarters was a Methodist minister. It was not unusual for a justice of the peace to be a barber. The leading minister of a certain thriving cow town, which experienced a " boom " in the early railroad days, eked out his scanty salary by working as a sign painter during the week. There seemed to the minds of the inhabitants of the country nothing incongruous in this mixing up of occupations, it being taken for granted that a man would endeavour to make a living in the ways for which he seemed best fitted.

In any early cow town or mining camp of the West there was sure to be a man from Leavenworth. No apparent reason for this curious fact seems ever to have been given, yet it is certainly true that no such town ever was settled without a man from Leavenworth to take part in the inauguration. He was apt afterward to be one of the town officers. He was nearly always a lawyer, or claimed to have once been one. He was sure to be the first justice of the peace, and in that capacity of high dignity presented an interesting spectacle. The early Western justice of the peace was a curious being at best. Apt to be fully alive to his own importance, he presided at his sessions with a wisdom and solemnity not to be equalled in the most august courts of the land. It was rarely that the justice knew much law, but he nearly always was acquainted with the parties to any suit and with the prisoner who happened to be at bar, and usually he had a pretty accurate idea of what he was going to do with the case before it came up for trial. It may have been such a justice as this of whom the story is told that he 'made the defendant's lawyer sit down when he arose to reply to the arguments of the prosecution, saying that the counsel's talk served to "confuse the mind of the court." Yet the frontier justice of the peace usually came well within the bounds of common sense in his decisions, as witness the ruling of that Texas justice who gravely declared "unconstitutional" a certain State law which restricted the sale of liquor in his town in many unwelcome ways, he holding that such a law must necessarily be contrary to public policy and against good morals. This man was later elected to the State senate.

The first female inhabitants of the town were also sure to come from Kansas. There seems to be no special reason for this curious feature of the fauna of the cow town in the early days, and it seems difficult to tell why all the men seemed to have left Leavenworth and all the women to have abandoned the State of Kansas, though the fact remained none the less apparent. The family from Kansas nearly always came

in a wagon, and among the family there were usually
two or three girls, sure to become objects of admiration for a large cowboy contingent in a short period
of time.   There never was a cow town which did not
have a family including "them girls from Kansas," and their fame was sure to be known abroad
all over the local range.   One by one the girls from
Kansas disappearead down the tortuous road of
matrimony, yet still the supply seemed unexhausted,
more girls coming from Kansas in some mysterious
way.

There was always a Jew merchant in any cow town,
who handled the bulk of the business in general supplies.   The infallible instinct of his kind led him to
a place so free with its money and so loose in its business ideas.   The Jew did not come from Kansas, but
dropped down from above, came up from below, or
blew in upon the wind, no one knew how, but he was
always there.   He advertised in the local paper, complaining about the rates, of course.   "Keep your eye
on Whiteman" read his advertisement, and "Geep
your eye on Viteman" was the burden of his talk to
his customers.   It was, indeed, a very wise thing to
keep your eye on Whiteman, though perhaps the
latter did not mean it in that way in his boastful
advice.

There was always a sheriff in a cow town, and he
was always the same sort of man—quiet, courageous,
just, and much respected by his fellow-men.   The public of the cow town had little real respect for the
courts, and the judicial side of the law was sometimes
farcical; but, by some queer inversion of the matter,
all had respect for the executive side of the law, and
indeed, recognised that side alone as the law itself.
The sheriff was the law.   He was worthy of this feel-

ing, for nearly always he was a strong and noble nature, worthy of an unqualified admiration.

There was always a barber in a cow town, and when
a town was so run down that it could not support a
barber it was spoken of with contempt. There might
not be any minister of the Gospel or any church, but
there were two or three saloons, which served as town
hall and general clubrooms, being the meeting places
of the inhabitants. There was no dentist or doctor,
though there might be a druggist, who kept half a
dozen or so jars and bottles. If a cowpuncher wanted
a little alum to cure a hide, the druggist charged him
at about the rate of ten or fifteen dollars a pound for
it, according to the extent of the need he had just
then for the money. If the druggist was playing in
fair luck at the time in the nightly poker game, alum
was cheaper.

There was always a little newspaper, a whimsical,
curious little affair, which lived in some strange fashion, and whose columns showed a medley of registered
and published brands and marks for the members of
the cattle association living in that district, this business being almost the only source of revenue for the
newspaper. Of news there was none, except such as
all men knew. The editor of the paper had a certain
prestige in political matters, but led withal an existence properly to be termed extra hazardous. The editor always drank whisky when he could get it, just
as everybody else did, it being quite too much to ask
that he should depart from popular custom; but the
paper was ground out from the hand press every week,
or almost every week, with a regularity which under
the circumstances was very commendable. Sooner or
later, if one paper began to make more than a living,
another paper came in, and then life assumed an added

interest with the inhabitants. Both papers were then
read, so that everybody might see what one editor was
saying of the other. The second editor was nearly
always a more vindictive man than the first one, and
he drank more whisky, and wrote worse English and
had a redder nose; but he added life to the town, and
he was sure of a fair showing until at some unfortunate
time he said the wrong thing. This wrong thing was
never far away in the journalism of the range. It behooved the editor to be careful in his criticism of any
one, and always to be sure to " boom the town," no
matter what else might be omitted.

One of the owners of the saloons was sure to be a
gambler as well as a dispenser of fluids. He had more
money than anybody else, and also a surer chance of
sudden death. He always killed one or two men before
his own time came, but his time came some day. He
was then properly mourned and buried, and the affair
was discreetly mentioned in the papers. If it seemed
that the gambler's partner was getting too " bad " to
be needed in the economy of the town, he was asked
to " move on," and this he was wise enough to do.
Another gambler came in then.

The lawyer of the town was something of a personage. His library did not amount to so much, con-
sisting probably of not more than two or three books,
not very many, for one can not carry many books
when on foot, and the lawyer nearly always walked
into town; but the lawyer had all the authorities in
his head, and so did not need a library. The lawyer
was naturally a candidate for the territorial council,
for county assessor, or anything else that had any
pay attached to it. Of strictly legal work there was
not much to do, but the lawyer always remembered
his dignity, and you could always tell him in a crowd,

for he was the only man in the town who did not wear " chaps " or overalls. The lawyer and the county surveyor sometimes had work to do in settling the lines of a homestead or some such thing when water rights were in dispute. He had no occasion to prosecute or defend any client for theft, for everybody in that country was afraid to steal; and burglary was a crime unknown. It was rarely that a man was prosecuted for horse stealing; never, unless the sheriff got to him first. A " killing " sometimes gave the lawyer a chance, but this was not a thing to make much stir about, and very often the killer was set free, because it was usually certain that the other man would have killed him if he could, and that is defence at law. Much more interesting was it when a man was shot and not killed, alike for the rarity of the occasion and for its probable consequences. Everybody wondered then which would be the one to get killed when he was well and around shooting again.

The cow town was very proud of any public improvements, very resentful of any attempt to cast slight upon such improvements, and very jealous of the pretensions of any other town of its neighbourhood. It being rumoured that a certain foothills city over toward the edge of the range was to have a railroad tunnel which would add to its attractions, it was gravely suggested by the citizens of a rival town located well out on the plains that the latter should also have a tunnel, and not allow itself to be surpassed in the " race of progress " by any " one-armed sheepherding village." The county surveyor lost popularity because he tried to point out how expensive it would be to construct a tunnel out on the prairie.

The first coal-burning stove, the first piano, the first full-length mirror to come to town made each an occa-

sion of popular rejoicing. At a time when all was progressing as usual in the leading saloon of such a town
one evening, two of the players at a card table, without
word of warning, arose and began shooting at each
other in the celeritous yet painstaking fashion of the
country. They were both caught by friends before
any damage was done to either man, but the aim of
one being disconcerted by the grasp upon his wrist,
his bullet missed its mark and shattered the stove door,
on the big new stove which was the boast of the community. For this careless shooting he received a general censure.

One time there came to a certain cow town on the
range a Missouri family who brought along a few hogs,
about half a dozen young porkers of very ordinary
appearance, but which none the less became the objects of a popular ovation, as being the first hogs ever
brought in on the range, and an attraction which it
was not pretended could be duplicated by the rival
town over in the foothills. These hogs were the pride
of the settlement for some time, until at an evil hour
they chanced to be spied by a drunken cowpuncher,
who was visiting town that day and enjoying himself
according to his lights. When the cowpuncher saw
these new and strange creatures in the streets of the
town, he at once went back to his horse, got his rifle
from his saddle, and forthwith inaugurated a hunt
after them, this resulting in the early and violent death
of all the "shotes." No one objected in the least to
his shooting in the streets, for that was the privilege
of all men, but it was voted a public offence to kill
those hogs. The cowpuncher was censured by some
of the citizens, including the druggist, who at that
time was pleasantly intoxicated himself, and he would
have killed the druggist had not the latter pleaded

17

that he was not armed. The cowpuncher, very fairly, it must be acknowledged, told the druggist to go back to his store and get his gun, and then to come on and they would have their little matter out together. With this invitation the druggist complied, and soon appeared at the corner of his cabin with a long six-shooter in hand, calling to the cowpuncher to come on down the street and be killed like a gentleman. The street was properly cleared for the accommodation of the two, a number of us stepping into the newspaper office, and standing well back inside the door, though with heads out to see what was going to happen.

At this moment there appeared on the scene the sheriff of the county, who had concluded that this was a matter of sufficient note to warrant his interference. The sheriff was a large, burly man, who spoke very little at any time and was now quite silent as he walked up the street steadily, without any hurry, into a line directly between the hostile forces. His hands, with the thumbs lightly resting in his belt, made no move toward the long guns which hung at each side. His face was quite calm and stolid, and with a certain dignity not easy to forget. As he passed the newspaper office, some one made some light remark to him—for all the time he was walking straight up to the rifle of the cowpuncher, who was warning him to step aside, so that he could kill the druggist, whom he appeared to dislike at the time. To the remark the sheriff made no answer, but turned his heavy, solemn face, with a look which said plainly that in his opinion a man ought not to be interrupted when he was in pursuit of a duty which might end in his death. The sheriff was not afraid, but he knew what was to be done. The deputy, who accompanied him, was white as paper and evidently badly scared. The two

walked on up the street slowly, the sheriff never hasten-
ing a step, until finally they reached the place where
the cowpuncher stood, the latter having been puz-
zled by the slow and quiet advance until he had forgotten to begin shooting, though the druggist continued to shout out defiance. The sheriff said nothing, and made no attempt to pull his gun, or to cover
his man in the style usually mentioned in lurid Western literature. He simply reached out his hand and
took the cowpuncher's rifle away from him, setting it
down against the side of a near-by house. Then he
said: "Now, Jack, you d—d little fool you, I don't
want no more of this. You go on down to my
house an' go to bed to onct, an' don't you come out
till you git plum sober. Go on, now." And Jack
went.

The sheriff then went on down to the druggist,
who had by this time slipped into his store and hid
his gun. Him the sheriff rated well as a disturber,
but did not take in charge at all. The loss of the
" shotes " was generally lamented, but on the following morning Jack apologized about that, paid for the
" shotes," invited everybody to drink to their memory,
and at the suggestion of friends both he and the druggist shook hands over the matter and forgot all about
it. This affair of course never got into the courts, as
indeed why should it? The settlement reached was
eminently the wisest and most effectual thing that
could have been done, and showed well enough the
sterling common sense of the sheriff, who retained
the friendship of all parties. His deputy, if left alone,
would have tried to " cover his man," would very likely
have been killed himself, and had he succeeded in getting his man to jail the latter would very likely have
killed the druggist as a point of honour as soon as he

got out. The peace and dignity of the town were far
better preserved as it was.

In the communities of the frontier men were sometimes apt to be a trifle touchy and suspicious of their
fellow-men, perhaps a bit ultra in their notions of personal honour and personal rights. A cowpuncher from
the Two Hat outfit was once heard explaining a little
instance of this. " It was this a' way," said he, speaking of the recent killing over on Crooked Creek of Bill
Peterson, who had been shot by his neighbour, a man
by name of Sanders. " Peterson an' Sanders had both
of 'em started hen ranches, allowin' to make plenty
o' money next year, when the hens had sort o' got used
to the range an' begun to do well on the feed. Sanders,
he come in there first, an' he 'lowed he wouldn't have
no one to buck aginst in the aig business, but Peterson he moves in on the creek too, and lays out his
ranch right up agin Sanders, an' that makes Sanders
plenty mad. Them two fellers, they got so blame
jealous of each other they used to be afraid to go to
sleep, for fear the other feller would think up some
scheme or other. The wild cats and coyotes got in
among the corrals like, an' before long they mighty
nigh cleaned up the whole cavvieyard o' hens fer both
of 'em, but they couldn't see it that way, an' each
accused the other of stealin' his hens, which of course
we knowed meant trouble some day.

" Fin'ly, these fellers got so jealous of each other
that one feller he'd stay out in his hen pasture all
day, a-herdin' back the grasshoppers to keep 'em
from goin' on to the other feller's range—which
them grasshoppers is shore good feed fer hens. Peterson, he consults a lawyer about this, and he comes
back and tells Sanders that grasshoppers is crit-
ters *ferry natoory*, or somethin' o' that sort, and so

they belongs to everybody alike. Sanders he says he don't care a d—n about that, he aint goin' to have Peterson's hens a-eatin' his 'hoppers, because he saw the place first. So they at last got to sort o' havin' it in fer each other. One day Sanders he come down to me an' ast me to lend him my gun, because his was out o' order, an' he had to kill Peterson purty soon. So I let him take my gun, which is a shore daisy, an' next mornin' he laid fer Peterson when he come out the house. Peterson he saw him, an' he come out a-shootin', but Sanders he was a leetle too quick fer him. Sanders he quit the ranch then, an' now you kaint get a aig in this whole country fer a dollar a aig, not noways."

In the rude conditions of the society of the frontier the man of "sand" was the man most respected. If one allowed himself to be "run over" by the first person, he might as well be prepared to meet the contempt of all the others. Sooner or later a man was put to the test and "sized up" for what sort of timber he contained. If he proved himself able to take care of himself, he was much less apt to meet trouble thereafter. The man who was willing to mind his own business was not apt to meet with the professional bully or bad man of the town. The latter was a person who understood the theory of killing and escaping the law. He was confident in his own ability to pull quick, and it was his plan to so irritate his antagonist that the latter would "go for his gun." After that it was a case of self-defence. In the great cities the man who draws a deadly weapon is severely handled by the law, but in the old days on the frontier the bearing of arms was a necessity, and their general use made all men familiar with them and deprived them of half their terror. The stranger in the cow town was at first much troubled when he heard of a " killing " next door to him, but soon he became accustomed to such things and came to think little of them. The fashions of a country are its own and are not easily changed by a few; the change is apt to operate in quite the opposite direction. It is not the case that all the dwellers on the frontier were brave men, but courage is much a matter of association, and comes partly from habit after long acquaintance with scenes of danger and violence. The citizens of the cow town all wore guns, and did not feel fully dressed without such appurtenances. There was but one respectable way of settling a quarrel. It was not referred to the community, but to the individual, for in that land the individual was the supreme arbiter. None the less, many a coward's heart has beaten above a pistol belt, and nowhere in the world was such a fact more swiftly and unerringly determined than in a primitive community such as that in question. Upon the other hand, the rudest of the inhabitants of that community would recognise the quality of actual courage very quickly, and the man who stood highest in the esteem of his fellow-men was he who had the reputation of being a " square man," not " looking for trouble," but always ready to meet it if it came.

A wealthy and respected cattleman of a certain part of the cow range had a niece who ran away and married a renegade ranch foreman against whom she had been warned. This man soon began to abuse her, and she returned to her former home. The quarrel was patched up, but the girl's uncle sent word to the husband that if she ever was obliged to come back home again, she should never again go away to live with him. The husband sent back word that he would kill the uncle on sight. To this the cowman made no reply, but he always rode abroad with a rifle across his lap. One day he had word that his enemy was about to waylay him, and accordingly he was upon the lookout for him. As he entered the edge of a bit of wood, he saw the dutiful relative waiting for him, but luckily looking in the wrong direction. The wind being in his favour, the cowman drove up within a short distance of the man who was seeking to kill him, and then calling to him, killed him in his tracks when he turned. In this act he was upheld by all the society of the range, and was never in the least called to account for it, as it was thought he had done quite what was right and needful. He was never molested by any more relatives after that. This incident was long ago forgotten in his history, and a quieter, more respected, or more useful citizen does not live than he is to-day, nor one more marked for his mildness and even-tempered disposition. He did only what in his time and under his surroundings was the fit and needful thing to do.

Such a man as this was the cowman who happened to be standing in a saloon one day, talking with some friends as he rested his elbows back of him on the bar against which he was leaning. The conversation was interrupted by a cowpuncher of the frisky sort, such as in those days occasionally materialized in the cow town for a little lark. This cowpuncher rode his horse into the saloon and up to the bar, declaring that both he and the horse had come a long way and were thirsty, and must both have a drink. His requests having been complied with, he began to shoot around a little, and drove everybody out of the saloon except this one cattleman, who still stood quietly with his back against the bar, leaning back upon his elbows, this directly in the middle of the room, which was only about twenty feet square. The cattleman stood there saying nothing, and finally the cowpuncher rode on out. When asked why he had not driven out the " old man " too, he replied that he had not seen him.

" You could shore of seen him if you looked hard," said one of his friends, " fer he was right at you there in the middle of the room."

" Well, I never did see him," said the cowpuncher gravely. " My eyes ain't allus as good as they ought to be, sometimes." As a matter of fact the reputation of the " old man " was such that the cowboy was very wise in not seeing him and undertaking to run him out.

Sometimes in the winter season society in the cow town would be enlivened by a ball. Such a ball was a singular and somewhat austere event, and one which it would be difficult to match to-day in all the land. The news of the coming ball spread after the mysterious fashion of the plains, so that in some way it became known in a short time far and wide across the range. The cowboys fifty miles away were sure to hear of it and to be on hand, coming horseback from their ranches, each man clad in what he thought was his best. The entire populace of the cow town was there, the ballroom being the largest room to be found in the town, wherever that might chance to be. Refreshments were on hand, sometimes actually cake, made by the fair hands of the girls from Kansas. A fiddler was obtained from some place, for where a few men are gathered together there is always sure to be a fiddler; and this well meaning, if not always melodious, individual was certain to have a hard night's work ahead of him.

Of course there was a great scarcity of lady partners, for the men outnumbered the women a dozen to one. No woman, whatever her personal description, needed to fear being slighted at such a ball. There were no wall flowers on the range. The Mexican wash-woman was sure of a partner for every dance, and the big girl from Kansas, the little girl from Kansas, the wife of the man from Missouri, and all the other ladies of the country there assembled, were fairly in danger of having their heads turned at the praise of their own loveliness. In the Southwest such a dance was called a *baille*, and among the women attending it were sure to be some dark-eyed *señoritas* with *mantilla* and *reboso*, whose costume made contrast with the calico and gingham of the " American " ladies. The dancing costume of the men was various, but it was held matter of course if a cowboy chose to dance in his regulation garb, " chaps," spurs and all. In the more advanced stages of society it became etiquette for a gentleman to lay aside his gun when engaging in the dance, but he nearly always retained a pistol or knife somewhere about him, for he knew there might be occasion to use it. Sometimes the cow-puncher danced with his hat on, but this later became improper. There are few more startling spectacles, when one pauses to think of it from a distance, than a cowboy quadrille in which there was a Mexican woman with only one leg, a girl from Kansas who had red hair, and two cowboys who wore full range costume.

Between dances the cowpuncher entertained his fair one with the polite small talk of the place; surmises that the weekly mail had been delayed by some mule getting " alkalied over on the flats "; talk of the last hold-up of the mail; statistics of the number of cattle shipped last year, and the probable number to be shipped this; details of the last " killing " in

the part of the country from which the cowpuncher
came, etc. Meantime the lady was complimented
openly upon her good points and those of her costume, not to her personal displeasure, for human
nature is much the same no matter where the ball is
held. It sometimes happened that the lady was not
averse to sharing with her escort of a bit of the liquid
refreshments that were provided. The effects of this,
the stir of the dancing, the music, the whirl and go
of it all, so unusual in the experiences of most of the
attendants, kept things moving in a fashion that became more and more lively as the hours passed by.
The belated range man, riding full gallop to town,
could see from a distance the red lights of the windows at the hall, and could hear afar the sound of
revelry by night. Excited by this, he spurred on his
horse the faster, answering to the dancers with the
shrill yell of the plains, so that all might know another man was coming to join in the frolic. He cast
his bridle rein over the nearest corral post, and forthwith rushed in to mingle with the others in a merriment that was sure to last to daybreak. Out of this
ball, as out of other balls, were sure to arise happiness,
heartburnings, jealousies, and some marriages. An
engagement on the plains was usually soon followed
by a marriage, and such an engagement was not made
to be broken; or if it was broken to the advantage of another man, there was apt to be trouble over it between
the men. Sometimes the night of the ball did not
pass without such trouble. Any such affair was apt
to be handled most delicately in the next issue of the
paper; although funeral notices were not customary
there, the papers being printed only each week or so.

The cow town was sure to have among its dwellers
some of the odd characters which drifted about the

West in the old times, men who had somehow gotten a warp into their natures, and had ceased to fit in with the specifications of civilization.   Such men might be teamsters, cowboys, or those mysterious beings who in some way manage always to live without doing any work—these not to be called tramps, for the tramp was something unknown in the cow town.   Such a man might have a little cabin of his own, with a fireplace and a bed of blankets.   Nearly all the male population of the town was made up of single men, and of these nearly all did their own cooking, living in a desultory, happy-go-lucky sort of fashion, with no regularity in any habits.   Some of these men were educated, and had known other conditions of life. Bitterer cynics never lived than some of these wrecks of the range.   There was Tom O——, a cowpuncher, apparently as ignorant and illiterate as any man that ever walked, but who had his Shakespeare at his tongue's end, and could quote Bryon by the yard. Tom's only song was—

"I never loved a fond gazel-l-e!"

The song rarely got further along than that.   A cheerful fatalist, Tom accepted the fact that luck was against him, and looked upon life as the grimmest of jokes, prepared for his edification.   No matter how ill his fortune, Tom never complained, even as he never hoped.   He had, too, a certain amount of enterprise in his character.   At last accounts he was headed for the Indian Nations, it being his expressed intention to marry an Indian woman and so become a member of the tribe, this being the easiest way open to fortune which offered to his mind.   He had several wives scattered over the range at different points, and at times he was wont to discuss the good and bad points of these

with the utmost candour and impartiality, thus showing himself a liberal and philosophical man.

The foreman of the O T ranch was a good cowman,
who stood well with the men of his own outfit and of
the neighbouring ranches.   This man never at any
time, either upon his own ranch or in town, was
known by any other name but that of " Springtime."
His accounts at the stores were run under the name
of " Springtime " and in no other way. His real name
one can not give, for it seems that no one ever thought
of asking him what it was. " Springtime " was a quiet
man, although, like Tom at times, given to medita-
tive song. As in the case of Tom, his song never got
beyond the first line, which ran—

" Whe-e-en the springtime cometh, ge-e-ntle Annie-e-e-e ! "

It never seemed to trouble him what had happened
or might happen in the springtime, and for him the
springtime never seemed to get any closer. Nor did
this fact give concern to his neighbours, who gave him
the name " Springtime " in all gravity, as being the
title by which he would be most readily and generally
known.

Other citizens of the cow town were One-eyed
Davis, and Hard-winter Johnson, and Cut-bank Bill,
and Two-finger Haines, and Straight-goods Allen, and,
of course, Tex and Shorty and Red, and all sorts of
citizens whose names never got further along than
that, unless in connection with their respective ranch
brands. Thus, in speaking of an event of interest,
down at the saloon or store, the proprietor would
say, " Yesterday, that feller Charlie, from down on
the Hashknife, he comes in here an' he says," etc.
And in course of reply some one else might cite what
Pinto, of the Hat brand, had said upon the subject;

all men knowing by those presents that there was meant a certain individual whose vast extent of freckles had by common consent earned for him the name of " Pinto." No one seemed to take amiss these clinging nicknames, and indeed it was as well to accept them without protest. A singular incident in a man's life, or a distinguishing personal peculiarity, was usually the origin of the name. In the simple and direct methods of thought which obtained it was considered wise to give a man a name by which he would be known easily and precisely. There might be many men by the name of John Jones, but there would be only one Overcoat Jones—a man who had the odd habit of wearing an overcoat all summer, for reasons which seemed to suit himself, and which therefore suited his acquaintances. There might be many Wallaces, but Big Foot Wallace was known from one end of the range to the other. There might, indeed, have been a certain courtesy in this plains nomenclature. It was one of the jests of the later West to ask a man, " What was your name back in the States? " but this was never seriously done in the cow country of the early times, because it might have been one of the things one would rather have left unsaid. Too much personal curiosity was not good form, and met with many discouragements. Under the system of the society of the cow town, it was quite enough to know a man by his local and accepted name, which should distinguish him easily; and the man was valued for what he was, not for what his name was, or for what that of his father had been. Some cheap persons of the later West bestowed upon themselves nicknames of rather ferocious sort for the purpose of impressing upon dwellers of the East a sense of their wild Western character; but the man who had his card engraved as Dead Shot Dick, or Charlie the Killer, or that sort of thing, did not make a practice of claiming his title when he was away from the new settlements and back in the society of the old cow country, where life was real and earnest in its lines, and assertions of a personal sort apt to be taken up for serious investigation.

In short, the cow town of the good old times was a gathering of men of most heterogeneous sorts, a mass of particles which could not mix or blend. Of types there was abundance, for each man was a study of himself. He had lived alone, forced to defend himself and to support himself under the most varying and trying circumstances, very often cut off from all manner of human aid or companionship for months at a time. Needing his self-reliance, his self-reliance grew. Forced to be independent, his independence grew. Many of these men had been crowded out of the herd in the States, and had so wandered far away from the original pastures of their fellows. They met in the great and kindly country of the old West, a number of these rogues of the herd, and it was a rough sort of herd they made up among themselves. They could not blend; not until again the sweep of the original herd had caught up with them, and perforce taken them in again among its numbers. Then, as they saw the inevitable, as they saw the old West gone forever, leaving no place whither they might wander farther, they turned their hands to the ways of civilization, and did as best they could. In many cases they became quiet and useful and diligent citizens, who to-day resent the raking up of the grotesque features of their past, and have a contempt for the men who try to write about that past with feigned wisdom and unfeigned sensationalism. Among those citizens of the old cow town were many strange characters, but also many noble ones, many lovable ones. A friend in that society was really a friend. Alike the basest and the grandest traits of human nature were shown in the daily life of the place. Honour was something more than a name, and truth something less than a jest. The cynicisms were large, they were never petty. The surroundings were large, the men were large, their character was large. Good manhood was something respected, and true womanhood something revered. We do very ill if we find only grotesque and ludicrous things in such a society as this. We might do well if we went to it for some of its essential traits—traits now so uncommon among us that we call them peculiarities.

A more curiously democratic form of society never existed upon earth than that of the old cow town. Each man knew his own place, but felt that that place was as good as any other man's. In the cow town, if anywhere, all men were free and equal. Perhaps no better instance of this curious independence in the genuine cowpuncher could well be found than in the story of a certain ranch foreman, whom we may as well call Jim, and his relations with his employer, who, according to the story, was a foreigner, an Earl of something or other, who had come to America to engage in the cow business. It seems that upon the first day they spent upon the ranch together Jim appeared at the dinner table without any invitation, and moreover without removing his hat. The earl objected not only to Jim's hat but to his presence, saying that he was not accustomed to dining with his servants. This was an error on the part of the earl, really a most unfortunate remark to make, but in extenuation it should be added that he was not to be blamed so much for it, for he was a newcomer in the cow country and had had very little time to become acquainted with its ways. But this fact Jim did not pause to consider. Without protest or parley, he drew his revolver, and so beat the earl about the head with it as nearly to kill him, though not so nearly, so says the story, as to prevent his apologizing freely.

"Why, that feller," said Jim, in a surprised and injured manner, when later speaking of the occurrence, "he put on more airs than a cook! . . . But," he added later, "he was all right after that, an' after a while he got to be a pretty good sort o' feller, fer a Englishman."

Over this vast, unsettled region of the old West the cattle of the cowman roamed, and this wild grazing was almost the only possible industry of the country. Therefore the employments of the cowman's occupation were practically the only ones open to a man in search of a means of making a living. Almost everybody had at one time or another tried his hand at "punching cows," and therefore the little town which made the headquarters of the surrounding country was sure to have all the flavour of the range. Its existence, of course, depended upon the trade of the great ranches which lay about it, at distances perhaps of forty, fifty, or even nearly a hundred miles. Distances had not the same values in that country that they have in the older States. A neighbour who was only fifty miles away was comparatively near. All the supplies of the town were freighted in perhaps a hundred and fifty miles from the railroad. The rancher thought nothing of driving sixty or seventy-five miles in to town to get his groceries. The cowboy would ride thirty or forty miles after the ranch mail, and think no more of it than one does of going down town on

the street car. The roads were usually hard and good,
and the air pure and stimulating. Either man or horse
can endure very much more physical exercise in the
country than in the city, because the air is better.
The atmosphere of the plains was very fresh and pure.

Now and then, therefore, the residents of the town,
who perhaps themselves had ranch interests or
" claims " somewhere out in the country, would have
the quiet of their daily lives broken by the visits of
the men from the cow ranches, near or far.   Then
the merchant sold his goods, the saloon keeper smiled
with pleasure, the editor had use for his pencil, the
lawyer stood in readiness, the justice of the peace
pricked up his ears, and the coroner idly sauntered
forth. The cowman was great. He was the baron of
the range. Cheap cattle and still cheaper Mavericks,
free grass and free water, with prices always rising
in the markets at the end of the drive—no wonder
that the cowman was king and that money was free
upon the range. No wonder that things were lively
when the cow outfit rolled into town, and that the
pleasantries of the men were tolerated. It was known
that if they shot holes in the saloon looking-glasses,
they would come in the next day and settle for the
damage, and beside throw the saloon open to the public. Those were the good old days—the days when one
cowman rode into a restaurant and ordered " a hundred dollars worth of ham and eggs " for his supper;
or when a certain cowman who had just sold his beef
drive to good advantage came home and " opened
the town," ending his protracted season of festivities
by ordering for himself at the little tumble-down hotel
a bath of champagne, filled with the wine at five dollars
a bottle. He said he wanted a bath, and that nothing
was too good for him at the time; and his wishes were

18

complied with cheerfully, though the last champagne of the cow town went into the bath.

One can see it now, the little cow town of the far-away country, a speck on the great gray plain, the mountains lying beyond it, blue and calm, all about the face of Nature looking on at it sleepily, through eyes half shut and amused, everywhere a strange, moving, thrilling silence, that mysterious, awful, fascinating silence of the plains, whose charm steals into the blood, never thereafter to be eliminated.

The cark of care, the grind of grief, the racking of regret—

all these things are gone, vanished from the face of this silent, smiling, resting land.

A dard-hued lizard on the dark-hued sand;
A rock; a short gray tree; an earth-built hut.
Around, an edgeless plain; above, an equal sky.
She sits and dreams. The whiteless blue of heaven
Comes down to meet the greenless gray of earth—
And compasses her dream.

It is high and glaring noon in the little town, but it still sleeps. In their cabins some of the men have not yet thrown off their blankets. Along the one long, straggling street there are few persons moving, and those not hastily. Far out on the plain is a trail of dust winding along, where a big ranch wagon is coming in. Upon the opposite side of the town a second and more rapid trail tells where a buckboard is coming, drawn by a pair of trotting ponies. At the end of the street, just coming up from the *arroyo*, is the figure of a horseman—a tall, slim, young man—who sits straight up on his trotting pony, his gloved hand held high and daintily, his bright kerchief just lopping up and down a bit at his neck as he sits the jogging horse, his big hat pushed back a little over his forehead. All these low buildings, not one of them above a single story, are the colour of the earth. They hold to the earth therefore as though they belonged there. This rider is also in his garb the colour of the earth, and he fits into this scene with perfect right. He also belongs there, this strong, erect, and self-sufficient figure. The environment has produced its man.

CHAPTER XIV.

THE NESTER.

THE destruction of the cattle range was a matter of doom. It was foregone that all these wide lands should at some time be claimed by those thousands of human beings who had taken fully upon themselves the compact of society. The cowman is a creature of unmeasured lands, of wide methods, of no multiplicity of laws or of acknowledged obligations. The husbandman is a man of small holdings of land, of eye jealous of his own rights, of reverence for the laws whose protection he covenants in the terms of his surrender of personal freedom to the society of which he has become a member. The cattle range is a womanless country. The farming country is a land of homes. Society is built up of homes, and the laws of society will sooner or later trend in favour of the man with the home and the yoke, the more willing or the more helpless slave.

The term "nester" was one applied in half contempt by the cattle men of the Southwest to those early squatters and homesteaders who first began to manifest a disposition to abandon the saddle for the plow, to cease ranching and go to farming. The nester might be a cowboy himself, who had met his fate in some pair of eyes that held him back from long journeyings. He might be some lean and sallow individ-

ual, whose wagon and team had brought him down
from some State where things were getting too much
crowded for him. Probably the first great accession
of numbers received by the cult of the nester came
from the settlements of Germans who, early in the
century, were colonized in large numbers in portions
of Texas. There are whole communities of these people in parts of that State to-day, and most of them
are valuable citizens, but many of them were hard
enough cases in the early days, and much disliked
by the native American population, from whom their
ways differed in almost every respect. The instinct
of these people was all for farming, and they retained then, as they do to-day, all their habits of economy, industry, and thrift. Added to this disposition
there was the wildness of nature acquired by years of
free life on the frontier in the early days. These foreigners kept pretty much to themselves, after their
clannish fashion, and each man was content to till
his little holding, perhaps by some water course or
spring, and concerned himself little about the affairs
of the great cattle baron whose herds roamed the
country at large. It might be that the homesteader
was really only a squatter, with no actual title to his
property at all, but possession was ten points of the law
in those days. Or it might be that he had taken up his
land under the State laws governing the matter (for
Texas was never subject to the United States land laws,
reserving title to her own lands when she entered the
Union), or who had bought his land from some earlier
owner and paid for it. Perhaps he had a few horses
and oxen, a few rude farming implements, a little flock
of sheep or goats. He had without doubt a " woman "
and a flock of children, some dogs, and a rifle. Surly
and inhospitable to a degree some of these foreigners

were, giving no welcome, perhaps, to the party of horse hunters who came over from the nearest ranch, sometimes refusing visitors the right to water or to camp in their yards, a thing unheard of in the annals of the land. What was thus refused them the rude and spirited range riders customarily took for themselves, telling the "Dutchman," as they contemptuously called their unwilling host, that if he objected too much they would hang him to a corner of his own corral. Sometimes, indeed, they did do such things, and that, with the original discourtesy, at times created hard feelings among the relatives of the departed, who viewed with sullenness every movement of the encroaching cattle men.

The vast lands of Texas could not fail to attract the attention of persons contemplating a venture in the cattle business, and at the time of the first "cattle boom" a great many men went into Texas for their operations, among these a number of wealthy foreigners who sought a place to use capital and younger sons. The country was fairly crowded with capitalists, who wanted possession of large bodies of land for the use of their herds. Such a cowman would look out a tract of land, perhaps twenty or thirty miles square, and would lease or buy it, paying perhaps a few cents an acre for some of it, or more for the better-watered portions. Public lands, school lands, railroad lands were taken possession of in large bodies. These tracts the cowman proceeded to fence in, not always being very careful how much he included in his fence, so that he was sure he had enough. Inside the sweep of his "pasture" fence he might have the little "nests" of dozens of the native small ranchers who had settled first on this land. These perhaps had their roads established, over which they went to town, or after their wood, or went hunting, or made any of their various trips away from home. This made no difference to the cattle man, who cut off the road, and perhaps left no gate within ten miles of it; nor did he serve notice on the nester where the gate might be found. This mattered little to the latter. He simply cut his own gate when he came to the fence. This first gap so cut was the sign of war—a war in which many lives were lost and much property hazarded before adjustment was found for the deep principles involved.

The big landowner went on with his fencing operations, and returned along the line some morning to find the fence gapped in half a dozen places. Perhaps he missed certain cattle whose range habits should have made them easy to find at a certain point. Perhaps he traced certain suspicious hides to the butcher shops in the towns. Of these things he made no complaint. But he stationed some cowpuncher, who was a good sure shot with the Winchester, at some gully near the trail over which the nester was apt to come some morning. The cowpuncher cheerfully shot the nester, and the cousin of the nester killed the cowpuncher, and that created a feeling of injury at the ranch for which the cowpuncher was working. Perhaps there was a little riding party the next day. Perhaps there were several nesters hiding out for a time. But the gaps continued to appear in the lines of the great wire fences, rendering them useless. Parties of cowboys lay out at night regularly watching the fence at suspected points, and parties of nesters lay out for the cowboys. Many on both sides were killed. One large landholder of foreign nationality put up twenty miles of fence in one line. He was disliked by his own cowboys as well as by the nesters, and all of them joined hands to destroy the fence. In the night time the men cut the fence in hundreds of places, and hitching their ropes to the long strands of wire dragged them bodily out upon the prairie. By morning the entire fence had disappeared.

The country had been free too long for a man to be hindered in his riding. What should one do who met this impassable wire when he was on his way across the wild country, riding by the shortest line, as had been his wont in the past? It was a dangerous thing, this fence upon the waterless country, which shut one off from the necessaries of life. There had never been bred in that land any respect for a law which cut a man off from the watering places, and from the right to travel across the open range. By no means was the "foreign" nester alone in his feeling against the fences. Natives joined him, and all men whose original liberties were transgressed. The cause of the nester grew in strength and became indeed a popular one.

It angered well-nigh to a point of frenzy many foreign and alien capitalists to learn that they had come indeed upon a land of the free; for the State of Texas had no trespass law. The remedy was to collect civil damages against the man who cut one's fence, and failing that, to kill him; the latter, a game at which he could also play, and often did. All sober-minded men began to see that the fencing of the country was obnoxious to the institutions which had long prevailed, and that there had been traversed the sense of justice in the hearts of a great body of the population. The question was one which demanded settlement, and at length the aid of the courts was invoked. In dozens and hundreds the nesters were arrested and brought in for trial. At one session of the court in a certain little Texas village, in the early '80's, nearly two hundred fence cutters were indicted by the grand jury. When their time came up for trial they were on hand—very much so. The town thronged with them. Each man of them had a Winchester and a revolver, and they held together in a great body of silent, watchful, determined men. The jailer of the town had a pair of valued hounds which he at occasion used in tracking escaped prisoners. Early in the day both of these hounds were found dead, poisoned by meat thrown over the jail wall to them. The jailer swore he would kill the man who poisoned the dogs. The sheriff, who was himself later killed, the United States marshal who had made most of the arrests, and who met death in the course of his duties at another time, together with the deputy sheriff, who was also killed later on, all at this time urged the jailer to keep quiet. The tension of the community was very great. All knew that if the limits of the law were enforced, the officers of the law would have to fight the whole body of their " prisoners." Really the court was in the hands of the prisoners, and had common sense enough to see it. One or two light fines were imposed, in cases where it was obviously just or feasible, and the other cases were dismissed or " continued."

Thus a state of wholesale war was temporarily averted in one section of the country. In other sections the war went on also, with varying results. The chief battles were fought upon the range, and many and bitter were the feuds in the outlying portions of the cow country. The name of the nester spread to other parts of the Southwest, and he was regarded with hatred or open contempt over the cattle country of New Mexico, where he too often turned up in legal possession of some choice bit of water front, which he misused, according to the cowman, by applying it to the purposes of irrigation. But everywhere the nester stood on his rights, legal and personal. He was as good a shot as any, and he had lived on the " front " as long as any, and he had all the wild frontier reliance upon himself and the swift hand of resentment for any injury. In the West it was never well to allow any man to " run over you," and he who suffered this forever lost caste. The nester was born to this creed as much as the cowman, and he lived up to it as sternly. Slowly the little wars went on, the underlying questions meantime receiving gradual adjustment in the courts. Naturally, a sort of compromise was the outcome, giving to each industry, so desirable of itself, a proper showing, and holding both to a stricter observance of the laws. To-day the original usages and necessities of the wilder past may be seen in some of the laws of the cow country. The great ranges of Texas are fenced, the land of the original source of the American cattle industry being the first to give up the " free grass " of the range. The great " pastures," as they are called, have fences running twenty, thirty, forty miles in unbroken line at times. But if one need to cross one of the great tracts of land, he shall have " wood and water right " to camp by the roadside wherever he may be. If the landholder fence in more than ten thousand acres of property in one body, one may treat it as if it were his to travel over and hunt over as he likes. The nester is almost forgotten now by his original name. The farmer is tolerated by the cowman, and the cowman by the farmer. They adjust their necessities each with the other, and the first phases of the question are decided.

But the homesteader, the man with the family,

the man with the small holding of land, is established in the cattle country of America, and will hold his own by a law greater than State law and greater than any national law; by the inexorable law of the growth and spread of the population of the earth.

CHAPTER XV.

THE RUSTLER.

As in the Southern cattle country the nester was an enemy to the interests of the cattle trade, so on the northern range was the man who represented his exaggerated counterpart, that somewhat famous Western character known as the rustler. There has never been upon the range a character more fully discussed or less fully understood. Many persons are familiar with the curious Western verb " to rustle," and know what is meant when one is asked to " rustle a little wood " for the camp in the mountains, or when it is announced that the horses should be turned out to " rustle a little grass," etc.; but they would be unable, as indeed perhaps many resident cattle men might be unable, to give the original derivation of the term " rustler."

Any one acquainted with the cattle country of the North would soon come to hear much of the rustler, and that in stories of the most confusing character. Thus he might hear of the murder of some dweller in an outlying camp, and be informed that the crime was attributed to " rustlers." A stage-coach might be held up, or a mountain treasure train robbed, and the act would be laid at the door of this same mysterious being, the rustler. He might hear that a number of men had been the victims of a lynching bee, and be advised that the men hung were rustlers. Thus in time he might come to believe that any and all bad characters of the West were to be called rustlers. In this he would be inaccurate and unjust. The real rustler was an operator in a more restricted field, and although it would be impossible to induce a cattle man to believe there was ever any such thing as a good rustler, it is at least true that there were sometimes two sides to the rustler's case, as there were two sides in that of the nester. In the later or acquired sense of the term, all rustlers were criminals. In the original sense of the word, no rustler was a criminal. He was simply a hard-working man, paid a little gratuity for a little extra exertion on his part. He got his name in the early Maverick days, before the present strict laws governing the handling of that inviting range product. He was then a cowboy pure and simple, and sometimes his employer gave him two, three, or five dollars for each Maverick he found and branded to the home brand. Then the cattle associations for a time paid any cowboy five dollars a head for any Maverick he found for the association. It behooved the cow-boys of those days to " get out and rustle " for calves, the word being something of a synonym for the city slang word "hustle," and with no evil meaning attached to it. The term passed through some years of evolution before it gained its proper modern significance, or the improper and inaccurate use which is sometimes given it.

Under the system of Maverick gratuities the cow-boy prospered on the northern range. Those were his palmy days. Any cowpuncher of active habits and a saving disposition could easily lay up considerable sums of money each year. As he was bred upon the range and understood nothing but the cow business, it was the most natural thing in the world for him to buy a few cows and start in business for himself, sometimes while still under pay of his former employer, and sometimes quite "on his own hook." He gradually began his herd, and had his brand registered as those of the cowmen of the district. Thus he ceased to be cowboy and became cowman; or rather he remained as he really always was, both cowboy and cowman, both herder and owner. In this way many young men who went on the range "broke" began in a short time to "get ahead" very rapidly. There were few better avenues to quick fortunes than those offered by the cattle business at this stage of its growth. The logical sequel followed very rapidly. From all parts of the country all sorts of men pressed into the business. There appeared upon the range a great many men of the sort known to the old-time cowmen as "bootblack cowpunchers," men who came from the Eastern country to go into the cattle business for what money there was in it, and who were not slow to see where the quick ways of making money might be made still a little quicker. There also came into the business a great many Eastern men of wealth and standing, who were wise enough to see that the cattle business offered profits fairly Midaslike compared to the possibilities of capital in the older country. The West was now settling up rapidly along all the railroads with a good class of citizens, men of culture and refinement among them, all pressing into the new West to "grow up with the country," and to take advantage of the great opportunities of that promised land.

Under this influx of mixed population and this access of new business methods there appeared a factor never before known on the great cattle ranges—that of com-

petition. Heretofore there had always been enough for
all. Now there came the stress of the multitude, and
with it the dog in the manger which belongs with the
ways of modern business life. By this time there began
to be hundreds of new brands upon the range, and the
wealthy cattle men saw some of their cowboys building
up herds in competition with their own. It always
grieves the heart of capital to behold a poorer man
begin to make too much money. In time there was
inaugurated upon the cow range the good old game
of the settlements, of dog-eat-dog, and the big dog
began to eat the little one. The big men met and combined against the little ones. They agreed that no
more Maverick commissions should be paid, and that
the cowpuncher need "rustle" no more calves for
himself, but should rustle them for his employer only.
Moreover, it was agreed that no cowboy should be
allowed to own a brand of his own. This all happened
just at the period of the passing away of the good old
times of the West. It was at the beginning of the
West of to-day—the humdrum, commonplace, exact,
businesslike, dog-eat-dog West—which, is precisely
like any other part of the country now, with as much
competition as any, and with as few special opportunities in business.

This blow at the welfare of the cowboy had a
curious effect. It was intended to stop "rustling,"
but it increased it a thousandfold. It was intended
to protect the herds of the big ranchers, but it came
near to ruining them. It was intended to stop an
honest business system, and it resulted in establishing
a dishonest one. It arrayed the written law against
the unwritten law which had in all the past been the
governing principle of the free West. It threw down
the gauntlet for that inevitable war which must be

waged between society and the individual; a conflict
which can have but one end. In this case that end
meant the destruction of all that free and wild character which had for a glorious generation been the distinguishing trait of a great and heroic country. Let
us admit that the rustler—who now began to brand
calves where he found them, Maverick or no Maverick
—was a sinner against the written law, that he was a
criminal, that he was the burglar, the bounds-breaker
of the range; but let us not forget that he acted in
many ways under the stern upholding of what seemed
to him the justice of the old West. At any rate, we
shall not be asked to forget him as the man who
watched out the flickering breath of that dying West
which not all our lamentations can now ever again
bring back to life.

The rustler was a cowpuncher, and one of the
best. He understood the wild trade of the range to
its last detail. Among cowpunchers there were men
naturally dishonest, and these turned to illegal rustling
as matter of course. They were joined by the loose
men of the upper country, who " were not there for
their health," and who found the possibilities of the
cattle system very gratifying. These took in with
them, sometimes almost perforce and against their
will, often at least against their convictions, some cowpunchers who were naturally as honest and loyal
men as ever lived. To understand their actions one
must endeavour to comprehend clearly what was really
the moral code of that time and that country. This
code was utterly different from that of the old communities. Under it the man who branded a few calves
for himself as an act of "getting even" with the unjust
rules of the large cow outfits and the big Eastern
syndicates was not lowered in the least in the esteem

of his fellow-men, but, to the contrary, was regarded as a man of spirit, and therefore entitled to the rough Western respect which had no eye for him who submitted to be "imposed upon." In some portions of the upper country, notably in a few counties of Wyoming, the rustlers, or men who took beef cattle or calves not their own, far outnumbered the men opposed to them. They were called thieves and cutthroats and outlaws, and so perhaps they were from one standpoint. From their own standpoint they were not, and there were so many of them that they really made the "sovereign people," which is supposed to be the ultimate court of appeal in this country. They elected all the officers and chose the judges in some counties, and they—the people—ran things to suit themselves. It was of no use for a syndicate man to try to get in one of those courts what he called justice, because he was sure to get what the people called justice, and the two were very different things.

To this organized rallying of the "little fellows," as the small cattle owners were called, there came all sorts of hard and dissolute characters out of the chaotic population of the West. The wild frontier life had attracted men of bold nature, who had taken on all the restless and unsettled habits of the country and were irked by restraint or law of any kind. Out of such population came many of the guides and scouts, who actually were such, as well as a deplorable number of a class contemptuously called "long-hair men" by the genuine Westerner. The man who lived on the "front" had to make his living as best he could. In the time of the buffalo a large class of men went regularly into the miserable occupation of "skin hunting," and it is due to their efforts that the innumerable hosts of the American bison were destroyed from the face

19

of the earth. At the close of the rapid season of butchery which was thus set on foot, there were thrown upon the settlements and outlying country of the cattle range a large number of these ex-skin hunters, men of hardy nature and of exact knowledge of the wildest parts of the country. These men scattered over the country and fell into such occupations as they could find. Some of them went to punching cows, and some went to the Legislature. Some lived in out of the way corners of the land, dwelling in the dugout or cabin which was their old-time home, and making a living no one just knew how. There was a little wild game left in the country, but not in the old abundance. After awhile there swept over the country, all around the dugout of the hunter, the great herds of cattle which inundated the northern range. Was it likely that this old hunting man would go without beef?

Thus it was that the cult of the rustler grew. The ranks were filled by cowpunchers wholly bad and only partly bad, by old-time cowpunchers and new-time ones, by ex-skin hunters and drifters of the range; in short, by all sorts of men who saw in the possibilities of the cow trade a chance to make a living in a way which to them seemed either excusable, expedient, or easily capable of concealment. The qualifications for the new calling, no matter what or who the man who filled them, were simply the best ones demanded by the calling of the cowpuncher. The rustler must without fail be a rider, a roper, a sure shot, and fully posted in all the intricacies of marks and brands. He must, moreover, be a man of " nerve." In viewing him we view the criminal of the range, but an open and unaffected criminal, and we are less than broad if we fail to see the extenuating circumstances for his crime which existed in the conditions which then obtained. Of course, if we can not claim acquaintance with those conditions, and know only those of the old civilizations, we must call him a renegade, a thief, and often a murderer. Under those names no one can be admired.

The rustlers of the upper country rapidly joined their forces and arrived at an understanding with one another. The true story of their operations has never been written, and would make stirring reading, as indeed would a description of many of the scenes and incidents of the cowboy's life. They had in a way a creed and a dialect of their own. A genuine rustler was called a "waddy," a name difficult to trace to its origin. He might also, when spoken of in terms of admiration, be called a "pure," meaning that he was a thoroughbred, a reliable man, with "sand" and ability in his chosen profession. He was sure to be a good plainsman, and probably a "straight-up" rider—i. e., one who could ride any bucking horse without a "bucking strap" to hang on to. The rustler, and indeed pretty much everybody in his country, lived on "slow elk," which is to say that they ate yearling beef belonging to some one else, probably some big cow outfit. It was held strictly a point of honor among these men never to touch an animal belonging to a poor man or a small owner. The big non-resident cattle companies were the chief sufferers through losses of their "slow elk." Sometimes the spring freshets would carry away from the little willow-covered creek valleys the skeletons or hideless carcasses of many "slow elk." Resident managers for Eastern companies were obliged to report a lessening yearly increase among their herds, which after a while became almost a decrease. The profit was nearly

taken out of non-resident cattle ranching by the operations of the rustlers in certain unfortunate parts of
the range. Sometimes the foreman of a ranch was
in open or concealed sympathy with the rustlers, and
very often some of the cowpunchers were friendly to
them. Perhaps some of the cowboys were a "little on
the rustle" themselves in a quiet way. Sometimes
such a cowboy would rope and tie out at some convenient place during the day a number of calves, and
would then slip out at night and brand them with his
own iron or that of some confederate.

Local sympathy was all with the rustlers and
against the Eastern syndicate men, and it was un-
popular to be too outspoken in condemnation of
the rustling operations. The small homesteader or
squatter who had made an attempt at a farm on
some water way out in the dry and inhospitable
country might not be much of a cowman, and might
not wish to mix up in any of these crooked operations
of the pseudo-cowman; but if a man came into his
house some morning and made him a present of a
quarter of beef, or sold it to him for half a dollar, who
was to be the wiser? It was difficult, and not always
safe, for the small settler to refuse. If he accepted,
and did so again a few times, he became tacitly recognised as bound to secrecy, and practically a friend
of the rustlers. After a time another man might
come along and ask permission to leave a few calves
in his pasture for a few weeks, and as he did not know
where the calves came from, he was perhaps not averse
to accepting the pay for this, unconscious of the fact
that the calves were only being made into artificial
Mavericks by being weaned away from their mothers,
so that no discrepancy of brands might be noticeable
between the mother and her calf. Thus also some-

times the corral of a sympathizer might be used at night to hold a few calves which were being run out of the country, or a bunch of horses which were going the same way. The very corral of the ranch from which the stock was taken might serve this same purpose. It was covertly understood by the majority of the population resident upon the cattle range of this section of the country that it was not well to watch things too closely. In this sentiment many cowboys joined who did not openly join the rustlers. The honest cowboys who remained steadfast in their endeavour to protect the interests of their employers were spoken of with contempt, and were referred to as being "*peoned* out" to their employers, and were accused of "living on bacon rinds, like so many jackasses." Sometimes they were called "pliers men," or "bucket men" by ex-cowboys who would have scorned to carry a "bucket of sheep dip," or to bother too much about mending a gap in a wire fence. Thus we see an entire perversion of the original cowpuncher love of justice, and his wish to give each man his own property. Instead of being ready to hang a cow thief or shoot a horse thief, we find our cowboys over a great strip of country sympathizing or conniving with such men. Such a pronounced change of principles surely requires a pronounced reason. In point of fact, this was not a change of principles, but a change of conditions. The cowboy remained true to the West, but he felt no loyalty for the East. He was true to his old code, but he maintained that the application of that code had changed in its conditions. Slowly he was to learn the new codes, and to become the cowboy of to-day.

If anything can be said in extenuation of the rustler, it is of that rustler who in certain parts of the range waged his fight against the big barons who, as he claimed, were oppressing the cowpunchers and depriving them of what had been a regular source of income. This was about the time of the forming of the Wyoming stock commission, and the appointment of the brand inspectors at the cattle markets, when the cattle men organized into a general State association for the purpose of protecting their interests against the lawless element. Long before that time this same question of cattle thieving had come up on the range, and under more virulent and absolutely inexcusable form. The range in Montana had been infested with cattle and horse thieves, who robbed indiscriminately all who owned property that came in their way, without show or colour of attempt at justification. These thieves lived in the out-country, each in his own cabin, and with only a very loose sort of organization, though if a visit of suspicion was made to the dugout of such a man, to see what was going on about his place, he was apt to be surly about it; and a second such visit might find him entertaining a few friends of his own, each a hard-looking man with a good gun and a clever way of using it. Long before the courts had become strong enough to be of use in meeting this outlawry, the cattle men of Montana banded together to crush it out by means of *vigilante* work. The description and abode of nearly every one of the cattle thieves were known, and a regular campaign of reform was begun, after the practical and thorough methods of that day. Some of the rustlers were asked to leave the country, and did so; and some who were thus asked to leave and did not comply, were shot or hung when next found. In this campaign the *vigilantes* killed between sixty and eighty of the rustlers. One railroad bridge one morning had thir-

teen corpses swinging to it. In the ten years from
1876 to 1886 the *vigilantes* of the range executed as
many men in Montana, Dakota, and Nebraska as have
been legally executed by the law in any dozen States
in all the time since then. It was the only way which,
in that part of the country and at that time, was practical. Capital punishment was a necessity, but jails
were an impossibility, and the population had not
yet had time to organize fully into the ways of the
older communities. We may call these lynchings
wrong also, and certainly they were as much against
the law as stealing cattle was against the law; but
it was here also a question of the unwritten as against
the written law. It is folly to apply the standards
of other times and places to the wild surroundings
of that rude early population. Far better might we
accord to them the right, which the American people
have ever been wont to claim and take, of governing
themselves according to their sense of justice under
the circumstances then and there prevailing. The
men of these times knew what we should always, in
our efforts to be just, remember also, that circumstances alter cases. Thus these opposing interests,
each lawless and each strong, fought out their battles
for themselves, and so arrived at eventual justice.

The rustler in those days was never to be accused
of "putting up a slow fight," or not "dying game."
He was very likely to be an individual of the sort
known as a "bad man with a gun." When he came
to town he usually wore two guns, and "wore 'em
low," as the saying went. That is to say, he carried
two revolvers, each swinging low down and pretty
well forward on his thighs, not on the hip in the less
efficient fashion. The scabbards, or holsters, of his
revolvers were attached at their bottoms to the man's

boot tops or to his trousers by buckskin thongs, so
that when a sudden jerk was made for the " gun " it
came out smoothly and did not pull the holster with
it, the latter being held down.   Nearly all the gun
fighters of the time had their pistol holsters thus tied
down to their clothing, even when the gun was worn
concealed by the coat, well around on the hip.   The
usefulness of this little device can be appreciated by
any one who has practised the handling of the large revolver both with and without it, and who remembers
the extreme value which each little shining moment
had in one of the rapid encounters of those days.
Sometimes the rustler showed fight when he was cornered by the *vigilantes*, but he was usually taken at
such disadvantage that he had little chance.   He rarely asked any mercy, for he was a practical sort of man,
and knew that it was not worth while.

"Excuse me, gentlemen," said one of them, as he
was led to the fatal tree, " but I'd just like to take a
chaw o' tobacco fer a few minutes before I leave."
His wish was granted gravely and politely.   " So long,"
said another, as he sprang boldly out from the end
of the wagon which made the death trap for his gal-
lows.   A few of these men broke down under the
memory of other days and scenes, but none of these
asked any aid or pity.   Some died cursing, not many
died praying.   They were hard, rough souls, these
fellows, but among them there were some men whose
splendid courage might almost have earned them a
right to longer life.

The *vigilantes* of the plains rarely made any mistakes in their hurried trials and executions, and though
they sometimes hung the wrong man it made little
difference, because it was a part of the optimistic
creed of the time that even if such a man was hung

under a mistake, he probably ought to have been hung
anyhow; so it was all right. It is only in the very
rarest of cases that a man who has ever engaged in a
lynching will speak of it to any one, even to a man
who has been of the same party with him. The act
is buried with its victim. It would be in bad taste
to quote any such confession even if it had been made,
but the case was different, at least in the popular
mind of to-day, when a man had simply acted as one
of a legal posse sent out under formal process of the
law to take a man, dead or alive. In either case the
method of making the arrest was much the same. The
practical Western mind early discovered that a man
must sleep, and that in time he must wake up again;
and these facts offered the suggestion for the manner
of either " getting " one's fellow-citizen as a private
matter, or " taking " him as a public matter. Such
an arrest was once described by a cowpuncher, who
had served upon a sheriff's posse for the capture of a
cattle thief.

" Reddy Patterson, the sherf," said the cowpuncher,
" he come to me an' he said he wanted me to go along
an' help take a feller.

" ' What feller? ' says I.

" ' Hank Ferris,' says he.

" ' What fer,' says I.

" ' Rustlin' cows on the Three X,' says he.

" ' Oh,' says I. So I goes an' gets my Winchester,
an' we all rides on over to Hank's place, about twenty
miles. Feller name of Parker was along. Parker he
taken up a hay ranch down clos't to town. Well, we
come to Hank's house, an' tied out a way from it an'
crep' into the bushes near the spring, fer we 'lowed
if Hank was home he'd come out perty soon to git
some water. We laid out fer a hour or more, an did'nt

see no sign o' nothin', till fin'ly we see a smoke start up in the chimbly, so we know'd some one was in there, sure.

"Bimeby Hank he comes out an' walks down towarts the spring wher we was a-lyin'. I could a-got him easy, but Reddy he holds me back, an' when Hank gets down clos't to us, Reddy steps out an' tells him to get up his hands. Hank he looks at him, an' don't put up his hands at first, an' yet so far as we could see he didn't have on no gun. I reckon he was plenty mad. Reddy he calls to him to get up his hands quick, and Hank puts 'em up then, though all the time he kep' a-backin' towarts the house. We all stood out and was goin' up to him then, thinkin' he might get some edge onto us, but jest as we got a'most up to Hank, blamed ef there didn't another feller run out of the house an' start to go 'round the corner. Parker he blazes away at this feller without no orders, an' blame ef he didn't get him, too!

"'What in hell you shootin' at?' says Reddy, who ain't give no orders. An' says Hank, 'D—d ef you ain't killed that feller! What'd you do it fer?'

"We all went to the other feller, an' he wasn't dead, only shot through the shoulder, an' he was mighty mad about it.

"'My frien',' says Reddy, 'who are you an' what you doin' yer?'

"'My name's Hanson,' says he. 'Who in hell are you?'

"'My name's Patterson,' says Reddy. 'I'm sherf o' this county. What made you run?'

"'I 'lowed it wuzn't safe,' says the feller.

"'It ain't,' says Reddy, 'er not always. Where'd you come from?'

"'Cheyann,' says he. 'I never was in yer before in my life. I wuz just visitin' Hank.'

" ' Is that so, Hank? ' says Reddy.

" ' Sure,' says Hank. ' That feller ain't done no rustlin'. D—n perty thing, you comin' an' shootin' him!'

"Reddy he thinks a while, and he says to the feller: ' Well, pardner, I reckon we was mistook about you, an' I ain't got no warrant fer you nohow. I'm mighty sorry we shot you.'

" ' That's so,' says the feller. ' It don't look quite right.'

"Then Reddy says to Parker, ' Parker, I reckon you better go on up to town ahead of us.—You mustn't mind him,' he says to the feller, meanin' he mustn't mind Parker. ' He's jest a leetle nervous, er he wouldn't a-shot you at all. I didn't tell him to, and I'm mighty sorry he done it, too.'

"That feller Reddy Patterson, he's shore a plum white man," said the cowpuncher in conclusion. " He don't mean wrong to no man."

The lawless life of the rustler, and the opportunities it offered for the easy and rapid accumulation of property, attracted many uneasy and loose-principled men from different parts of the country. Some of the men publicly known to belong to the rustlers in the Wyoming factional troubles of less than a decade ago were men who had respectable ranch properties. They had good cottonwood log-houses built, with permanent improvements, corrals, etc., just as the legitimate cowmen had. They had good herds begun, principally without the trouble of buying any cattle at the start. One of them was thought to be worth seventy thousand dollars, and had a herd of several hundred head of good horses, some of them as fleet as " ever looked through a bridle " ; for it was well for the rustler to own fast horses. This man was " doing

well," when he was shot and hung one day by unknown parties, his body not being discovered until
some time later. Tom W—— will do for the name
of this man. "Stalker Smith" will come near enough
to the name of another successful man in this line of
business; for now we come down to times less than
half a decade old, and could easily touch upon some very
tender memories, which may as well be left untroubled.
The team of Stalker Smith came home one day, and
in the wagon was the driver, shot through the neck
and dead. No one ever knew who did it.

The successes of some of these rustlers, and the
general sympathy in which rustler principles were held,
offered temptation to many ambitious young men to
go into the same business, in spite of the risk of it.
In the Big Horn country of Wyoming it was for a time
a toss up when a new cowboy came on the range
whether he would go in with the cowmen or join the
rustlers. Sometimes the new man had sudden occasion to regret his departure from the strict ways of
rectitude. One recalls one such instance which was
especially sad. There was a young cowpuncher who
came up from Kansas and became fascinated with the
sort of cowpunching he found going on in his adopted
country, a trade in which it was not necessary to have
any capital to get cattle, or even any iron to own
them. He fell in with two men whom we may call
Jimmy and Spoke for short, these at least being names
which will serve the purpose. These men told him
that they were engaged in a very risky occupation,
and did not encourage him to go in with them, but
the new cowpuncher insisted that he wanted to be
as bad a man as anybody, and was bound to try this
new way of getting along rapidly in the cattle business. The result was that the three went out one day

after "slow elk," and shot down half a dozen cattle in a little hollow, where they thought they would not be observed by the ranchers' men. Their confidence in this latter belief was ill-placed, for they had not half finished the skinning of their illegal beef before they were surprised by a party of cattle men and officers, who rose up from the edge of the hill above them and ordered them to throw up their hands. Instead of doing this, all the rustlers threw themselves flat on the ground, each behind the carcass of an animal. The oldest of the three ordered the others to lie close and not to show a head until they got an idea of what to do, but the Kansas cowpuncher could not get the better of his curiosity. He stuck up his head over the back of his dead cow, and was at once shot square through the forehead and instantly killed. Thus ended his aspirations as a rustler on the very first day that he went out.

Spoke jumped to his feet to run to his horse, pulling at his revolver as he rose. He was shot through the right wrist and his pistol dropped. He picked it up in his left hand and was shot through that wrist as he ran. He and Jimmy none the less got to their horses, but Jimmy's horse was shot down just as he sought to mount. Spoke turned to him and said, " Here, Jimmy, take my horse. I'm shot so I can't ride anyhow, and we can't both get away. You get on and ride, and keep on a-ridin'." So Jimmy took his comrade's horse and rode away under fire. His mount was a grand one, and in less than thirty-six hours he was a hundred and twenty-five miles away, and never has been caught yet. His plucky fellow-rustler was captured, tried, and imprisoned, but it is enough to say that he did not remain in prison very long and is to-day a free man. In regard to the location of this rude little drama, which did not occur so very long ago, it will do to say in the rustler vernacular that it happened " where the winds come from."

As there is but an inaccurate popular knowledge in regard to the character of the rustler himself, still less exact is the understanding in regard to his occupation and the manner in which he carried it on. Indeed, perhaps there are not a few experienced cattle men whose mode of life has not made them familiar with all the tricks of the rustler's trade. Really the rustler needed to be the most expert of all cow handlers, for he had to deceive the most expert of the legitimate followers of the trade, and was forced to outwit, outride, and outbrand—sometimes even to outshoot—the cowmen who had perhaps been in the business all their lives. He needed to know the range brands thoroughly, and to know the manner in which they could most successfully be changed without detection.

It might be supposed, for instance, that the branding iron of the rustler was simply a straight " running iron," with which he wrote over the former brand on an animal his own brand; or it might be supposed that he simply impressed his own hot stencil upon the hide of the creature, thus blotting out the original brand. This would be very clumsy work, apt to be easily detected by the nature of the wound left upon the hide of the creature, which would in such a case often slough off and leave visible proof that there had been tampering with the brand. The rustler who was a past master in his art was very fond of a bit of hay wire, or better yet, of telegraph wire, as a branding tool. This could be folded up and put in the pocket, so it could be easily carried without much chance of detection. Upon occasion, it could be twisted into the form of almost any of the set brands of the district, or made into shapes which would cunningly alter such original brands, and yet leave no trace of the original by which it could be proved. It should be borne in mind that the rustler was branding after the round-up in some cases, and it would not do for him to claim a calf showing a sloughed-off brand at a date when all calves were fairly to be supposed well of their spring branding and with the hair clearly showing the mark of the brand wound. After the rustler had used his bit of wire, the whole altered brand had the appearance of having been a genuine brand and all made at the same time. The fresh burn fitted in with the older and heavier burning in such way that it was impossible to tell legally that there had ever been any attempt at change—at least it was legally impossible to do so in any of the courts sitting in rustlerdom!

Another favourite way of easing down a brand was by means of branding through a wet blanket. The heavy iron could then be used, and yet the wound would not be so severe as to " give the thing away," as the saying of the range ran. Experts were divided as to the merits of these two methods of blotting brands, but the easily concealed hay wire had its advantages. It was so easy to pull a bit of crooked wire out of the pocket, heat it red hot, and by simply laying it upon a given point of the calf's hide acquire title to that calf, which alone would represent a pretty fair day's work for a poor man.

There were different ways in which the rustler operated. He might be rustling calves for his own ranch, or he might be rustling beef for the markets, and he might work a little differently at different times in either specialty. Of course he had always to overcome that great unerring instinct by which the cow and her calf always kept together for nearly a year of the calf's life, an instinct which has been explained as a part of the whole foundation of the cattle business. The rustler must separate these two in order to get the calf. Sometimes he shot down the cow, and simply took away the calf with him, branding it as his own. This might be before the round-up or after it, and the calf might be already branded or not branded. Or he might make up a bunch of calves and hold them in corrals or pastures away from their mothers, and so finally drive them away to another part of the range, these calves either branded or not branded as the case might be.

If the rustler wanted any beef, he simply shot down any animal he fancied and skinned it, carrying away the meat. As he might not care to have the incriminating hide found in his keeping, with its telltale brand to speak against him, he might burn up or destroy the hide or throw it away where it might not be found. It was a very big and wild country, and not many persons would be apt to cross his trail in the course of a day or a week.

It was not considered any crime at all for the residents of the country to kill what beef they wanted for their own use, provided it was beef that belonged to the big cattle companies. But the rustlers were not content with this. They wanted to do a little more than live. So they began to regularly market this free beef. A great many of the butcher shops in the ragged little frontier towns would take all the risk of handling such beef, especially if this happened to be in one of the recognised rustler towns, where a trial involving the title to beef always went one way, and that not in favour of a non-resident or a big cattle company.

Under these conditions the rustler was able to make a living and a little more than a living, and had not much cause to complain; or as he would probably have phrased it, he " had no kick coming." But presently there appeared upon his horizon a change of condition which offered him a still better chance to get on in the world, and gave his occupation a veritable "boom." Across the cattle range of Nebraska and Wyoming came the advancing arm of a railroad, the C. B. & Q. extension into Montana. The camps of the railroad contractors, where hundreds of men were employed and had to be fed, made a most enticing market, one right at the door of the rustler, a most accommodating and pleasant thing to have occur. The rustler was a boon to the railroad camps, and the latter were a boon to him. At once a fine traffic sprung up in free beef, and whole communities were benefitted by the new line of trade. In some way or other the rustler always managed to part with what money he made, and rarely became a very successful business man, but during the railroad days a number of the rustlers got hold of considerable amounts of money. It was all so very simple. Here were the cattle. Here was the market. There was no complicated system of round-ups and drives and shipping and inspecting, and, best of all, a man did not need any money to go into business. All he required was a rifle and a wagon. It was no wonder that under so flattering a prospect a great many men went in with the clans of the resident rustlers. The result was so wholesale a stealing of the range cattle of non-residents and of large resident outfits that the industry of cattle raising received a terrible blow. All the

20

profits of the ranches were going into the hands of the rustlers, and the herds instead of increasing were standing still or decreasing. Of course, this state of affairs could not long prevail, and there ensued the determined fight upon the rustlers which resulted ultimately in the breaking up of their practices, or reducing them to an endurable extent.

It may be curious information to some to learn the exact manner in which brands were changed by these light-fingered persons, so that one brand was made into another without leaving proof behind it of the change. We now come upon a delicate field, as the rustling operations in consideration all transpired within a few years back, and a great many of the men who assisted in them might not like to have their names and signs manual appear in print. It is not alleged that any or all of the brands given herein are actual or genuine, or that the alterations shown were ever actually made by any persons, and no accuracy is claimed for the names of the different brands mentioned. They are simply given, as the " retired rustler " who reviewed them remarked, to " show the possibilities of the cow business in a good climate." There may or may not be certain cattle men or certain ex-rustlers who might recognise some of the brands shown, but these no doubt would understand the motive to be simply one of accurate explanation of the subject in general and not in particular.

Thus, we may say, one of the first brands to appear on the upper ranges after the first Southern drives was the old **IO** brand. Numbers of cattle men bought cattle of that brand to stock their ranges, and, of course, needed to rebrand the cattle. It was an easy thing to think of the **IOI** brand, and this was one of the largest outfits on the range. But let us suppose a rustler wanted to brand one of the **IO** cows for his own private purposes. He simply took his little iron or wire, and put a little top to the figure 1, making it into a 7. It then appeared thus: **70**—quite a different thing! Still more different was it written with a letter S after it, thus: **70S**. The owner would not recognise his own cow thus disguised. Neither could the owner of a **IOI** cow very well prove his property when he found it wearing a brand which said **70I**. The matter would be still more difficult by the time the next rustler had made it **70L**, and the original **IO** cow would be very difficult to recognise under the evolved brand **ЯOB**. It should be borne in mind that the brand mark as it actually shows upon the hide is not so sharp and clearly defined as it looks upon paper.

There was a brand known upon the range as the Wrench brand, thus: **)—(**. By the time the rustler was done with it it appeared thus: **O—O**. Or it might assume this form, **O╫O**, and be called the Bridle-bit brand. The brand **21** was easily made to read **26**. Without much trouble **999** could appear quite differently, as **888**. The hair of the cow would cover up any little defects of penmanship.

A brand which was a simple **V** was easily altered, as thus: **◊**; but the skilful rustler would have been wise enough to put a straight line across it, thus: **◆** covering up the junction mark of the two brands. Of the old brand with the curious name of the Wallop, **X**, there might possibly have been constructed the brand appearing **8**.

The man who invented the Pipe-bowl brand, ▬U, had reason to believe he had a good brand till he saw it written thus: Ω ; and then thus: 8. The originator of the following brand, ∞, was contented with it until he saw it changed into the ∞▬, and called the "Fiddle-back" brand. Bar T, written ▬T, was readily made into 크I ; and finally it might have appeared thus : [Ⅲ].

The open A U was written thus : ᴧU ; but it came to pass that a brand appeared on the range which read thus : ᴧ℧—quite a different thing ! Another reading of the ▬T might be ❹▬B. The L brand might become the Block brand, thus : ❑. The brand TOT might have a second story put underneath it, and so become P8B. A gentleman by name of Kid A—— is said to have discovered that the DHL brand, ❹▬L, looked better thus : ❹▬B. The 2I brand was very pretty when made into the Tin-cup brand, thus : ☎. The Bar-ll-Bar (▬ǁ▬) brand was much improved in the estimation of some by being inscribed ♯, under which form it was called the Hog-pen brand. The owner of it is said to have gone over the divide. The brand ᑫI might be pleasant as reminding some Eastern cattle man of the year he went into the cattle business. A few years later he might be looking for some cows marked in that way, and would not know them when he saw them, for they might be marked ᑫb. Or they might also be marked ᑫᑭ. The brand originally made thus, ✳, was easily made into the Wheel brand, thus: ⊕ The original brand ǁ

could have been changed to ⋃, and then into ⊔F. It is not stated that any such change ever was made, but it might have been made along with any of the above. The letter S, alone or in combinations, was one of the hardest brands for the rustler to change successfully.

But perhaps the best instance of the brand-blot-ter's or " brand-blotcher's " art, one which shows alike his ingenuity and his grim sense of humour, was the alteration of the brand of the Liverpool and Suffolk Cattle Company, a wealthy English corporation who went into business in Wyoming with a view to gaining American money and American experience. The latter they actually got. The brand of this company was known as the " Guinea brand," in token, perhaps, of the many guineas of profits which were to flow into the company's coffers. It was written thus on the recorder's books : £. But some of the cattle of the English company changed their guinea stamp. The cow was the cow for a' that; but it bore the mark of the good old American dollar, and was called the property of the " Dollar brand," whose sign was thus : $. This was something which the Englishmen could not understand for a long time.

Reference to the cuts will show the process of evolution of some of the rustler brands, and will afford a clear idea of the means by which the intention of the old-time identification marks of the cow trade was perverted by dishonest individuals. Of course this was all a serious injury to the legitimate trade—indeed, a blow at its fundamental principles and a contravention of the original principle of justice among cowmen. Those of the ranchmen who were suffering, together with those who were opposed to all such dishonest methods, soon joined forces to crush out this growing evil, which must else have put an end to the cattle trade. The whole sanctity of the brand was going, and there was danger that the idea of its integrity as a sign of owner-ship would lose alike legal and popular value. The height of these depredations was reached at a time well within modern days and modern methods; none the less the law of force was invoked, as well as the law of the land, and this upon both sides. Two or three ranch foremen who remained loyal to their employers' interests were forced to leave the country, and one or two others were killed outright by the rustlers. Sev-eral non-resident cattle men found it unsafe to live upon their ranches, and so returned to their homes in the States. Upon the other hand, a few of the rus-tlers were killed, and many were warned or threat-ened. Finally came the climax of affairs, which ul-timately resulted in the waning of the star of the rustler and the general establishment upon the range of those principles of justice which were agreed upon by all as best for the interests of all. The cattle asso-ciations attained the practical control of the cattle busi-ness. Cattle men held the most responsible positions of public life, and were acknowledged to be among the most important citizens of the State, and to represent the State's most considerable industry. Since then the cattle business has become one of business methods and high organization.

The rustlers were wrong. They were lawless men— refugees and outlaws many of them. Yet there is a certain picturesqueness in their story, intimately blend-ed as it is with the story of the cattle trade and of the cowboy, a romantic interest which we should not overlook. It was the rustler who held the last pinnacle in the fight for the old days and the old ways of the West.

Since his fight was doomed of necessity to be a losing one, let us at least endeavour to be just to him. He was the burglar of the range; but, unlike the burglar of the cities, he very often thought that he was justified in what he did by the precedents of his country. When he came to see and to believe that he was wrong, he in many cases reformed and never again went back to the old ways. There should be no stigma allowed to rest upon the name of as honest and hard-working a class of men as any of the country, and so there should be no confusing of the rustler with the cowboy; yet it is none the less true that some of the most skilful and most trusted men now engaged in punching cows upon the range are men who at one time were "a little on the rustle," and who are by no means anxious to cover up their past. Nor is their past a barrier to them, even in these days, in the open-hearted country of the range.

CHAPTER XVI.

WARS OF THE RANGE.

AT times there have been wars upon the cattle range—conflicts between armed bodies of men of such numbers as to lift the matter above the field of mere personal encounters. These wars occurred when the interests of one class of men interfered with those of another. They might be classed as wars between sheepmen and cattle men, between factions of cattle men, or between the cattle men and rustlers or cattle thieves. In all these affairs the cowpuncher was the private soldier, the rank and file of the firing line, so essential in any fighting. In his capacity as armed retainer we shall see him in yet another light.

Of these three great sources of armed interferences, the difference of interests between sheep men and cattle men is the one which has attracted the least attention, but which is the most serious of all. This is a war not only of men, but of conditions. The sheep are bound to drive out the cattle from much of the range held by them to-day. This range is limited and is growing less. It will be cut into more and more by farmers and by irrigation, and on such part of the wild range as is left the sheep have as good right to the free grass as have the cattle. As they can live on less, and as they destroy the life of the range for cattle as they pass over it, it is sure they will have the best of the final argument. The cattle men resent this thought even to-day. What must have been their feelings in the early days, when the idea was first presented to them? One may readily find the answer when he considers the customs and precedents which then obtained. The great remedy for trouble in those days was the gun.

When the great herds of sheep were heard of as approaching over the feeding grounds of a certain district, the cowmen hurriedly met and took action. A delegation was sent to the men in charge of the sheep bands, warning them to come no further. If the sheep outfit felt strong enough, which was rarely the case, it sent back its defiance, and said that it would walk its sheep over any part of the free earth that seemed most convenient. The cowmen then sent to town for extra ammunition.

As the sheep worked in over the country, passing sometimes over high and dry mountain plateaus and across the rocky foothills, the herds were watched constantly by the cowboys of the nearer ranch outfits. The solitary sheep herder, sitting with head downcast on some mountain side, might hear the sing of a bullet. His own rifle, rusted and full of grass and sand, might fail him even if he tried to use it. He might take the hint, or again receive the final hint, and indeed go over the range," never more to return. The sheep, sometimes driven by the cowboys into some box cañon or defile, were butchered in hundreds and thousands. One sheep outfit, if memory serves correctly, lost nearly four thousand sheep one afteroon in a little cañon where they were crowded up, their bodies being left where they were shot down and their attendants driven out of the country. The law of might was the only one held in respect in those days. The general consensus of opinion was that no man engaged in walking sheep could be a decent citizen. He was a low down, miserable being, whom it was quite correct to terrify or kill. A popular contempt was entertained for " sheep meat," and any one addicted to the habit of eating it was considered of degenerate tendency. The little cow town hotel at times served this meat on its tables, but the very waiter girls had scorn in their voices when they called to the cook through the kitchen window their order for a " plate of sheep."

Of all the wars of the range, the greatest and bloodiest was the Lincoln County war of New Mexico, a mere factional war, in which there was no principle at stake, and no motive except the desire of robbery and personal revenge. This bloody partisan contest was carried on at a time before the modern ways of gathering news had penetrated so far as the remote country which was the scene of the disturbances. Did that country remain to-day as wild and unsettled as it was then, and as far from railroad and telegraphic communications, the best of the newspapers of to-day might have no inkling of equal sensations occurring there until weeks or months after they had happened. Europe, Turkey, the Soudan, are not so far as was, about the year 1880, the little-known country between the Rio Grande and the Pecos River. The Lincoln County war raged for a couple of years or more in spasmodic virulence, until the whole cattle community was ranged in factions, one half against the other, and each man doubtful of his neighbour. It was supposed that this war resulted in the death of two or three hundred men, but no one will ever really know how many men were killed in this guerilla fighting, until the tally-book of the recording angel shows how many skeletons are lying out in the mountains of that calm

Southwestern country, where even to-day the deer
hunter may find a human skull, or the scattered members of some disjointed thing whose nature he perhaps
fails to recognise. Yet recent as was the occurrence
of these terrible events, they are already shrouded in
apathy and buried in forgetfulness. The public never
knew of this war, and does not know of it to-day. The
newspapers of the cities never got hold of the facts in
any actual accurate state. Most of the men of the country did not care to write or tell all they knew. The
greatest war of the range has passed into the oblivion
which broods above the cattle country. Yet were the
book of this little drama written, it would be in its
way a series of hero tales, full of the bravery and determination, the faithfulness and hardihood of many;
of the fiendish cruelty, the lust of blood, the insatiable
vindictiveness of others. Human life was never cheaper than in the Spanish Southwest. In this time of
outbreak it seemed that all the smouldering passions of
generations, all the uncentred hate, the misgrown men-
tality, the distorted love of blood, and the reckless love
of danger for its own morbid pleasure had accumulated
and broken forth in a volcano of blood and crime. The
only society was one of armed conflict, the only fellow-
ship was that of mutual danger or mutual criminality.
There were no law courts in the region at the time
fit to bear such name, and such as there were remained
helpless. The Territorial authorities were no less
helpless. The Governor of the Territory was disposed
to quell the disturbance, and it is related of him that
in pursuance of his military training he intended to
send troops and cannon down into the desert to fight
these cowboys, though this perhaps was related with a
bit of the grim humour of the times. Prices were
put on the heads of some of the most dangerous men,

and then for years the merry chase of man-hunting went on until most of the gangs were broken up. Many of the men were killed, and those remaining alive dispersed into Old Mexico. During the prevalence of the war the whole country had been terrorized by continual scenes of violence and death, and so indiscriminate had been the murderous spirit of the worst of the outlaws engaged in this fighting that no man knew when he was safe from some one or other of the many gangs which infested the country.

The cause of this great war lay primarily in the loose state of society at the time. Far down in the Seven Rivers country, at the lower portion of the Pecos Valley, was the ranch of old John Chisholm, who had ventured in there when few other men had dared to try the country. He had become very wealthy. That was the day of Mavericks, and as the country was very wild and unknown—perhaps it is less known to-day than any country of equal size in the United States—the Chisholm herd soon grew to number anywhere from thirty to sixty thousand, and Chisholm and his brother lived the lives of veritable cattle kings. Under them at times were large numbers of cowboys, and among these were some of the hardest men that ever threw a leg over a saddle, as indeed they had need to be.

The whole region was full of horse thieves and outlaws, the worst of these being under the leadership of the notorious cutthroat, Billy the Kid, a name famous even yet along that border. Billy the Kid died at the ripe age of twenty-three, and at that time had killed twenty-three men, committing his first murder when he was but fourteen years of age. He and his men inaugurated a reign of terror, which made his name a dread from one end of the country to the other.

They lived on their earnings as robbers, and glad
enough were the Mexicans of the remote *placitas* to
give them anything they asked in return for life.   This
young fiend and his gang at one time shot down in
cold blood a party of seven Mexicans whom they found
encamped at a water hole, declaring later that they
did this " just to see them kick."   Twice captured by
the bold officers sent after him, the Kid escaped, in
the last instance killing his two guards in the county
jail, and then openly parading on the platform before
the court house for half an hour before he deigned to
move off upon a horse which he took from a passer-by.

The gang of the Kid made a practice of raiding
the little white settlements then just coming into the
country, and each such raid was apt to mean a life
or two.   Once they thus visited the village of White
Oaks, and at night amused themselves by shooting at
the lights in the windows of the houses.   It chanced
that there was a family living in one of the houses
among whom were some women, almost the first that
had ever come to the camp.   The stern men of the
frontier might pass over the shooting at their own
windows, but they would brook no ill treatment of
the women of the community.   A band of pursuers
was made up, and the Kid was besieged at a ranch
house some miles north of White Oaks.   The self-ap-
pointed leader of the pursuers went into the house
with a flag of truce and was detained there.   Later he
tried to escape from the house and was shot down by
the Kid as he ran, this breaking up the siege with Billy
still in possession of his fortifications.   It seemed that
the Kid would never be killed or taken, and he and his
men became more and more daring and outrageous.
Yet it is a curious fact, showing well the condition of
the society of the times, that the Kid was perfectly well

known by nearly everybody living in the country, and had many warm friends and adherents. A great many others entertained him when he called, and professed for him a friendship which they did not feel, but dared not deny. If a man was suspected by the Kid as apt to convey undesirable news to undesirable parties, the Kid never made any accusations, asked any questions, or waited for any denials. He simply shot the man, laughed about it, and rode on. A wilder or more lawless part of the earth never lay out of doors than this portion of New Mexico at this time.

It was the habit of these gangs of the Kid's people to make a living from the country in the easiest way possible. Some of them knew all about the Chisholm outfit, and it seems to have been agreed among them that it would be a desirable thing to kill the owners of the ranch, take possession of the property, and settle down to being cattle kings themselves, counting upon the remoteness and untravelled nature of the country to protect them in this crime, as it had in hundreds of others. There may have been some disagreements over Maverick matters and that sort of thing which never came to light, but the conclusion on the part of the gang was to make a wholesale killing and stealing.

There was one obstacle to the carrying out of this little plan of taking the Chisholm herds and killing John Chisholm, and that was the objection John Chisholm had to both phases of the proposition. Instead of submitting or running, he sent out word and in a short time had about him as good a little army of fighting men as ever got together. These men were paid about five dollars a day apiece, and had arms and ammunition furnished them. In a short time there were practically two armies scattered about over the country looking for somebody to kill. As neither party had

any uniform or distinguishing mark, it was difficult for
a man to tell his friends from his foes. When two
parties of these armed riders met, it was known there
must be a statement as to sides, for all the country was
forced to take one side or the other. The wayfarer
who saw a body of men approaching was obliged to
guess, and guess very quickly, which side he favoured.
If he guessed wrong, the coyotes had another meal.
The victim was left lying where he fell. The mountains were full of dead men, and each camping place
by the infrequent water holes had its tale of blood and
horror. One man after another was killed thus by
men of one side or the other, sometimes men who were
entirely innocent of any connection with the trouble
in hand. If a paid fighter was killed, another man was
hired to take his place.

Neither faction knew how many men the other
had arrayed against it, nor did it care, for there
was no regular force on either side and no general meetings of the opposing clans, the little
straggling bands of fighters being scattered about
as the case might be, not only near the Chisholm
ranches, but over the whole of a county which is as
large as the State of Pennsylvania. At one time there
was a sort of pitched battle waged at the county seat
of Lincoln County, and some of the Kid's men "holed
up" in a 'dobe house until driven out by fire, meantime
making deadly rifle practice upon any of the enemy
who chanced to show a head anywhere along the street
of the tiny 'dobe town. Upon the hillside back of
the courthouse one of the opposing force attempted
to run to the cover of a big rock, from which he could
command the windows of the 'dobe fortress of the
Kid's men. As he ran there spoke a heavy buffalo gun
from the window, and he fell shot through the back

at four hundred yards. He was not killed at once, and lay upon the hillside all the rest of the afternoon waving his hand for help, but no one dared go near him; and there he died, one of the cowboy victims of this war—a death inglorious enough, but met in pursuance of what the poor fellow thought was his duty.

Many were the stories of the bloody incidents of the Lincoln County war one heard upon the scenes of their happening and within the year or so following their occurrence, but it would be sickening to tell the full details of this great feud, or enter into the long story of its history of open or secret assassinations. It is enough to say that the outlaws who were at the bottom of it were gradually defeated. The officers of the land were as brave men as ever lived, and they never ceased in their killing or capturing until they themselves were killed, and then their deputies took up the work. Prices were put on the heads of the leaders, and this made traitors of many of the men, all the arts of State's evidence and the like being employed by the courts, now gradually becoming stronger in the country. Gradually the war died away in a series of personal feuds, which resulted in many killings years later. Some of the hired fighting men left the country when it began to get too hot for them, and some of these may be living now on the Northern cow ranges, not telling all the things they know about the past. Indictments were out for many men who never had service of warrant made on them.

Pat Garrett, the man who had been elected sheriff for the express purpose of killing Billy the Kid, and who had sent word to him that one or the other of them must be killed—to which Billy gave a cordial assent—finally got track of the little ruffian just as he was about to leave the country for Mexico. It was reported that Billy was to call at night at a certain ranch to say good-bye to his sweetheart, a Mexican *señorita*, and Pat Garrett went to the house and secreted himself behind the bed of the ranch owner in the room nearest the entrance. After dark Billy came to the house, passing two of Garrett's men half suspiciously as they sat on the ground outside the door. He apparently was about to repent of having violated his customary rule of shooting first and inquiring afterward, and had pulled his gun from the scabbard and was looking out at the men as he came backing into the door, with his boots in one hand. Garrett saw and recognised him, and at once shot and killed him; none too quick, for Billy heard him as he rose from behind the bed, holding the scared ranchman down with one arm as he fired. Billy turned swiftly about and made a quick but ineffectual shot, for he was dead even as he fired. Pat Garrett to-day is a respected ranchman, as pleasant a man as one would ask to meet. All that country now is trying to forget its earlier history, and little is ever done to diminish the general ignorance in regard to the most serious and most bloody factional war ever known upon the cattle range.

The last of the important cattle wars was the somewhat famous " rustler war " of 1892, in which a campaign was made by the cattle men of Wyoming against the rustlers of Johnson County, Wyoming. This " war " was not without its opera-bouffe aspects, though it was ventilated for each day for over three weeks in the daily press, and heralded to the corners of the world. It was very much an affair of going after rustlers with a brass band, and it did not result so successfully as was hoped by the leaders of the pro-

21

ject. Only two men were killed in this "war," yet
the matter attracted far more attention than any
similar clash that ever occurred in the cattle country. This was simply because of the newspaper no-
toriety it had. An old cowman covered the case perfectly when he said: "There might be twenty-five
men killed each day down in Lincoln County in the
old times, and it wouldn't make half the stir that is
made nowadays if one man shoots at another in Wyoming. The newspapers make all the difference." The
full force of such a remark can never be felt unless it
has been one's fortune to live, at some time or other
in his life, in a country where there were no newspapers and no law. He is then back at the beginning
of the world, antedating civilization, and in a position to see the crude and grim forces underlying this
human nature which pretends later to compose itself
with the ways of society, but which has really a snarl
and a claw not far away.

The newspaper accounts of the rustler war of 1892
were in many respects incorrect, the despatches coming
from Buffalo, in Johnson County, the seat of the rustler element, being entirely contradictory to those
emanating from Cheyenne, the headquarters of the
big cowmen concerned in the raid. One gathers his
beliefs in regard to the situation not from the newspaper accounts, but from thorough review of the matter upon one hand with a cowman who was one of the
participants in the raid, and upon the other hand with
some rustlers who were at Buffalo and thoroughly concerned in all the incidents which occurred on that
side of the "war."

For a long time the rustlers had been making life
a burden to the legitimate cowmen of the counties of
Johnson, Natrona, and Converse, until they had nearly

brought to a standstill all the proper operations of the cattle industry. Before the establishment of the live stock commission and the brand inspectors, it was impossible for a ranchman to tell whether he was going to come out at the end of the year with any cattle left or not. Practically the whole country was living on stolen beef, and not content with this and with serving notice on the cattle companies that they would no longer be allowed to hold their round-ups, the rustlers began to ship beef by car-load lots to the markets of the East. As there were no brand inspectors there to detect the fraudulent nature of such shipments, there was imminent danger that the illegal cattle men would entirely ruin the legal ones. The extent of the losses suffered by the cattle men may be inferred from the fact that within the first year after the appointment of the brand inspectors at the markets they sent back to the commissioners of the State $127,000 of "estray money" on cattle passing to market from the Wyoming range. The commissioners found proper ownership for all but $14,000 of this, but refused some of the funds to rustlers who openly claimed dues therein. This appearance of the action of the new cattle laws was extremely unsatisfactory to the rustlers, and it resulted in a practical solidification of the various rustler factions, and made of the county of Johnson a rustler settlement, where the cattle men had no voice. In four years the cattle men brought one hundred and eighty suits in Johnson County against rustlers for stealing beef or calves, but no jury could be found which would convict a man, and the only case in which a rustler was ever punished was one in which a thief had killed a cow and taken home a quarter of the beef, for which he was convicted of petty larceny and assessed the value of the beef, about eighteen dollars.

The rustlers posed as small stockmen, and did all they could to array the interests of the actual small stockmen against those of the " barons," or ranch capitalists, claiming that the fight was one of wealth against men in moderate circumstances, and asserting that as to the methods practised in acquiring cattle, the big ranchmen were no better than they should be. In this latter statement there was colour of truth in many instances, for the fortune of more than one man engaged in the raid against the rustlers was more than probably laid in the early and active efforts of their foremen with the branding iron. When such foremen sought to carry on the old methods for themselves which they had practised for their employers, the latter made objection, feeling that there had been a change in the former relations of *meum* and *tuum*. There is large undercurrent of unwritten history on both sides of the question in this rustler war. Be that as it may, there was much bitterness felt on both sides, and no doubt both sides thought they had some partial justification in many things which they did or attempted to do.

Early in the spring of 1892 a number of the large cattle owners met at Cheyenne and resolved upon a general raid against the rustlers, they having the names of about one hundred and twenty-five men whom they claimed to know were engaged in the rustling business, some thirty-five of whom they agreed among themselves either to kill or drive out of the country. In this movement to invoke the old-time ways of the range were several men prominent in State affairs, a member of the Legislature, a member of the stock commission, and some two dozen wealthy cattle men, several of whom were practically non-resident Easterners who had large holdings of cattle in Wyoming.

There never was a more select, or a more inefficient, lynching party started out across the plains. Nearly all the cowmen of the movement were men of culture and refinement. Two Harvard graduates were among the outfit. There was a young Englishman along to see the fun—which he saw—and all in all the gathering was, socially speaking, everything that could be asked. It was incidentally remarked in one of the newspaper reports that one of the select lynchers while asleep in camp one day chanced to toss out his hand over his blankets, thus displaying two large diamond rings which he wore as part of his range costume. It is not justly to be said of these men that they were not brave and determined, and it probably never occurred to them that they would fail of carrying out their programme as arranged in detail without experiencing any great hindrance on the part of the men they were intending to hang, shoot, or drive out of the country. They had read of such things being done, and agreed that it was desirable they should do some of those things for themselves. That one of their number who tells this story of the raid admits frankly that they made a great mistake. They were all new at that sort of business, Eastern men who had not been reared in the hard school of the old times, and who, while they might have been fit for privates in such an enterprise, were absolutely unfit for leaders; in which latter capacity there seems to have been a general willingness to serve. The men who should have been in charge were the men who were hired by the day to serve as privates—twenty fighting Texans, cowpunchers from the lower range, who were imported for this purpose and paid five dollars a day and expenses to go along and see or assist in the hanging, shooting, and driving out. Had the leader of the cowboys been the leader of the party, the result might have been, at least in some respects, different; for here was a man with followers who, though they had not accumulated enough funds to afford to wear diamond rings when going to a lynching, had none the less served in the rude apprenticeship of Western life on the plains, and knew far more about partisan campaigning than all the men who acted as the leaders of this raid.

The party as finally organized numbered forty-three men, including the twenty Texans, and their outfit was as perfect as money could buy. They had three wagons and plenty of cooks, and evidently intended to travel in perfect comfort. Secretly embarking their outfit on a train at Cheyenne at night, early in April, 1892, they went by rail to Casper, Wyoming, arriving there the following night. Thence they started with their horses and wagons overland across the wild country, something like one hundred and thirty miles, which lay between them and the seat of war. The first serious business of the expedition was at the K. C. ranch, occupied by two well-known rustlers, Nate Champion and Nick Ray. The raiders held up this ranch at daybreak, and early in the morning took prisoners two freighters who happened to be stopping at the house, and who came out of the house to go toward the barn. The house was then surrounded by a firing party of twelve men, it being supposed that Champion and Ray would soon miss the other men and come out to see what had become of them. Presently one of the rustlers, Ray, stepped to the door, and at once fell under the rifle fire of the men who lay concealed and waiting for him. The participants in this raid are very reticent in regard to the names of those who did any shooting, but one of the freighters taken prisoner afterward said that it was a smooth-faced boy, one of the Texas fighters, who took the first hurried aim and shot Ray down. Ray was shot again as he crawled back into the house. The other rustler, Champion, remained game till the last and refused to come out, keeping up his fire upon his besiegers whenever opportunity offered. Champion was finally driven out by means of fire. A wagon load of hay was pushed up against the ranch house and set on fire, so that the cabin was burned over the head of the rustler defending it. The body of Ray was later found burned and charred.

When the heat became too much for him, Champion ran from the burning house, endeavouring to reach a little gully near by. He was shot as he ran, and it was later said that twenty-eight wounds were found in his body. The rustler side in this war claim that when Champion was first shot down he was only wounded, and asked the men who came up to him not to shoot again, but that one of the party placed his rifle to Champion's face and deliberately shot him as he lay upon the ground. The body of Champion was left with a card pinned to it bearing the inscription, " Cattle Thieves, beware." In Champion's pocket, after his death, there was found a roughly written memorandum of the events of the day as they appeared to him as he was shut in his cabin by the invading party. He told of the suffering of his comrade Ray, stated the hour of Ray's death, mentioned his efforts to get a shot at the men who were firing at him, stated calmly that he did not think he could hold out much longer, and mentioned the appearance of the wagon-load of hay which he knew was to burn him out. Then, as though in deliberate address to his fellows of the range, he wrote, " Boys, I guess it is all up.

Good-bye." Had the fact not been established clearly enough otherwise, it might have been seen from the simple nature of this pitiful little scrawl that the rustler Champion was a brave man. He had long been known and dreaded by the cattle men.

While the siege of the K. C. ranch was in progress, two men came along the trail with a wagon, and owing to the poor management by the leaders of the raiders, these men were allowed to escape, which they did at full speed on the horses which they took from the wagon. It happened that one of these men was Jack Flagg, a man whose brand, ⌐ℬ, was odious in the eyes of more than one of the cattle men who could here have held him prisoner. Flagg was one of the prominent men among the resident range people who were accused of rustling. His escape meant the ruin of the raiders' expedition. Flagg never drew rein until he had alarmed his friends from the K. C. ranch to the town of Buffalo. In twelve hours all Rustlerdom was alarmed and hurrying to the combat. The town of Buffalo, the county seat of Johnson County, and the headquarters of the free-range element, was at once aroused into that deadly fury which among Western men means but one thing. Immediate war was to be given those who had carried war into this country.

Nor was this war upon the side of the rustlers to be without show of legal justice. It is all very well to say that the principle of the majority is a dangerous principle in the hands of dangerous men; yet how can this principle legally be set aside in any of the forms of this Government, whether in the election of officers national or municipal? Legally speaking, the county of Johnson was as regularly organized as any, and a man who lived there had as good a right to vote

for the officers of that county as has any man of any
part of the Union. The residents of Johnson County
had legally elected as their sheriff Red Angus, who
therefore wás the recognised agent of the law. As
sheriff, Angus summoned about him a posse of the citizens of Buffalo and vicinity, in numbers sufficient, as
he thought, to accomplish the arrest of the invading
party of raiders, who of course had no legal status
whatever in that country, and who were breaking laws
of a nature always held to be higher than those laws
which they accused the rustlers of violating. Surely a
more dramatic or more involved situation never appeared upon the cow range than this, when two armies,
each armed, each able and anxious to kill, met each
other to decide an issue—an issue in which both were
wrong! In no country but the West of the cattle
days could any such situation ever have arisen.

The sheriff had a vast posse at his back when he
started forth from Buffalo to arrest the band of cattle
men. The latter, knowing what would be the result
of their mistake in allowing the two men to escape and
spread the news, pushed on as fast as they could into
the country where they expected to find others of the
men whom they had upon their list as men to be shot,
hung, or driven out of the country. They seem
little to have known the seriousness of their undertaking, or the sternness of the men against whom they
were proceeding, among whom, wrong as they were,
were some of the best cowpunchers and hardiest plainsmen of the entire cattle range. The raiders kept their
wagons with them as long as they could, and then
pushed on ahead, leaving their supplies behind them.
In a little while after that the rustlers swarmed in
upon the trail, seized the wagons, and took prisoners
the teamsters. From that time the invaders ceased to

be the pursuers and became themselves the pursued. They stopped at the T. A. ranch, by this time discovering what the circumstances really were. Here they stood at bay and were surrounded by the forces of the rustlers. There were three hundred and nineteen men in the body which besieged the cattle men at the T. A. outfit, the force being made up of rustlers and rustler sympathizers, with perhaps a great many others who were afraid to refuse the invitation to join the fight.

The cowmen were outnumbered, although they claimed that they expected re-enforcements from a body of Montana cattle men within the week. Yet they were brave as any, and moreover they had intelligence and skill upon their side. They quickly fortified the T. A. ranch with regular rifle pits, barricaded the buildings with logs, made firing stands out of more logs, and really had things in fine shape for a long siege or hot attack. The rustlers constantly increased in numbers and were determined to kill or capture the entire party. Firing was kept up at long range on both sides, though without much damage. One old fellow by the name of Boone, a plainsman with a big buffalo gun, was on the rustlers' side, and was extremely accurate with his fire. He would throw a big bullet against the ranch door or through a window nearly every time he shot. There were twenty-six horses killed in one day in the T. A. corral by the rustler fire, and it must have appeared to the cattle men that they were soon to be set on foot in the middle of a very hostile country. It was never admitted that any of the rustlers were killed in this long-range firing, and the cattle men will not admit that they had any one killed in the fight, though they say that two of their men were accidentally killed. One of them was thrown by his horse and his rifle accidentally discharged, shooting him through the thigh so that he afterward died. A second man, while hurrying out of the door of the ranch house to go after some water, knocked his own revolver out of its holster, and was so shot through the abdomen, dying later.   One of these men was still living at the time of the surrender, and both of them came from the ranks of the cowpunchers who were hired to do the fighting.   The siege lasted for three days, the firing being kept up more or less steadily on both sides.   The cattle men claim that they knew many of the men in the rustler party were small stock men who were really not in sympathy with the rustlers, and who took pains to fire high when shooting at the ranch house.

While all this was going on, the entire civilized world knew every detail of the combat from day to day.   The commanding officer of Fort McKinney, which lay so close to the T. A. ranch that the firing could be heard distinctly all the time, was asked by the county authorities to assist in the capture of the cattle men.   This he declined to do, and he also declined to lend the sheriff a cannon or a Gatling gun for use in carrying the barricaded ranch house.   The rustlers then began plans for blowing up the ranch house with dynamite, they having found in the captured wagons one hundred pounds of that article intended for use against themselves, and having concluded that it would be well to show the cattle men still more fully the unwelcome situation of being hoist by one's own petard.   The commander at Fort McKinney wired his superior officer as to what course he should pursue, and the Government at Washington replied through the general in charge of the Department of the Missouri, stationed at Omaha, that the officer in command at Fort McKinney should put an end to this armed disturbance, and should turn over his prisoners to the proper authorities, but should not deliver any prisoners into the hands of the opposite faction.   On the third day of the siege a troup of cavalry rode out from Fort McKinney carrying a flag of truce, to which the cowmen answered.   Their surrender to the United States forces was demanded, and to this they gladly agreed upon the assurance that they would not be turned over to the authorities at Buffalo, which all knew meant the same thing as death. The sheriff demanded these prisoners of the United States troops, but was refused.   There was then talk among the rustlers of taking away the prisoners by force and holding them for civil trial at Buffalo.   No forcible attempt of this nature, however, was made, although there was very bitter feeling among the rustlers at seeing their invaders escape from them.

The officer in charge of the prisoners was instructed to take them away from the scene of conflict, removing them to Fort Russell, about one hundred miles below.   Here, about three weeks after their outset from Cheyenne, without their outfit, without their horses, with two of their fighting men killed and two of their teamsters missing, they arrived at Fort Russell, not in the character of victorious returners, but as prisoners in charge of the United States troops.   In condition they were somewhat different from that under which they had started forth.   Some of them were sick, all were weary and bedraggled, and all the leaders were willing to admit that they had had enough of *vigilante* work for the time.   They admitted that they had been mistaken and had not known what was before them, but still contended that their movement had of itself been just and right.

As every detail of the fight at the T. A. ranch had been given the public through the daily press, so was the report of each day's march of the return given to the world by the press correspondents. The inglorious little " war " attracted a national attention, and was for months the one theme of discussion in the State of Wyoming, where it figured for a long time in State politics, the two factions continuing their fight after they had been obliged to lay down their arms. By one party it was urged that these men should be taken back to Buffalo to be tried there, at the scene of their offence; but all knew what that meant, and the wealth of the cattle men was brought into the legal fight which contested any such dangerous contingency. The men were finally taken by the civil authorities to Laramie, and there succeeded in obtaining what they coveted, a change of venue to Cheyenne, where they were among their friends and on their own ground. The methods of modern law, which they had but a few months ago violated and held in contempt as unsuited to themselves, they now hailed fervently as the one thing to which all men should submit, and gladly enough availed themselves of it as their only means of salvation. So far from desiring to be set free, they clung with ludicrous eagerness to their prison, and actually paid their own expenses to be allowed to remain in jail! This they did for three months, knowing that it would bankrupt any of those scantily populated counties to keep so large a party of prisoners, and they being desirous of anything rather than the boon of liberty just then, since liberty meant danger and imprisonment offered them safety! Their plans were successful, and that law which they had scorned, and under which they now cowered, took care of them better than they perhaps deserved.

It was now the time not of the old West, but the new West. All the wealth and influence of the most heavily populated portions of Wyoming were with the cattle men, and it was foregone that they would not be convicted. When finally heard in court, these men were all set free upon their own personal recognisance, each man charged with the murder of two men, Champion and Ray, and each offence made bailable in a very large sum of money, the total of bail for the forty men or so tried amounting into the millions. This the cattle men were able to produce or to pay if necessary, but of course the Texas fighting men were not. The latter, acting under advice of counsel, left the country, " jumping " their bonds. During the trial of the cause the cattle men were practically given their liberty, being asked to attend at court at certain hours of the day. A list of over one thousand possible jurymen was called, and at a time when not even half of the peremptory challenges of the accused had been exhausted, it became apparent that it would be impossible to get a jury. It was actually seen that the affair was too big for the courts of the State to handle. The prosecution for the State *nolle prossed* the cases. These men were therefore never tried, never acquitted, and yet can not be again arrested on the old charges. There are few of these cattle men who care to speak much about this matter nowadays, and probably most of them still remain enthusiastic supporters of the law of the land to-day; or at least they should if they possess the trait of gratitude. Indeed, the law has gradually taken sway in Rustlerdom as the country has grown older, and now the battles are referred to the courts by both parties to much greater extent. Some of the rustlers have become bold enough to openly forswear the old ways. Some have turned State's evidence. Yet others are now employed by the cattle men, and make the best cowpunchers possible to be found. In the odd conditions of the range it has already been agreed between these late armed foes that bygones are to be bygones.

Thus ended the last of the great wars of the range, and the only one that has ever been a ludicrous one. It might not have been so much smiled at had it succeeded, but success on either side might have been a very unfortunate thing. The attempt failed partly because the men who made it were not suited for such work. Not plainsmen themselves, they undertook the methods of plainsmen. They might far better have clung to the ways under which they had been born and brought up, and to which they so gladly returned when they found they could not negotiate the ways of the old West. Indeed, their fundamental mistake was one of chronology. Suddenly it had grown too late for the old ways. The old West was gone.

The story of this last attempt at the revival of the past fashions of the West does not make to-day the pleasantest of reading, but it serves after all to show something further of the character of the cowboy. Misguided and impulsive perhaps, he was always eager to be where the fighting was thickest, and there he conducted himself as a man according to the creed under which he had been reared. Creeds change about us; creeds of morals, of religion, of ethics, as the history of the past shows must continually be the case, everything being always relative to some other thing. It may have been a creed outworn which served the cowboy upon the one side or the other of this ignominious little war. Yet it is a singular fact that, ignoble as the part of a hired fighter has always been held to be, no one has ever smiled at the part played by the cowpuncher supernumerary in this little drama of the range. The centre of the stage was occupied by figures larger financially than himself, but he alone out of all those engaged played through to the end the part for which he had been cast.

CHAPTER XVII.

BEEF AND FREEDOM.

THERE is very great temptation in writing of the American cowboy to tell only the thrilling stories of his life, to paint only the vivid pictures, the material for such treatment being so abundant and the demand for it so pronounced. Yet, perhaps, we can afford to be more just to the man and the country he represented, can afford to read at least a short lesson which would show the cowboy not as a freak, but as a factor. A factor he certainly was in the development of the West. He was precisely the right man in the right place. Therefore he was a factor in the building of America, and as such he deserves a just and definite place in the history of the country—a place where he can be viewed not so much with amusement as with pride, where he can be recognised for what he was, one of the great essential citizens of the land. The cowboy did not make two blades of grass grow where one had grown before, but he caused double the number of cattle to graze upon the unutilized grass which made one of the resources of the land. He was not only a product of the country, but a producer for the country, and he distinctly added to the total of the crude natural wealth quite as much as the farmer who digs such wealth up out of the soil. He brought into the reach of the citizen of America his share of those incomparable resources which have made that citizen the most fortunate man of the earth. He played his part in that national development which made the American citizen not only the luckiest citizen of the earth, but also the best citizen, the citizen best fitted to uphold a nation's honour and prosperity.

It is no mere catch phrase to say that beef and freedom go together. Compare the beef-eating English with the rice-eating natives of India, or the fruit-eaters of Africa, whom they overwhelm so easily. It is a matter of nationality in the first place, to be sure, but of nationality plus long generations of better food. To go further, both logic and history warrant the conclusion that there is not upon the face of the globe to-day a better fighting man than he who by birth and residence is entitled to be called a citizen of America, because he has been the best-fed man on earth. The cowboy has helped feed that man. He has added to his wealth. For this he deserves an industrial credit as much as does the farmer who also produces wealth, the sailor who carries it, the soldier who defends it. It was the part of the cowboy to aid in the production of food of the most desired and valued sort, a food which but small portions of the inhabitants of the world have ever been able to afford. America has sold beef to the world, but she sold of her surplus and did not stint herself to sell. She gave to Europe what was left over from her own table. Happy has been the American—perhaps how happy he does not stop to think, and perhaps why happy he does not pause to ask. Much of the measure of his good fortune lay in the vast, the apparently inexhaustible treasures of the West. The measure of his ignorance of that good fortune may be seen later on in the history of the nation; seen too soon, perhaps, when the mines of this wealth shall have been laid open and laid bare, when the American, rich and unreckoning, shall have shared with all the world, and that to his own disadvantage, the wealth that was his native heritage.

The beef of the cattle range makes up but a small percentage of the total of the beef which now comes into the great cattle markets of the United States, for the " granger " has won his fight, and from this time on the farms and the herds will be smaller and smaller. But it is not in the least fanciful to take into estimate the relations of American free beef and American free institutions as well as the American free and fearless character. The beef herders and the beef eaters of history have been winning peoples as far back as we can find in history, and it is not asking too much of history to expect that she shall repeat herself. It is not impossible to predict the quality or the names of those nations which from now on will divide the world among them. These will not be the vegetarian nations. The latter will be eaten up, as the lion eats up the deer.

Almost an overwhelming proportion of the population of the globe, even of the population of Europe, is vegetarian, not by choice but from necessity. The American citizen who goes to Germany for a year's residence learns that in that country many things are held as luxuries which in America are necessaries, expected as matter of course by every American citizen, no matter how poor he be. How often can the German peasant afford even the most miserable bit of inferior meat for his table? It is a feast for the family of such a man if they chance to have that which the American labourer eats as his daily and expected portion. America throws away out of her back door more than would make the German peasantry de-

liriously happy. Moreover, America can afford to
do it.

The great bulk of the English lower classes, though
the English are the greatest meat-eating nation of
Europe, rarely see a bit of beef upon their tables. The
labourer of that country may make ten to twenty shil-
lings a week, out of which he is to support himself and
family, if he be conscienceless enough to marry and
raise a family, as usually he is. Both beef and freedom are far beyond such a man, dreams in which he
has no part. Compare the chain forgers and other
metal workers of England—men, women, and children, whole families fettered to the bellows and anvil
year in and year out, hopeless, continually hungry
for even one satisfying meal of but the coarsest bread,
to say nothing of a particle of meat—compare such
beings with the free cowboy of America. Which
should be the better citizen? Whose the better blood
to have in a nation's veins? Take the slaves of England's collieries, whose terrible and hopeless lives are
passed truly beneath the heel of their civilization, and
apparently beneath the consideration alike of hope
and of humanity; compare such men with the wild
rider of the range, who lives under the big blue sky,
who fears no thing that breathes, who has health and
energy fairly to throw away in mere surplus of vitality.
Which is the better sort of citizen to have behind a
nation in the shock of arms or in the shock of years?
Well may the slaves of the older civilization long for
the beef and the freedom of the West. And if that
West be gone, well may we sigh for it ourselves!

The Hindu eats rice and grain, and he sits dreaming by the rivers which have mirrored his same apathetic face for ages. The Russian lives upon wheat
and corn, when he is lucky enough to have it from

his own soil or as the gift from rich America to the
starving; and behold the children's children of the
Russian in sheepskins, and unable, as their fathers
were, to do more than make the sign of the cross and
the gesture of submission.   The Chinese live upon
rice and what else they may find; and what are they
among the nations?   What do such peoples know
either of beef or of freedom.   We may be too proud to
ask a comparison between such men and the inhabitants of this rich and favoured land of ours.   No land
of the earth has ever been more fully or more variously
favoured than this; and never has any, in all the history of the world, shown the sudden expansion and the
permanent growth into all the richness of things valuable in national prosperity.   It has been a wonderful
country, this rich, free land.   It has won its wars,
and outlived its wounds, and builded well its cities
and great works, and bred a race that will live through
the centuries.   France remembers to-day the benefi-
cence of that monarch the sign of whose wiseness was
a public prosperity which enabled every citizen to
" have his chicken in the pot."   America has put upon
every poor man's table as much as that and more, and
for that it thanks no sovereign at all.   Its treasure-
house for such store was largely in the West—that
glorious, abounding, open, manly West, where there
never was a throne except the saddle—the land *par
excellence* of beef and freedom.

CHAPTER XVIII.

THE IRON TRAILS.

THE settlement of the West went forward by leaps and bounds, along projecting tongues of civilization, which extended far in front of the main body of the population. The demon of unrest drove the American frontiersman to move a dozen times in a generation. The settlers who pressed over the new land rolled on and over in long waves, like a flock of feeding wild pigeons, those in the rear rising and alighting ahead of those who had preceded them; and, moreover, they did this along lines determined by the same reasons which governed the wild pigeons. They went in the line of the least resistance; that is to say, where they could find their food most easily. There is no push so irresistible as that of advancing civilization. The frontiersman dreaded a neighbour, and would be moving yet if there were any place to which he could move. In his journey to the West he followed the farming lands, the hunting regions, the rain belt, and the places where the Indians were least prohibitory in their numbers. Thus his progress was a series of broken leaps, of concentrations and expansions, always forward, and for the most part along the line of latitude upon which he had been born. Of later years the tide of interstate immigration has begun to move from the North to the South, but this has occurred only since the Western lands suitable for cultivation have been taken up, and in search of the cheap Southern lands which still remain unoccupied.

There came a time in the history of the West when the projecting arms of civilization which extended into the West were crossed at right angles by the scanty population which came up from the southward with the cattle trade as it spread swiftly over the northern range. Thus the open lands of the Northwest and middle West were assailed from two directions at once. It was a singular population which took possession of that wild country, and one whose like we shall hardly see again at any corner of the world. Hunter and trapper, skin hunter, gambler, horse thief, capitalist, cowman, farmer, merchant, artisan, money lender, professional man, desperado and tenderfoot—all mingled in an eddy and boil of tumultuous, vigorous life. Into this new population there came pushing up steadily from the South the cattle of the trail and the men who cared for them. Thus there came yet other new inhabitants, with new customs and a new industry. That was the time when the two trails met, the long trail of the drive and the iron trails which crossed it on their way to the Western ocean.

It was not foreseen what tremendous changes these iron trails would make in the features of the population and the pursuits of the West, nor how unspeakably rapid would be these changes in their coming, yet the changes came so swiftly as to forestall prophecy. Each railroad acted as an irrigating ditch to carry the stream of population out over the unsettled lands. Each little town was the gateway for a series of smaller ditches through which the flood trickled out and around. Far out into the rainless region the wave of people rolled and lessened and trickled, until fairly swallowed up by the ultimate earth, a soil which refused to yield them a living.

The railroads crossed the continent once, twice, thrice, and yet again. They began to build spurs and side lines, reaching out into all places where there were merchantable things to be carried in or out of the country. It was not long until the railroads saw what a carrying trade there was in the cattle industry of the West. These many thousands of great creatures, the range cattle which came North at the expense of a season's time and a sad per cent of loss, could be handled in a much quicker and safer way. The railroads could do in a few days what the trail outfit needed months to do, and could deliver the cattle with less loss and in better condition. The railroads no longer followed the law of latitude. They took the suggestion of longitude. The iron trails bent down and ran North and South along the old footworn trails of the great cattle drives. In the year of 1896 there was but one trail outfit driving cattle North from Texas. Before the days of the railroads there had been hundreds.

Over the iron trails there went out ploughs and mowing machines and harrows and other things strange and unheard of upon the old cow range. The grain lands pressed into the grass lands, and to these growing grain lands, as well as to the remaining range region, the railroads began to carry the horned cattle from the South, from the East, from every direction. They carried cattle from the North to the South, changing the whole breed of the latter country. They carried cattle from the South to the North, changing another breed in turn. Moreover, they carried out wire for fences, and so they sewed the shroud of the old cattle range.

Into even the farthest corners of the cow range
the railroads crept. Towns sprang up over the
plains; towns where there were steeples, and where
houses had paint upon them, something hitherto unheard of in that country. The cow town dwindled
away or became disgustingly decorous, its place being taken by the smart and pretentious little city of
the new West. A horde of lawyers, doctors, mer-
chants, thieves, and other necessaries swept into each
town as quickly as it was organized. Life on the waning frontier became more colourless and less picturesque. Again new customs came in. Hospitality
became less generous and suspicion more general.
There were locks on the doors.

The wire fences and the fields of the farming man
came into evidence wherever stony-hearted Nature
would allow the latter to hold his own for a season or
so out of every half a dozen; for the Western farmer
above all things was hopeful and enduring. The
farming communities, or "granger settlements," as
the cowmen called them, fed little towns of their own,
such towns taking also for a time the trade of the stockmen. Then the cattle trade began under the influence
of the railroads to settle and centralize into big permanent cities of much more import and permanence
than the old cow towns of the frontier. One heard of
Sherman, Denison, Henrietta, Fort Worth, in the
South; of Miles City, Laramie, Cheyenne, in the
North.

And then there came another time in the history
of the West. The iron trails had brought all sorts
and conditions of men to this Western country, prom-
ising them all sorts of things in addition to those
things which they in their ignorance promised themselves. Some of these found the West not so hospita-

ble as they had thought. The "rain belt" proved a most unsatisfactory thing to count upon, though it looked well enough in Western railroad literature to say that it had steadily moved westward and was now shedding regular and beneficent showers alike upon the just and the unjust over such and such lands in the arid portions of the West. The farmers found that corn would not ripen on the high bleak table-lands, that wheat would not do well once in a half dozen plantings. The nights were too cold for some crops, and the days too warm for others. The "rain belt" yielded no rain. It needed the deepest of wells to reach unfailing water. There was no fuel within hundreds of miles. There ensued some seasons of want over great stretches of the newly settled country, and some winters in which hundreds of the "grangers" actually froze to death in the severe storms which found them unprepared. Back from large areas of Dakota, Nebraska, and Kansas the discouraged settlers began to sweep, and the antelope resumed the feeding grounds from which they had been temporarily driven.* The cowboy followed the antelope back again over some of this natural range. Then in time came the resultant of all these many forces, the "sag" in the

---

* A newspaper paragraph printed in May, 1897, has the following information, *apropos* to the above: "The towns of Woodsdale, Moscow, Springfield, and Fargo. in Kansas, which had a population of 1,100 in 1890, have now only a population of eighteen, according to a correspondent of the United States Investor. Hugoton has three families out of the 400 that used to live there. Nine children go to the $10,000 schoolhouse, and there is standing, like a monument of folly, a water-works system that cost some Eastern plutocrat $36,000. The town never paid a cent of principal or interest on all this and never will."— E. H.

cattle business, and the final readjustment under the exacter system of later days.

The edge was worn off the frontier by the grind of the wheels of civilization. It became fashionable to speak of law and order, of city improvements, of Eastern capital, of future growth of the city, and all that. Politics began to be considered, and all the ways of older society came into effect. The men of the wilder and freer West who made a good part of the new population were not the ones to oppose all this. As they had made it possible, so now they aided in making it permanent. The old citizen of the West became the new citizen. Changing with his fellows, the cowboy now became a steady, quiet, faithful, and hard-working man, following his trade as he had learned it in the past, though now under conditions very different.

The centre of the cattle industry had now shifted entirely from the South to the North, Wyoming and Montana furnishing the bulk of the range beef instead of Texas. Always the cattle in the long train loads going to the markets had shorter and shorter horns. Always the hatband of the Northern cowboy became narrower and narrower. Far down in the Spanish Southwest, in the remote and desert country where even the boldest granger dared not venture, the ways of the past were slowest to yield to change, and the cowpuncher retained more fully something of his old-time picturesqueness; for there the iron trails met iron customs and the stony apathy of centuries of calm.

If the cowpuncher lost something of his old-time picturesqueness as a Western type, the change did not rob him entirely of his innate traits and characteristic habits, nor did it change materially the routine of his duties. The old ways of the range, the ways invented by the unknown old Spaniard centuries ago, remained somewhat or much the same. The mark and the brand were still the title of ownership, and the round-up still the recognised means of establishing the cow-man's wish for justice. The day's routine, the work of the drive, the round-up, the corral, remained much the same. Then, as ever, the life of the cowboy was one taking him far from the settlements and into such narrow solitudes as remained. He still needed his traits of courage, skill, and independence of action. He was still a cowboy. All the nation knew him now. His vogue was greatest at the beginning of the end of his short day. Changed though he was in minor extent, he had now blended with the life of his country. He had become a citizen. He was a part of the warp of an interwoven web of humanity, though still he made a dash of colour upon the growing monotone.

CHAPTER XIX.

SUNSET ON THE RANGE.

THE great law which rules all animate life compels all creatures to wage continual war with their surroundings, yet teaches them that they may best win in that war by compromise with the surroundings. Each creature partakes of the soil that bore it. We are all not ourselves, but the reflection of that which was about us.

The great West, vast and rude, brought forth men also vast and rude. We pass to-day over parts of that matchless region, and we see the red hills and ragged mountain fronts cut and crushed into huge indefinite shapes, to which even a small imagination may give a human or more than human form. In the " frozen music " of the broken buttes there may lie models for some future architect.

That same great hand which chiseled out these monumental forms and phases laid its fingers upon the people of this region. Rude and ironlike, their nature simulated that of the stern faces set about them. Into their hearts came the elemental disturbance of the storm, the strength of the hills, the broadness of the prairies. They lay in the cradle of solitude, swung by the hand of calm. These babes of the West were giants, because that was a land of giants. Among their own people, who stood about them unseen and

337

unknown, they grew to their full stature. Never shall that stature lessen! Never shall they pass away! The Indian, the hunter, the plainsman, the cowboy will not die. They will but pass back among their people, whence they came. They will vanish again upon the edge of the plains. They will look down upon us from the hills in some immortal form!

Of all these babes of the primeval mother, the West, the cowboy was perhaps her dearest, because he was her last. Some of her children lived for a century, others for half that time; this one for not a triple decade before he began to be old. Knowing for him that which he did not know, the West foresaw the time when he too would ride away into the hills and never come back again; yet none the less she smiled upon him, with the slow smile of elemental mysteries— that smile which rests upon stone lips by the banks of the Nile, and upon the lips of the faces in the Rockies.

What was really the life of this child of the wild region of America, and what were the conditions of the life that bore him can never be fully known by those who have not seen the West with wide eyes. Those who did not, but who looked superficially and superciliously, remembering only their own surroundings, and forgetting that in the eye of Nature one creature is as good as another if only it prevail where it stands, were content with distorted views of that which they saw about them. Having no perspective in their souls, how could they find it in their eyes? They saw colour but not form in these wild men of the wild country. They saw traits, but did not see the character beneath them. Seeking to tell of that which they had not seen, they became inaccurate and unjust. Dallying with the pleasant sensation of exciting themes, they became grotesque instead of strong in their handling of them.

The cowboy was simply a part of the West. He who did not understand the one could never understand the other. Never was any character more misunderstood than he; and so thorough was his misrepresentation that part of the public even to-day will have no other way of looking at him. They see the wide hat and not the honest face beneath it. They remember the wild momentary freaks of the man, but forget his lifetime of hard work and patient faithfulness. They insist upon the distorted mask, and ask not for the soul beneath it. If we care truly to see the cowboy as he was, and seek to give our wish the dignity of a real purpose, the first intention should be to study the cowboy in connection with his surroundings. Then perhaps we may not fail of our purpose, but come near to seeing him as he actually was, the product of primitive, chaotic, elemental forces, rough, barbarous, and strong. Then we shall love him; because at heart each of us is a barbarian too, and longing for that past the ictus of whose heredity we can never eliminate from out our blood. Then we shall feel him appeal to something hid deep down in our common nature. And this is the way in which we should look at the cowboy of the passing West; not as a curiosity, but as a product; not as an eccentric driver of horned cattle, but as a man suited to his times.

The study of the cattle trade is essential to a study of the cowboy, and hence the wish to speak broadly of the varying conditions of that trade. Finally we must come to those widespread changes of condition which have changed or will soon have changed fundamentally the entire industry. We have seen the forces working against the permanency of the great industry of cattle ranching. The small land-holder, the sheep herder, the fence builder and the irrigator are the great enemies of the cattle man. Perhaps of all these the one most to be dreaded is the last one. The man who brings water upon the arid lands of the West changes the entire complexion of a vast country, and with it the industries of that country. This irrigation may be by means of artesian wells or by use of the natural streams. Already there are thousands of acres of soil as rich as any of the world which are now redeemed from the desert and changed into fertile farming lands. These are added to the realm of the American farmer. They are stolen from the realm of the American cowboy. The valleys of Montana and Wyoming, when placed "under the ditch," produce corn as good as any of Iowa or Illinois, wheat as good as that of Dakota, oats and barley in similar abundance, and fruits of like size and excellence. Wherever such things are possible, good-bye to the days of grass feed and cattle driving, for their time is past. The old Spaniard who taught us the cattle trade also taught us irrigation; but he handed us the two together, little thinking that the one would destroy the other.

Not all the open range will ever be farmed, but very much will go under irrigation which is now thought to be irreclaimable. The great artesian wells which have been sunk in Dakota, Colorado, and other parts of the West have produced results so strangely vast in their significance that it is impossible to predict where they may finally arrive. Artesian water was first used to open up thousands of acres for the cattle man; but it will take all these acres away again, and many more, and give them to the farmer of the

future. The constitution of the chief cattle State of
the Union safeguards the title of the running water
to the people as a gift of Nature; yet eventually the
water will be used by many instead of a few. Each of
these will take his share of the wild farm of the cowboy. These factors remain as yet unformulated, but
their suggestion is very strong in its trend, and a review of them can lead to but one conclusion.

Singularly enough, at the time of the writing of
these lines, there is in progress at a city in western
Nebraska a great " irrigation fair," the first of its kind
in the history of that part of the country. This fair
exploits the possibilities of the soil when under irrigation. Thousands of people have come together there,
among these many Indians and cowboys and old-
time men of the plains. In faint imitation of the
days of the past, the town is run " wide open." It
is reported that the scenes of '69 and '70 are repeated. The cowboys are riding their horses into the
saloons as they did in the days of the early drives. It
is sought to revive the spirit of that old West which
is really dead beyond the reach of all our lamentations.
Do many pause to consider how dramatic a scene this
really is, this irrigation fair at which the cowboy is
asked to attend as a curiosity, as an attraction? Does
he himself know what it is that they are asking him to
do? They ask him to disport himself in a Titanic
shadow-dance, and to close his play by blowing into
its final flare the dwindling flame of his own candle.

The West has changed. The old days are gone.
The house dog sits on the hill where yesterday the
coyote sang. The fences are short and small, and
within them grow green things instead of gray. There
are many smokes now rising over the prairie, and they
are wide and black instead of thin and blue.

23

As we look out in the evening light from where we stand, we may see the long shining parallels of the iron trail reaching out into the sunset. A little busy town lies near, flanked with fields of grain ready for the harvesting. There are cattle; not those of "deformed aspect," which Coronado saw when he walked across this country in the gray of other days, but sleek, round beasts, which stand deep in crops their ancestors never saw. In the little town is the hurry and bustle of modern life, even here, upon the extreme edge of the well-settled lands. For this is in the West, or what is now known as the West. It is far out upon what may now, as well as any place, be called the frontier, though really the frontier is gone. Guarding its ghost, watching over its grave, here stands a little army post, once one of the pillars, now one of the monuments of the West.

The routine of the uncomplaining men who make the army goes on here still, as it does all over the land. One has seen the forming of the troops to-day, over there, upon the parade ground. As evening comes he can hear the song of the trumpets, music to tingle in his hair. As the sun drops to the edge of the plains there comes the boom of a cannon at the fort, and fluttering down its staff falls the flag which waves over East and West and South and North alike, alike over the present and the past.

Out from the little "settlement" in the dusk of evening, always facing toward where the sun is sinking, rides a figure we should know. He threads the little lane among the fences, following the guidance of hands other than his own, a thing he would once have scorned to do. He rides as lightly and as easily as ever, sitting erect and jaunty in the saddle, his reins held high and loose in the hand whose fingers turn up daintily, his whole body free yet firm in the saddle with the seat of the perfect horseman. His hat still sweeps up and back in careless freedom of fashion. It is dusk, and we may not see his trappings. Let us hope his belt is still about his waist, his spurs still jingling as he rides. His pony is the same or much the same as when we saw it many years ago coming up the street of a very different town. It trots steadily forward, with the easy movement of the animal accustomed to long distances. The two, man and horse, show up strongly in the unreal light of evening on the plains. They seem to rise and move strangely as one looks, seem to grow strangely large and indistinct. Yet they melt and soften and so define; and at length, as the red sun sinks quite to the level of the earth, the figures of both show plainly and with no touch of harshness upon the Western sky.

The cowboy as he rides on, jaunty, erect, virile, strong, with his eye fixed perhaps on the ridge miles away, from which presently there may shine a small red light to hold his gaze, now looks about him at the buildings of the little town. As the boom of the cannon comes, and the flag drops fluttering down to sleep, he rises in his stirrups and waves his hat to the flag. Then, toward the edge, out into the evening, he rides on. The dust of his riding mingles with the dusk of night. We can not see which is the one or the other. We can only hear the hoof beats passing, boldly and steadily still, but growing fainter, fainter, and more faint.

ADDENDA.

Page 40.

In the early days of the northern range the rancher had a double reason for the dirt roof which he put upon his house. It was not only the warmest and most easily constructed roof possible for him in his remote part of the world, but it was also the safest. In the frontier times the outlying ranch houses were often attacked by Indians. Even yet there are ranch houses standing on the range whose sides are pierced by the loopholes which were once so necessary. Against the dugout of the cowman the Indian was well-nigh powerless. He dared not approach under the deadly rifle fire of the defenders, nor could he set on fire the roof of the ranchman's castle, one of the sturdiest and most effectual fortresses that ever formed the outposts of a civilization. Sometimes the cowman had a tunnel dug back from his dugout, connecting it with another building not far away, or leading farther back up the hill to a better fighting place. Such precautions were not common, but they instance the skill and determination of these men, who never intended to relinquish their grip upon the land they had discovered.

As time wore on the old-time cowman might be so wedded to the dirt-covered house which had served him in the past that he would never seek to change it. The cowman who remained an "old batch" was very apt to find his dugout or his cabin good enough for him. If, however, he married and was urged to take a step or so up in the world, he might build him a better ranch house, perhaps making his roof on the home ranch building of shingles or using sawn lumber about the place to an extent which would have been impossible in the early days. The new

345

man from the East, who had not grown up in the cattle trade, and who had been accustomed to better houses in his youth than had the old-timer, would be very apt to go to some extent of expense and trouble to put himself up a ranch house a little more ambitious than the dugout or the rude cabin, this more especially for the home camp where he intended to reside when on the range. The line camps or out-dwellings for the men would still be of the old style—the walls perhaps of logs or sod, the roof being perhaps laid with rude half tiles hollowed out of divided saplings, and laid so that they " broke joints," the edges of two convex ones fitting in the hollow of one concaved, so that the water would thus be carried off as it is on a tiled roof so fitted. A covering of dirt usually completed this rude provision for the shedding of the rain. In the later days boards were used in fitting up a roof, but the commonest way was to lay a rude covering of small logs or poles, then a thin thatching of willow boughs and grass, covering the whole with a layer of dirt. Such a roof was very apt to leak, but, as the cowboy had not very much need for the roof at best, he did not mind so trifling a thing as that.

Page 48.

It is a peculiarity even of the wildest range cattle that they must have water at frequent intervals. The more they lose their wild quality, the more often they need water, and the wilder they are the safer they are in their contest with the elements. The horses will paw through the snow, but the cattle will not. The horses will stay out on the hills, where the snow is thin, feeding there and not crowding down to the valleys and creek beds after water. The cattle have not so much sagacity, and it is a common sight to see the valleys of the water ways crowded with them during the winter time at the very points where the snow lies deepest. Here they will huddle up and silently starve, hanging about the watering place and refusing to go out on the hills to feed. A part of the work of the cowboys at such a time is to drive these animals away from the valleys up to the broken country back from the streams, where they can find a little feed. Sometimes trails are broken up from the valleys by the cowboys, who ride their plunging ponies back and forth and finally form a roadway over which the cattle can be driven out from the death trap into which they have come and which they refuse to abandon. It has even been the case in more recent days that a rude snowplough has been made and used to open a trail for the cattle back from such a deadly valley where they were perishing. The instinct of the cattle thus appears to be not always a wise one. Sometimes, in their eagerness to get at the coveted water which is sealed away from them by the ice, they crowd in numbers out upon the ice of a considerable stream. It has happened that the ice in such an event has broken, many scores of cattle thus being drowned.

The salvation of the cattle upon a wide extent of the northern range lies in the Chinook wind, that strange, warm current of air which sometimes in the winter season comes over the summit of the upper Rockies, suffusing far out to the east of the mountains the mild breath of the Japan current of the Pacific Ocean. Its effect may be felt perhaps nearly across the State of Montana, and in some cases as far south as Wyoming or parts of Colorado. When the ranchman who has been witnessing his cattle perishing about him in the snow sees the mountain tops begin to look black and ominous, he sighs in relief, for he knows that the "black wind" of the Indians is coming. Violently this wind blows, and suddenly all the air is soft and mild. The snow does not melt, but simply vanishes, passing away as though by magic. Then the cattle may drink and may feed. It is the armistice offered them by Nature. Feebly the living abandon the dead and seek to gain what strength they may for the continuance of the battle when it shall again close in upon them.

Page 214.

If it be during the springtime, the cowpuncher may meet yet another curious feature of the range life as he rides on his daily round. As he passes over a patch of the short gray sagebrush or a bit of grass longer than the average, perhaps even a piece of ground apparently almost bare, his trained eye may catch a glimpse of an object which the inexperienced observer would never note at all. Something in the look of the motionless, shapeless thing lying flat on the ground invites a second and sharper gaze. The cowpuncher dismounts, and pulls up by the ear a little young calf, which has been lying sprawled out as close to the ground as it could lie, making not the slightest sound or movement to attract the attention of any creature passing by. The cattle of the range are almost as wild as the elk or antelope or deer, and their ways are very similar in many respects. The mother of this little calf has perhaps found it necessary to go five or ten miles to water, and she has told the calf to lie down and keep perfectly still, no matter what may happen, knowing very well that this is the safest way for it to escape the eye or the nose of the wolf, the coyote, or any other enemy which would be apt to assail it during her absence. Thus does the mother deer or antelope "*cache*" her offspring while away feeding or at water, and it is astonishing how effective is this ruse of the mother heart. The hunter may pass within a few feet of the little antelope and never see it, so closely does it blend in colour with the surrounding tone of the landscape. The young calf may be betrayed by its redder coat, but it will be as motionless as the antelope kid. The cowboy picks it up with his rude playfulness, but as soon as he lets it go it falls flat and motionless again, hugging the ground as tightly as it can and obeying to the letter the injunction of instinct. But the little calf has not yet learned more than what instinct has taught it. Its mother has been gone for some time, and in its confused young mind it thinks that perhaps this other big creature has come to take charge of it in place of its mother. If the cowboy stays about the calf long, picks it up several times, or pays it much attention, the little thing will after awhile come toddling along after him, its long legs wobbling and stumbling as it walks. At times the cowboy finds it wise to earmark this calf where it is found, if he be clear in his own conscience that it belongs to his outfit; but even after the cutting with the knife the little calf may not understand that it should not follow away this big creature, and will come after the cowboy even after he has mounted and started to ride away. Then the cowboy gets down again from his horse and pushes the calf down on the ground again, and teaches it as well as he can that it must stay there and wait for its mother. He knows how quickly the young of wild animals, the antelope, the deer, or even the buffalo, will lose the instinctive wildness at this period of its life, and follow away a captor without any compulsion. The writer has seen young buffalo calves, which were left loose and were suckling domestic cows about camp, refuse to run away and join the wild buffalo, a herd of which were standing less than a quarter of a mile away. Two weeks later one of these calves would follow the wagon without being tied, and showed no disposition to escape. A hunter who takes young wild animals for the Zoölogical Gardens at Washington says that a fawn which is found *cached* by its dam will often follow its captor within a few moments, and that the kids of the antelope need but very little attention to make them entirely docile and reconciled to captivity.

But if it chances that the cowpuncher finds his calf *cached* near by a little bunch of cattle, or perhaps sees several calves surrounded by a few cows or a number of other range cattle, he does not get off his horse and attempt to handle the calves. He knows that should he do so he would be charged furiously by the band of cattle, and that he would be fortunate if he escaped serious injury. If he is thus charged, his one concern is to get to his horse as fast as possible, for once he is mounted the cattle will leave him alone. They understand him then, though when he is on foot he is to them simply a wild animal and a probable enemy.

(21)

THE END.